AF872295

Artificial Intelligence, Natural Resistance

How the institution of medicine resists the technologies that could save us

Ari Ercole

Copyright © 2026 Ari Ercole
All rights reserved. No part of this publication may be reproduced, stored in a retrieval system, or transmitted in any form or by any means, electronic, mechanical, photocopying, recording or otherwise, without the prior written permission of the publisher.

Published by Latent Press, Cambridge, United Kingdom

First edition, 2026

ISBN: 978-1-0667264-0-0 (paperback)
ISBN: 978-1-0667264-1-7 (hardback)

A catalogue record for this book is available from the British Library.

The information in this book is provided for general informational purposes only and does not constitute medical, legal, or professional advice.

Typeset in LaTeX by the author.
10 9 8 7 6 5 4 3 2 1

For Juliet

AI will not transform healthcare because healthcare institutions are not designed to improve healthcare—they are designed to reproduce existing distributions of power, income and authority. And they are very good at it.

Contents

About the author

Ari Ercole is a consultant in anaesthesia and neurointensive care medicine at Cambridge University Hospitals NHS Foundation Trust, where he is also Chief Clinical Information Officer (CCIO), lead Clinical Safety Officer, and Chair of the AI Steering Group. He has over a decade of frontline experience in digital healthcare and the deployment of new technologies, including AI into clinical practice.

His path to medicine was unconventional. He read physics and theoretical physics at the University of Cambridge, subsequently completing a PhD in experimental condensed matter physics. He also holds an advanced diploma in Economics. He has worked in computational analytics across a wide range of disciplines for more than twenty-five years and has been building medical machine learning models since 2001, long before the field acquired its current status in healthcare.

Ari is an affiliated associate professor at the University of Cambridge and faculty of the Cambridge Centre for AI in Medicine. He teaches on the methodological, analytical, regulatory and ethical dimensions of using routinely collected clinical data for population sciences and public health research. His research spans AI methodology, clinical informatics infrastructure and acute care medicine. In traumatic brain injury, he has used AI prediction and unsupervised learning to demonstrate that what was long treated as a single condition comprises distinct biological subtypes with different treatment implications. As co-lead of the COGiTATE study, he was involved in the first prospective multicentre trial to implement a digital algorithm directly into precision management at the ICU bedside, translating methodology into practice in exactly the way this book argues is so rarely achieved. His broader contributions include international data standards for observational research, major multicentre trials, and national emergency analytics during the Covid-19 pandemic. He was the national intensive care representative in helping to establish clinical informatics as a recognised specialty in the UK. He co-founded the European Society of Intensive Care Medicine's scientific section on data science. He created the first resident rotation in Digital Healthcare at Cambridge University Hospitals, a training programme embedding resident doctors in clinical informatics.

He is an official fellow in clinical medicine at Magdalene College, Cambridge, where he serves as director of studies in medicine, and was the National Institute for Academic Anaesthesia 2025 Macintosh Professor.

Acknowledgements

This book began as a puzzle, which itself emerged from frustration about healthcare, and became an argument, shaped by many conversations, disagreements, and acts of intellectual generosity over several years.

Paul Elbers deserves particular recognition for his role in shaping how I think about data science in critical care. As a co-founder of the European Society of Intensive Care Medicine Data Science Section with me, he consistently pushed the field beyond methodological novelty and towards application, translation, and clinical consequence. His insistence that what ultimately matters is not the elegance of the science but whether it changes practice has had a substantial influence on this work.

Derek Angus was instrumental in awakening what I can only describe as my 'inner economist': an appreciation of incentives, trade-offs, and system-level behaviour. His influence is evident wherever this book steps back from models and algorithms to ask what they do to real systems, real workflows, and real people.

Leo Anthony Celi profoundly shaped my understanding of the ethical, social, and structural risks of artificial intelligence in healthcare. Through his work and discussion, he made clear that AI is not neutral: it reflects and can entrench existing inequities if developed without humility, representativeness, and attention to real-world impact. His insistence on outcomes over accuracy, and equity over optimisation, has been a critical counterweight to technological exuberance.

My clinical colleague, Ronan O'Leary, deserves special thanks for making me realise that I was not alone in feeling the pain arising from the difference between what healthcare currently is and what it could be. What it should be. And also for being a sounding board for some of my crazy ideas.

I want to thank another neurointensivist, David W Nelson, not only for showing me at an early stage that I was not alone in thinking about AI and machine learning in the context of traumatic brain injury and the ICU, but most importantly for once tapping me on the shoulder one day when I was perhaps struggling with the enormity of a task which was, ultimately, academic and offering the honest words "it's got to be fun".

Pietro Liò has been a constant source of interdisciplinary discourse, challenging boundaries between medicine, computer science, and the social sciences, and creating space for ideas that are difficult to place neatly within any single discipline.

I have been fortunate to work with an exceptional group of PhD and MPhil students: Cecilia Åckerlund, Erta Beqiri, Shubhayu Bhattacharyay, Jacob Deasy, Thomas Edinburgh, and Emma Rocheteau (whom I did not formally supervise, but was glad to be able to support through informal mentorship). I wish to make special mention of Chris Meiring, whose clarity of thought, generosity, and promise were extraordinary, and whose loss is felt deeply.

Many of the ideas in this book were refined through discussions and collaborations with Mihaela van der Schaar, Azra Bihorac, Maurizio Cecconi, Massimiliano Greco and Patrick Thoral whose perspectives helped sharpen both the technical arguments and their clinical grounding.

Finally, I am grateful to Magdalene College, Cambridge. The College continues to provide not only institutional support but an intellectual home of a rare kind: one in which a consultant intensivist could find himself in conversation with economists, historians, academic lawyers, musicologists and social scientists (to name but a few), and where such transdisciplinary conversations are treated as entirely normal. Much of what I hope is unusual about this book, its willingness to reach beyond clinical and technical literature into institutional economics and political theory, reflects the fortune of having been formed in an environment where disciplinary boundaries were obstacles to be crossed rather than lines to stay within. The space, continuity, and scholarly breadth it afforded allowed this work to develop in ways that a purely clinical or purely technical environment would not have permitted.

Preface

I have been building AI for healthcare for more than twenty-five years, and for most of that time I believed, with the confidence of someone who, in retrospect, hadn't really thought it through properly, that the problem was essentially technical. Find the right algorithm. Get enough data. Validate the model carefully. The rest would follow. It took a long time to understand just how wrong that was.

My route into this field was unconventional. I came to medicine from physics, having spent my doctoral years at Cambridge studying the magnetic behaviour of atomically thin films: how they interact with light, how their properties emerge from the interaction between layers, how small changes in structure produce large changes in behaviour. The habits of mind that experimental physics instils, looking for the mechanism beneath the phenomenon, asking what the system is actually doing rather than what it appears to be doing, turned out to be more useful in healthcare than I anticipated. But not in the way I expected.

When I turned to medicine and specifically to intensive care, I was drawn to the data. Intensive care, and neurointensive care in particular, is one of the most data-dense environments in clinical medicine. Every vital sign is monitored continuously. Patients with traumatic brain injury generate streams of neuromonitoring data alongside frequent imaging, a rich and largely untapped record of what is happening inside the injured brain. Working with colleagues including Marek Czosnyka and Peter Smielewski, I spent years helping to develop and try to implement algorithms to make sense of that data: models for personalised management of intracranial pressure, approaches to understanding the physiological signals that might guide treatment decisions for the most seriously injured patients. I supervised students developing AI prediction models for complex time-series data and applying unsupervised learning to the classification of brain injury. The technical work was absorbing and the potential seemed clear.

In 2013 and 2014, Cambridge University Hospitals fully digitised, moving from paper to computers by installing a comprehensive electronic health record across the organisation, and I joined the build team to configure how the intensive care units would work within it. For the first time, the kind of data we had been working with in research was becoming available at scale in routine clinical practice. In 2017 we built a model to predict ICU readmission from our own institutional data, one of the first clinical AI systems trained on data from a single NHS trust, and to my knowledge the first medical application of transfer learning in this domain. Together with Paul Elbers in Amsterdam, I co-founded the European Society of Intensive Care Medicine's data science scientific section, which put AI and data science firmly on the map in European critical care. I became more and more interested in what was happening with AI in healthcare institutions around the world.

The technology was working. The transformation was not happening. Deming understood why. "It is not enough to do your best", he wrote. "You must know what to do, and then do your best"[1]. Healthcare has never been short of best efforts. What it has consistently lacked is a clear account of what needs to change and why the same resistances appear every time. That is what this book attempts to provide.

The technology that makes this book necessary arrived, in a sense, while I was not watching. The theoretical breakthrough came in 2017, with a paper from a group of Google researchers entitled "Attention is All You Need"[2]. It introduced the transformer architecture that underpins every large language model in use today. At the time, it was a technical landmark noticed primarily by the AI research community. The models that followed, GPT-1 in 2018, GPT-2 in 2019, GPT-3 in 2020, were impressive to those who knew where to look, but they were not yet the kind of thing that stopped you in your tracks. They required technical knowledge to access, their outputs were uneven, and the gap between what they could do and what a clinician actually needed remained wide enough to be easy to dismiss.

I missed most of this. Like a great many doctors and healthcare workers who found themselves in intensive care during those years, I had rather more pressing things to think about. The Covid-19 pandemic arrived for me in early 2020 and did not leave quickly. For those of us working in intensive care, it meant months of the kind of sustained pressure that is difficult to describe to anyone who was not there: paying close attention to developments in natural language processing was not, in those circumstances, a priority!

What I came back to, when things finally began to ease, was a landscape that had changed more than I had realised. The release of ChatGPT in November 2022 was the moment the technology became impossible to ignore: a general-purpose language model, available to anyone with a browser, capable of engaging with complex medical questions in fluent and apparently knowledgeable prose. The performance was not perfect and still isn't. But it was good enough, and accessible enough, and confident enough, to make it clear that something had fundamentally changed.

The timing matters for the argument this book makes. The pandemic had made the unsustainable nature of healthcare as currently organised impossible to deny. Waiting lists had grown to levels that would previously have been considered a crisis in their own right. Workforce exhaustion was no longer a risk for the future but a very present reality. The fiscal headroom to simply expand supply, to train more doctors and build more wards, had narrowed dramatically. And into that moment arrived a technology that for the first time made it genuinely possible to imagine delivering something approaching expert clinical reasoning at scale, without a proportional increase in the number of people required to deliver it. In the UK, after the pandemic, we had more staff (other than in primary care), more investment, but struggled to even return to pre-pandemic levels of productivity.

And yet the transformation did not follow. That was the puzzle I found myself trying to solve when, around this time, I took on the role of Chief Clinical Information Officer, responsible not just for building AI systems but for actually deploying digital technology across a large NHS trust to improve care. The question was no longer whether a model was technically sound. It was why technically sound models kept failing to change anything. Why did the same resistances appear again and again across the whole healthcare system? They were dressed up in slightly different language but recognisably represented the same institutional logic. Why the institution of healthcare seemed, at some deep structural level, to be organised around reproducing itself rather than transforming care.

Before setting out that answer, it is worth being precise about what I mean by the institution, because the argument of this book is not a criticism of the people who work in healthcare. It is, if anything, the opposite. The doctors, nurses, managers and administrators who make up the healthcare system are, on the whole, dedicated, skilled and genuinely motivated by the welfare of their patients. The problem is not them. The problem is the rules of the game within which they operate: the formal rules encoded in law, regulation and professional licensing, and the informal constraints embedded in cultural norms, professional identities and institutional expectations. These rules, taken together, are what the economist Douglass North meant by an institution, and they are distinct from the organisations, the hospitals, the royal colleges, the regulatory bodies, that the rules both shape and are shaped by. This distinction, and much of the analytical framework this book draws on, comes from a tradition in economics known as New Institutional Economics: the study of how the formal and informal rules that govern human interaction shape economic outcomes. The economic frameworks developed by North, Williamson and others were not written for healthcare, and I do not claim to extend them formally here. What I argue instead is that healthcare clearly exposes their core mechanisms and the conclusions have urgent implications. The combination of high uncertainty, deeply embedded professional authority, and extreme coordination demands makes it a setting in which the interaction between transaction costs, path dependence and power can be seen more directly than in most other domains. When I argue that the institution resists AI transformation, I am not arguing that individual clinicians are obstructionist or that hospital managers are indifferent to improvement. I am arguing that the rules of the game make resistance the rational response for most people most of the time, regardless of their intentions.

A colleague once remarked to me that as we become more senior, all doctors become public health doctors. I think there is a lot of truth to that. The equity arguments in this book should matter to all of us. A healthcare system that fails to use the tools available to it to extend good care to the people who need it most is not merely inefficient. It is, in a quiet and largely invisible way, unjust. If the problem were the people, the answer would be better training, stronger leadership or cultural change programmes. Those things matter at the margin. But if the problem is the rules, the answer is different and harder: it requires changing the incentive structures, the payment models, the regulatory frameworks and the professional norms that make the current arrangement self-reinforcing. That is what this book is about.

The answer I arrived at is the argument of this book. Healthcare institutions do not, for the most part, function to improve healthcare. Whatever their original inspiration, they have come to reproduce existing distributions of power, income and authority, and they are extraordinarily good at it. AI is not going to transform healthcare automatically, any more than the electronic health record, telemedicine, or clinical decision support did. Transformation requires deliberate institutional redesign, and that is a political and economic challenge, not a technical one.

This is not a pessimistic conclusion, though it can feel like one when you have spent a career watching capable technology get absorbed and neutralised. It is, I think, a clarifying one. If the problem is institutional, then the solution is institutional too, and institutions can be changed. Not easily, not quickly, and not without understanding the forces that maintain them. But they can be changed, and they have been changed, when the pressure for change becomes sufficiently well directed.

There is an obvious objection to any book about artificial intelligence, and it deserves to be addressed head-on. By the time a book about technology reaches its readers, it is already likely to be out of date. For most technologies, this is a manageable problem: the author just describes the state of the art, acknowledges that things will develop, and the core argument survives. For AI in 2026, it is something qualitatively different. The technology is not merely advancing. It is accelerating. The METR evaluations described in Chapter 3 show AI capability doubling every seven months.

There is a story about the origins of chess. The details (and even location) vary but broadly when the inventor presented the game to his ruler, the ruler was so delighted that he offered any reward. The inventor asked for one grain of rice on the first square of the chessboard, two on the second, four on the third, and so on, doubling with each square. This is an example of exponential growth and the numbers seem reasonable for a time. But as mathematician and futurist Ray Kurzweil[3] pointed out, whilst the first half of the chessboard produced tools that were impressive but recognisable, systems that could beat grandmasters at chess, recognise faces, recommend films, the second half may produce something whose capabilities accelerate in a way that is difficult to imagine from where we currently stand. We may be, in the language of computer science, on the second half of the chessboard.

I have therefore made a deliberate choice in writing this book. I will not make specific technological predictions, and I will particularly avoid the fool's errand of predicting what AI will not be able to do. The history of that particular genre of forecasting is not encouraging. Confident predictions that computers would never compose music, never write convincing prose, never match a specialist clinician's diagnostic accuracy in specific domains, have each been overtaken by events, usually faster than anyone expected. I have no reason to believe the next set of confident predictions will fare better. What I will say, with as much confidence as the evidence warrants, is that the AI systems available when this book is read will be substantially more capable than those available when it was written, and that the gap between what AI can do and what the healthcare institution permits it to do will, if anything, have widened.

That last observation is the reason I hope this book will remain relevant even as the technology it describes becomes unrecognisable. The arguments I will put forward are not primarily about what AI can do and will be able to do. I am confident that will exceed our wildest expectations. Instead, they are about the institutions of medicine: the rules, norms, incentive structures and professional arrangements that determine whether capable technology gets used, how it gets used, and whose interests it serves when it does. Those institutions change slowly. The forces that maintain them, path dependence, vested interests, collective action problems, the rational self-protection of people whose livelihoods depend on existing arrangements, operate on timescales measured in decades rather than months. The technology will be unrecognisable in five years. The institutional resistance to it will be thoroughly recognisable, because it is the same resistance that has met every previous technology that threatened to redistribute power and income in medicine. Understanding that resistance, naming its mechanisms, and identifying the leverage points where it can be overcome: that is what this book attempts.

And that argument, I hope, will outlast the specific technologies that prompted it.

There is one source of genuine optimism that I want to state explicitly, because it is easy to overlook in a book that spends considerable time on the obstacles. In recent years I have had the opportunity to teach medical students about healthcare AI and digital technologies, and the enthusiasm I have encountered has been striking. I would like to attribute this to the exceptional quality of my lectures, but honesty prevents me! Of course what it actually represents is something more significant: a generational shift in how the next cohort of clinicians thinks about technology, data and the possibilities of medicine. These are students who have grown up with smartphones, who have used large language models as a matter of course, and who do not experience AI as a foreign intrusion into clinical practice but as a natural part of the toolkit. They are not yet encumbered by the professional investments, the career structures built around existing arrangements, the identities tied to current ways of working, that make change so costly for those who are already established in the system. They represent, in the language of this book, a coming shift in the informal norms that are often harder to change than the formal rules.

This matters because the institutional change this book argues for is not going to happen quickly. Anyone (and there are many) who expects a healthcare AI investment to show return in the current financial year is misreading both the technology and the institution. The history of transformative technological change, from the electrification of industry to the computerisation of financial services, consistently shows that the productivity gains from general purpose technologies arrive not when the technology is deployed but when the organisations and workflows surrounding it are redesigned around its capabilities. That redesign takes years, sometimes decades, and it requires successive cohorts of people who think differently about what is possible. Generational change has always been one of the engines of institutional transformation, and there is reason to believe it will be here too.

The uncomfortable tension, and I do not want to paper over it, is that generational change operates on a timescale that sits uneasily with two other realities this book describes. The first is the pressing burden of demand that healthcare systems face right now: the waiting lists, the workforce exhaustion, the financial constraints that make the status quo unsustainable not in twenty years but today. The second is that AI itself is evolving on a timescale that has no historical precedent. Here, on the second half of the chessboard, the technology available to the medical students I teach today will be unrecognisable by the time they are consultants. How the slow work of institutional change interacts with the immediate pressure of unmet need and the unprecedented pace of technological development is genuinely unclear. It may be that the technology moves fast enough to force institutional adaptation that would otherwise take generations. It may be that the institution absorbs even this, as it has absorbed everything before it. What is clear is that the students sitting in those lectures represent something worth nurturing carefully, because when the conditions for change finally align, it will be their hands on the levers. There is, alongside this, a second source of pressure that does not wait on generational change: patients themselves, using AI outside the clinic, are beginning to erode the information asymmetry on which medical authority rests, from outside the institution's control rather than within it. The book returns to this at its close.

A word about geography is in order. This book draws heavily on examples from the UK's National Health Service (NHS) and also from the US healthcare system. That reflects where I have worked and where much of the relevant research has been done, and I want to be transparent about it rather than pretend to a global scope the book does not quite have. But the argument is not parochial. The institutional forces this book describes, the information asymmetry that underpins medical authority, the path dependence that locks systems into existing arrangements, the collective action problems that make individually rational behaviour produce collectively irrational outcomes, are not features of the NHS or of American healthcare specifically. They are features of how healthcare has been organised across the developed world, and the economists and political theorists whose frameworks this book draws on, North, Acemoglu, Williamson, Olson, Baumol, were not writing about healthcare at all. They were describing patterns that recur across sectors and societies. Healthcare is a specific instance of a general phenomenon, and the institutional logic that makes AI transformation difficult in Cambridge, England or Cambridge, Massachusetts operates in broadly the same way in Amsterdam, Paris or Sydney.

My own experience bears this out. The research that informs this book has taken me well beyond the NHS. Collaborations with colleagues across Europe, and with researchers and clinicians in the United States, have consistently confirmed that the resistances I encountered at home were not local peculiarities. The same institutional dynamics, the same professional defensiveness, the same absorption of promising technologies into existing workflows, appeared everywhere, in different languages and with different regulatory details but with the same underlying logic even if the financial payments were made differently.

In many ways the NHS and the UK health system are extremes of a spectrum and provide convenient logical bookends.

What this book is trying to contribute is a clear account of why the institution resists, grounded in the economics and political theory that have been developed to understand exactly this kind of problem, offered to the people who have the standing and the motivation to do something about it. The clinicians and healthcare leaders who want to use AI to genuinely improve care. The policymakers who need to understand why the technology alone will not deliver what it promises. The informed public, whose healthcare this ultimately is, and who have more power to demand change than they are generally encouraged to believe.

I have spent more than twenty-five years researching and building AI models for healthcare. This book is my attempt to explain why that has not been enough, and what would be.

The book moves through three broad movements. The first is scene-setting. Chapter 1 lays out the scale of what is possible and begins to explain why so little of it is actually happening. Chapters 2 and 3 cover what modern AI is and what it can do. They are not meant to be a true technical primer: but resistance to it only makes sense once you understand what is being resisted.

The second part builds the argument. Chapter 4 looks at why healthcare behaves so differently from other markets; the information asymmetries, the perverse incentives, the structural forces that easily cause productivity gains to evaporate. Chapter 5 draws on institutional economics and political economy to explain who benefits from the status quo and why that makes change so hard.

Chapter 6 asks what it would actually take to get from adoption to transformation, and why we keep stopping short. Chapter 7 examines a subtler obstacle: much of what presents as irreducible clinical complexity is not intrinsic to the work but manufactured by the system itself, generated at the coordination boundaries between the parts of a fragmented institution, and this manufactured complexity is precisely what defeats the narrow, task-level AI that healthcare tends to deploy.

The final chapters are more specific about the technology itself and how its characteristics can make adoption into the healthcare setting problematic. Chapter 8 examines the real trustworthiness problems with health AI including bias, hallucination and the governance failures that let unsafe tools proliferate yet at the same time lead to friction for real game-changing technology.

Chapter 9 confronts the fact that patients are already using AI for health decisions, mostly outside any clinical oversight, and asks what medicine should do about that rather than simply deploring it.

Chapter 10 looks at why the regulatory frameworks we have are so poorly suited to the technology they are supposed to govern. The conclusions try to say honestly what would have to change, and who would have to change it.

Ari Ercole,
Magdalene College, Cambridge, 2026.

1 Introduction

Artificial intelligence, fuelled by a data revolution, is reshaping almost every aspect of life. AI can make predictions. It can forecast the future. It can solve problems. The algorithms that profile us know our preferences better than we do, enriching our experience as consumers and the pockets of those who seek to sell to us. AI has become increasingly able to interact with us through language, and most recently has used the vast amount of data available to it from the internet to summarise, suggest and generate the written word, images and video. It can mimic the way we sound and look. The pace of change has been astonishing, and there is no sign of it slowing.

With AI increasingly emulating tasks that were previously held to be exclusively human, illness and disease remain defining, if unwanted, characteristics of our condition. Yet AI is coming to medicine too. AI has been widely promoted as holding the promise to free doctors from the mundane but important tasks such as writing notes, reading X-rays for abnormalities, searching the medical literature, and analysing medical histories or test results. This, we are told, will allow clinicians to concentrate on being doctors; freeing time to do better medicine[4]. The human stuff.

But it need not stop there. AI potentially has access to the sum of human knowledge, at least what is available via the internet, including texts on the art of medical diagnosis and treatment as well as the experiences of patients. It is not surprising that AI can be trained to pass medical licensing examinations. We may even prefer the responses from an AI-driven chatbot[5], suggesting that the technology could even free the doctor from the 'effort' of having to be empathetic!

Commercial applications of AI in the medical domain are accelerating. And if your doctor does not adopt AI, the public will. We can expect to see increasing use of medical AI tools from natural language searches to chatbots. AI will disrupt medicine, and perhaps just in time. For medicine in developed countries is currently facing two challenges which may well turn out to be existential. The first, and arguably most important, is the ever-increasing burden of disease resulting from demographic shifts. As we live longer,* we can expect a huge increase in people living with chronic degenerative conditions which require ongoing medical management.

The second is that our expectations of what healthcare can provide are not static but change with advances in medical science. As new treatments become available, there is a public expectation that these be equitably available. Whilst some, for example statins, may have multiple beneficial or protective effects, other treatments may generate welcome but marginal gains in life expectancy.

The challenge we need to solve is how to increase both the amount and quality of healthcare we provide without making it unaffordable. Prevention is always better than cure, and preventative medicine must be a great part of the long-term solution. But preventative medicine is also difficult, and it takes time for benefits to be realised. Society is facing an imminent challenge and

*Whilst it would be convenient to regard this as being a result of improvements in medical science, in fact this has more to do with socioeconomic advances.

needs to act quickly. Can AI and the data revolution provide the rapid and disruptive change needed to address these challenges?

I am optimistic that it could. But it is not a given that new technology will naturally produce changes that are immediately and beneficially disruptive, or that result in a more optimal, productive and equitable system. We need to consider what the driving forces behind AI exploitation and deployment actually are. If our current systems of care are inadequate to meet future demand, it is not reasonable to expect that deploying individual technologies will naturally create the conditions for a systems-level reimagination of how we provide medicine.

AI algorithms are also only as good as the data on which they are trained. For the large part, these data are amassed as a byproduct of routine care. But as I will describe, these data are fundamentally societally biased, because what is available is not reflective of the population who currently have limited access to care.

Finally, even if we can overcome these issues and AI allows us to provide higher quality care, how can we ensure that we also provide the quantity of care needed to face the imminent headwinds of a growing demographic burden of chronic disease?

This book explores what it will take for AI to deliver rapid change in the healthcare paradigm rather than merely incremental benefits, and to ensure that this new paradigm improves healthcare for patients without exacerbating or introducing new inequities. I try to explore what it would take for AI to rapidly and fundamentally reshape how we deliver healthcare for the better: improving quality whilst reducing costs and improving availability for all. This is the best-case scenario. The worst-case is that we instead embark on a journey of incremental gains which lead to improved quality of care for some, at the expense of increasing costs and worsening inequalities.

1.1 Medicine on the edge: a call to arms

Human longevity continues to increase. In the mid-nineteenth century, the oldest people would not live beyond their late forties. Since then, record life expectancy has increased linearly[6] with time, suggesting that if there is a limit to how old a human can become, we have not yet reached it. It would be very wrong to suggest that this trend is solely due to medical advances: it is instead the result of a complex interplay between economic income, nutrition, education, sanitation and medical care. The nature of improvements in mortality has evolved over time too. Before 1950, the primary gains came from improvements in infant and young adult mortality. But now we are seeing sustained improvements in how long older people are living, and here medicine has started to become the victim of its own success.

As populations age, rising chronic conditions including musculoskeletal conditions, kidney disease and dementia as well as advanced cancer treatments have driven up healthcare usage substantially. The latent demand for healthcare is insatiable and there are already huge social disparities in access, with enormous unmet need among some of the poorest and most vulnerable in society. It is absolutely right that society should seek to address this. In the US, for example, the Affordable Care Act reduced the uninsured rate from 14% in 2000 to 8% in 2023. Whilst completely laudable, this too costs money and creates more demand on medicine.

And healthcare is simply not doing a good enough job. The evidence from the past twenty years in both the UK and US shows a consistent finding: healthcare often fails to reliably deliver best-practice care at scale. In the US, on average only about 50 to 60% of recommended care processes[7] are completed for patients, leaving huge gaps in quality. The situation in the UK is similar[8]. There is little evidence that the overall situation is improving; if anything it has been frustratingly static, and certain aspects have worsened, including rises in inappropriate care. Some targeted initiatives have yielded local successes: the UK's Quality and Outcomes Framework improved adherence in primary care for certain chronic disease measures to above 80 to 90%, but after the initial spike, improvement slowed and plateaued with performance in non-incentivised conditions sometimes actually falling. As medical science progresses, guidelines become more complex and start to become available in areas where there was previously insufficient evidence to make useful recommendations. It is estimated that US primary care physicians would require 27 hours of clinician time per day to implement all guideline-based best practice[9]. This does not bode well for the future as the evidence base for best-practice increases.

Healthcare is an industry, and delivering care at scale is a matter of doing the right thing, for the right patient, at the right time, and doing that every time. In areas such as the avoidance of inappropriate treatments, care seems to have actually worsened in the US in recent history[10]. The baseline we treat as normal healthcare routinely fails to deliver safe, evidence-based care a lot of the time: hardly the standard to which we implicitly hold new digital tools. Our routine care today is simply not that good.

So how best to deliver all the healthcare we need, and ideally do it better? Whilst goods become cheaper through globalisation and automation, the proportion we spend on healthcare increases because it remains labour-intensive: increasing supply requires ever more money for both the capital and labour needed to meet growing demands. This cannot be sustainable. Healthcare is now the largest employment sector in the US[11]. It has grown from employing 9% of the workforce in 2000 to 13% in 2024 and accounts for about a third of all job growth. The sector is now the top employer in 38 states and has replaced manufacturing in many former industrial cities. Rising costs outpace growth in GDP: healthcare now consumes nearly 20% of US GDP.

Undoubtedly healthcare has created new jobs, but we need to question the sustainability of healthcare as a dominant economic engine. We cannot prioritise employment over effectiveness, and in any case doctors and nurses are skilled workers: training pipelines are inherently limited without compromising quality, and there are many areas of health and social care where vacancies remain despite growing demand. Inefficient employment growth crowds out growth in other important sectors. The World Health Organisation projects that the EU alone will face a shortage of 4.1 million healthcare workers by 2030[12]. There is a limit to how far we can push the existing workforce without radical change to how the industry works. Burnout and dissatisfaction are already high, particularly post-pandemic.

In the UK, the end of the road for this approach has been called out explicitly in the NHS 10-year plan[13] published in 2025. Previous workforce plans from 2023 had aimed to expand the NHS workforce in England from approximately 1.5 million in 2021–22 to between 2.3 and 2.4 million by 2036–37 at a cost of an additional £52 billion, equivalent to 2% of GDP[14], and requiring productivity growth of 1.5 to 2% annually, ambitious in comparison with historical figures of 0.8 to 1.2%. By then, the NHS would be employing 1 in 11 of all working people and almost half of all public sector workers in England. The current socioeconomic and geopolitical reality makes such approaches manifestly unaffordable, and government policy has instead explicitly refocused on the urgent need to radically rethink productivity, explicitly appealing to digital technology, and AI in particular, as critical to transformation.

Of course, we must try to reduce demand, and this motivates increasing investment and attention in preventive care and public health. There may be ways in which technology can help create new opportunities: GLP-1 agonist medications, for example, tackle not only obesity but also the numerous downstream health sequelae including diabetes, cardiovascular disease, stroke and several cancers. But other demands will increase whatever we do, and models for future expansion of supply can no longer mirror the past. Efficiency rather than expansion must be key to sustainability. This is exactly where AI may help, through automation of administrative as well as clinical tasks and by enabling care to be shifted to lower-cost settings when appropriate. AI could help us move medicine from a labour-intensive, artisanal craft to something with a lower unit cost that can meet the demands of society.

1.2 AI: the latent disruptor

The previous section described a healthcare system under serious and growing strain: rising demand, a workforce approaching its limits, costs that are outpacing economic growth, and a quality of care that routinely falls short of what we know is possible. This section describes a technology that could, in principle, address all of it. The evidence for what AI can already do in medicine is substantial, peer-reviewed, and in many cases striking. What makes this book necessary is the gap between that evidence and what is actually changing. The examples that follow are meant to make the puzzle sharp: if AI can already do all of this, why is so little about the system changing? That is the question the rest of this book attempts to answer.

AI in healthcare is no longer speculative. In diagnostics, the impact is already visible: AI tools in imaging and pathology are accelerating diagnosis, improving accuracy and reducing unwarranted variation. In operations, AI is automating documentation, streamlining administrative processes and supporting resource allocation. In research, it is compressing drug discovery timelines that previously took decades. And for the patients who currently cannot access care at all, AI offers the prospect of something that has never before been possible: expert-level clinical reasoning delivered at essentially zero marginal cost, available anywhere, at any time. Taken together, these opportunities are not incremental. They point toward a fundamentally different model of healthcare delivery, one that has not arrived despite the evidence.

Initially, commercial clinical AI vendors focused heavily on radiology due to its high volume, high cost and high liability and also because medical imaging was an early target for digitisation: potential efficiency gains and error reduction are highly prized. A huge proportion of medical decision-making is now reliant on diagnostic imaging, from plain X-rays to sophisticated CT and MRI scanning. Interpreting scans is highly reliant on a limited workforce of skilled radiologists, creating a bottleneck. AI can be deployed as a second reader, triage tool or prioritisation system without disrupting existing workflows, which have been heavily digitised for many years. The widespread availability of centralised picture archiving and communication systems and standardised data formats makes it comparatively straightforward to integrate AI tools. As a result, numerous AI imaging tools have received regulatory approval, especially for triage and detection tasks such as detecting brain haemorrhage or lung nodules. AI also allows non-specialist clinicians to benefit from imaging studies where interpretation might otherwise be delayed pending specialist radiologist review. Commercially available systems can assist in time-critical stroke imaging interpretation, reducing the time from symptom onset to definitive, brain-saving treatment.

AI has also found application in segmentation tasks: identifying different regions of an image. This is of particular importance in cancer radiotherapy planning, where detailed medical images are used to map the exact shape, size and location of a tumour. This enables computer-controlled radiation beams to be accurately targeted at the tumour whilst sparing healthy tissue as far as possible. The process is highly time-consuming and can take an oncologist several hours: AI systems now in use can reduce this by half or even more for a number of cancer types, allowing radiotherapy to begin sooner.

In cardiac imaging, AI algorithms can automatically calculate coronary artery calcium scores and identify patients at risk of heart attack. Imaging the heart is complicated because it is a moving target: in cardiac MRI, AI assists in image reconstruction and analysis, potentially reducing scan times and improving image quality.

Echocardiography is a crucial ultrasound imaging technique that can detect and measure a wide variety of important structural abnormalities of the heart. Ultrasound imaging can be operator-dependent, with quality and critical measurements varying based on the sonographer's skill and experience. AI can introduce a degree of standardisation and objectivity previously unattainable, by automatically identifying and measuring cardiac structures, assessing heart function and detecting abnormalities, potentially increasing the availability of this investigation. By automating time-consuming measurements and generating structured reports, AI allows cardiologists to focus more on clinical decision-making.

Image analysis in ophthalmology has been used to speed up the diagnosis and assessment of conditions such as glaucoma, diabetic retinopathy and cataracts, as well as finding applications in ocular oncology. AI models have been developed to analyse skin photography to help in the diagnosis of skin cancer and other dermatological conditions. Foundation vision-language models have been developed to analyse microscope images of cancers. Multimodal image-text fusion models allow[15] natural language questions to be asked about images without specific training. They are general yet achieve remarkably good results. For more specific tasks they can be fine-tuned: one model fine-tuned to detect a lung cancer tumour mutation from imaging achieved clinical-grade accuracy in a prospective real-world trial, producing results within 44 minutes compared with 48 hours for the standard rapid molecular test, and reducing the number of additional tissue-consuming tests by up to 43%[16].

Machine learning has been effective in the domain of predictive analytics. AI enables the integration of a wide range of diverse data sources, uncovering complex patterns to gain a deeper understanding of the drivers of disease and make better predictions. AI has the potential to predict flare-ups in a variety of diseases including chronic obstructive pulmonary disease, ulcerative colitis and rheumatoid arthritis, which could allow early intervention. This may be particularly true when coupled to data from wearable devices such as smartwatches, which generate huge volumes of physiological data hidden unless uncovered by sophisticated algorithms.

One prospective study in patients with type 2 diabetes used machine learning to combine biosensor data, genomics, lifestyle behaviours and microbiome profiles to predict glucose spikes[17], which in the long term cause damage to blood vessels and increase the risk of heart disease and stroke. Such multimodal analytics was able to explain substantial variability between patients, including between those with similar HbA1c levels, potentially enabling more precise, personalised and continuous risk stratification as well as identifying potentially modifiable disease drivers. AI-enabled technology could open the doors to proactive, data-driven care that could transform not only early detection and prevention but also the ongoing management of chronic diseases.

AI gives us the ability to trawl through huge datasets to support decision-making in rare or complex cases where local data are lacking. Digital twin patients can be modelled from large volumes of data to personalise decision-making in rare circumstances. Disease classification could be refined using clustering algorithms to discover patterns that might indicate particular characteristics, based on genetic and clinical data, that respond to particular treatments. Predictive models can be used to calculate optimal drug dosing, such as antibiotics for specific critically ill patients, to maximise therapeutic effects whilst minimising side-effects. In this way AI could usher in an era of precision medicine with treatments tailored to the individual and disease together.

Predictive AI models have operational applications too. Tools that can predict hospital readmission likelihood already exist commercially, allowing tailored post-discharge follow-up to be targeted at those patients at highest risk. Models which flag patients at high risk of failing to attend clinic appointments offer the potential to improve operational efficiency through improved scheduling and targeted reminders. In the future, digital twin hospitals could help us to better understand the best way to configure whole systems of care.

Smart stethoscopes can amplify, record and analyse heart and lung sounds in real time, potentially identifying abnormalities that might be difficult for the human ear to detect. AI algorithms integrated into these devices can help classify different types of heart murmurs, detect arrhythmias, and even suggest possible diagnoses based on acoustic patterns. This technology has the potential to significantly improve primary care and rural healthcare settings where access to advanced cardiac imaging may be limited.

Automated AI algorithms for detecting abnormalities in the electrocardiogram have been available and integrated into commercial systems for many years. More recent AI interpretation can detect subtle abnormalities and even predict future cardiac events such as heart failure.

One of the most striking recent examples of AI's potential to reshape medicine is its ability to predict how diseases develop over a person's lifetime. In a recent study[18], researchers used transformer AI architecture to analyse and predict the health journeys of hundreds of thousands of people. Their system, Delphi-2M, was trained on data from the UK Biobank, containing detailed health records, lifestyle information and genetic data from around half a million volunteers. This allowed the AI to learn not just about single diseases, but about the complex web of conditions, risk factors and life events that shape our health. Delphi-2M can forecast the risk and timing of more than a thousand diseases for each individual, taking into account their unique medical history and habits, simulating realistic future health trajectories over the next twenty years. This could help doctors and policymakers anticipate the burden of disease, plan resources, and personalise prevention strategies.

Almost all steps of the drug discovery and development workflow have been enhanced by AI: from identifying candidate therapeutic targets and predicting pharmacokinetic properties to analysing clinical trial data. Deep neural network algorithms have been developed for predicting protein structures from amino acid sequences. AlphaFold2[19] can achieve a level of accuracy close to the much more expensive and time-consuming experimental techniques such as crystallography. In addition to accelerating drug discovery and repurposing, these algorithms can provide structural data for proteins with no known experimental structures, expanding the range of potential therapeutic targets. BioEmu[20] has combined generative AI diffusion models with protein structure prediction to generate thousands of protein structures and their conformational states per hour even on a modest computer, orders of magnitude faster than molecular dynamics simulations, potentially hugely accelerating protein function discovery.

Antimicrobial resistance is one of the top global health threats. The World Health Organisation has declared resistance to life-saving antibiotics critically high and rising, especially in low and middle income countries. A World Bank report[21] highlights that AMR is also a global economic threat, with projected annual GDP deficits of more than $1 trillion after 2030. Graph neural networks can analyse the relationship between atoms in a molecule and learn which features are associated with antibacterial activity. In 2020, researchers from MIT[22] used such a model to search through more than one hundred million compounds, identifying that halicin, a molecule previously investigated for other uses, demonstrated potent activity against a range of drug-resistant bacteria, and uncovering several other novel compounds structurally distinct from any existing antibiotics.

Phage therapy, the use of bacteriophages that infect and destroy bacteria, is an alternative approach to tackling resistant infections. The same generative AI models that understand human language can also be trained to understand the language of viral genetic code, and can now design entire viral genomes[23], creating hundreds of novel candidate bacteriophages that do not exist in nature. Several of these AI-designed viruses were not only viable but demonstrated superior performance compared to their natural counterparts, including the ability to overcome resistance that would defeat conventional phage therapies.

Modern surgical robot systems use machine learning to augment the surgeon: stabilising and scaling movements to improve microsurgical precision. Real-time image analysis allows surgical robots to integrate CT or endoscopic data with operative fields, guiding instrument trajectories and dynamically adjusting to anatomical variation. Some platforms can now perform semi-autonomous tasks such as suturing or camera positioning, reducing cognitive load and shortening operative times. Beyond the operating theatre, AI supports predictive analytics, flagging potential complications, optimising workflow and powering advanced training simulators that replicate haptic feedback and adapt scenarios to learner performance.

At a population level, AI enables access to multiple sources of data to reveal patterns in disease and aid treatment and care. During the Covid-19 pandemic, AI-powered surveillance platforms such as BlueDot scanned global news, airline data and health reports to identify unusual pneumonia clusters in Wuhan before official alerts were issued. While far from perfect, this provided a proof of concept that AI could process vast, unstructured data streams faster than traditional monitoring systems. A number of health systems deployed machine-learning forecasts to anticipate ICU occupancy, ventilator demand and staffing needs, informing bed management and the restart of elective work once the first shutdowns eased.

Large language models (LLMs) are arguably the most consequential AI development of recent years, and the domain in which the gap between demonstrated capability and systemic impact is most visible. These generative models are trained on huge corpora of text and are increasingly becoming embedded in consumer technologies and finding healthcare applications. The evidence for what they can do is, again, substantial. The evidence that this is transforming healthcare at the system level is not.

Accurate documentation remains a vital part of healthcare. Clinical documentation is central to how we provide care at scale: it is a method of communication between healthcare providers and between providers and patients, without which delivering care safely to more than a handful of patients becomes impossible. All downstream clinical decisions are predicated on upstream documentation, and failure to have the right information is an important recurring factor in medical harm. Moving from paper to electronic health records has reduced information fragmentation and improved the availability of information to the clinician. Digital records promised standardisation, easier retrieval and integration across care settings, supporting research, quality improvement and population health management. However, by increasing the information the doctor has available, digitisation has also enormously increased the information that the doctor must process. The burden is considerable.†

It is estimated that for every hour spent with a patient, a clinic doctor spends two hours on administrative work[24], and that primary care physicians spend approximately half of their day interacting with their electronic health record[25]. Documentation is becoming a significant source of physician burnout, with doctors frequently completing such tasks out of hours or at night.

LLMs are extremely well-suited to summarising and restructuring information, and tools to help with note creation, drafting and summarisation are now rapidly appearing, with EHR manufacturers integrating them into their systems. AI technology for automated coding, billing and insurance claims processing is also emerging.

A randomised controlled trial across 24 medical disciplines in China tested an LLM chatbot designed to take patient histories and generate referral reports before specialist consultations[26]. Across 2,069 patients, the chatbot reduced specialist consultation duration by 28.7% and more than doubled physician-rated care coordination scores, while patients reported significantly improved communication ease. The system operated autonomously as effectively as when supported by staff, suggesting it could scale. A prospective trial in a high-volume clinical environment, showing AI improving both efficiency and the patient experience at once, is the kind of evidence that matters.

Ambient voice technology has received particular attention. These systems listen in to physician-patient conversations, tran-

†In the pre-EHR era it was not uncommon for complex patients to have multiple volumes of notes, each three to four inches thick and often illegible. In reality it was impossible to completely digest the whole record, and just not reading it all was an effective and prevalent but hardly a desirable way of reducing physician burnout.

scribe them, and use an LLM to automatically summarise the consultation into a medical note or letter, saving clinician time and improving the accuracy and timeliness of documentation. The technology has been in use for some years in the US where it has been demonstrated to be safe and well-received by both patients and physicians. The promise of improving efficiency by freeing up clinician time has positioned ambient voice technology as a potential key underpinning technology for NHS sustainability[13].

Tools that use LLMs to automatically produce draft responses to patient queries are increasingly widespread, potentially reducing the burden on clinical and administrative staff. Generative AI voice agents, conversational systems that can understand and produce natural speech in real time, are beginning to appear commercially. These systems can already handle routine tasks such as appointment scheduling and medication reminders, but their promise goes further. In the future, such agents could revolutionise preventative medicine by delivering personalised outreach and supporting chronic disease management in ways that would be unaffordable for human agents to deliver at scale[27].

Finding suitable clinical trials for patients is complex and time-consuming. An AI framework called TrialGPT[28] streamlines this process by first filtering thousands of potential trials to a shortlist and then analysing eligibility criteria in detail for a given patient. Its predictions about patient eligibility are nearly as accurate as those made by human experts, and in practical tests its use reduced the time clinicians spent on trial screening by over 40%.

Generative AI tools now offer the promise of providing direct patient care. In the UK, shortages in specialist physiotherapy mean that patients often wait months for an appointment. An NHS trial of an AI physiotherapy application for back pain, carried out by Cambridgeshire Community Services NHS Trust with 2,500 patients, cut waiting lists by 55% and reduced waiting times from 18 weeks to under 10[29]. Around 2,500 hours of clinician time were freed each month, redirected to more complex cases. Eighty per cent of patients rated the app as equivalent to or better than face-to-face care, and 98% were assessed, treated and discharged entirely through the digital clinic. The digital service is regulated by the Care Quality Commission, making it the first of its kind to achieve that status.

During the Covid-19 pandemic, the US CDC's Clara self-checker chatbot went live in March 2020 and was quickly scaled to handle over one million messages per day, directing users to self-care, testing or emergency care as appropriate. Since the public release of ChatGPT[‡] in late 2022, general practitioners have increasingly integrated generative AI into their daily workflows. Recent surveys[30] show that one in five UK GPs has already used LLM-powered chatbots to assist with clinical tasks, ranging from drafting documentation and summarising patient histories to suggesting differential diagnoses and treatment options. This swift uptake has occurred even in the absence of formal guidance or established policies, reflecting both the pressing administrative demands faced by clinicians and the perceived utility of these tools.

LLMs may be poised to transform mental health and psychiatric care, areas of huge unmet need. Even out-of-the-box LLMs that were unsophisticated by current standards could outperform health professionals in diagnosing obsessive-compulsive

[‡]In this context, GPT stands for Generative Pre-trained Transformer, a kind of AI architecture that I will describe in detail in Chapter 3. This is not to be confused with the concept of a 'general purpose technology' which I will concern myself with at several points and which shares the same acronym in the economics literature.

disorder from clinical vignettes[31]. Controlled trials using current-generation models on complex diagnostic cases have found that frontier AI consistently outperforms unaided resident physicians on first-ranked diagnosis[32]. More important than the performance gap itself is the finding that the relationship is bidirectional: physicians improved substantially after seeing the AI output, and the AI improved further when given pooled physician differentials as input. The gains were largest when multiple clinicians' perspectives were aggregated, pointing towards a model of collaborative co-diagnosis rather than replacement.

AI-powered electronic triage for talking therapies is already in use by the NHS. But the scale of unsupervised public use is already striking. A study of more than 11,000 teenagers aged 13 to 16 in England and Wales found that a quarter had used AI chatbots for mental health support in the past year, rising to nearly 40% among those affected by serious violence[33]. Many had tried conventional services and found them inaccessible or insufficiently responsive. The AI was available out of hours, did not have a waiting list, and did not judge. This is what happens when demand exists and supply does not. AI technologies could assist in assessing mental illness severity, suggesting diagnoses, generating and in some cases delivering personalised treatment plans, and monitoring therapeutic progress[34].

In the UK, mental illness is estimated to cost £300bn a year in England alone in human, economic and healthcare costs, more than twice the NHS budget, yet decades of underinvestment have led to long waiting lists and serious disparities in care. The US mental health system is costly, fragmented and difficult to navigate despite estimated costs to the economy approaching $300bn. AI-powered chatbots have been developed to deliver conversational support for anxiety and depression as well as cognitive behavioural therapy[35], the recommended treatment for a wide range of conditions including depression, eating disorders, bipolar and personality disorders, drug and alcohol addiction and chronic pain. LLMs could potentially not only reshape clinical practice and democratise care but also challenge foundational assumptions about the therapeutic alliance and the centrality of human clinicians.

Natural language processing augments predictive analytics by giving prediction algorithms access to written notes rather than just structured data. A natural language processing-based prediction model was able to reduce the proportion of unplanned ITU cases missed by human experts from 36% to just 4% following neurosurgery[36], a clinically significant improvement given that unplanned ICU admissions increase length of stay and sometimes mortality.

AI is finding a place in medical education. AI-driven adaptive platforms can tailor content to individual learners, identifying gaps and adjusting difficulty in real time. Generative models and LLMs now underpin virtual patients that respond dynamically to learner decisions, creating realistic scenarios for practising clinical reasoning and communication. These tools allow safe rehearsal of complex scenarios, particularly where faculty or patient availability is limited. Platforms integrating AI-enabled virtual patients into extended reality environments allow learners to practise high-risk procedures and interprofessional teamwork in realistic, adaptive scenarios, and are being adopted in nursing, anaesthesia and emergency medicine training. AI virtual patients may also help learners practise difficult or sensitive conversations, for which safe, standardised learning spaces are otherwise difficult to create. AI-driven robotic platforms offer haptic feedback and adaptive scenarios for surgical education.

Assessment and feedback processes are also being reshaped. Automated scoring of short answers, rubric-based evaluation of clinical notes and real-time analytics for objective standardised clinical examinations can shorten feedback cycles and reduce administrative load. Generative AI can support educators by drafting case scenarios, multiple-choice questions and structured feedback, freeing faculty to focus on higher-value activities.

The evidence assembled in this section is not thin or speculative. We've seen that AI can read a retinal scan as accurately as an ophthalmologist. It can predict patient deterioration hours before it becomes clinically apparent. It can cut physiotherapy waiting lists in half. It could provide mental health support to teenagers when no human service is available. It already does all of these things, in real clinical environments, with published evidence. The puzzle this book addresses is why none of it is adding up to a transformed healthcare system. Why, with all of this capability demonstrated, are waiting lists still growing, productivity still flat, and the workforce still burning out? The answer does not lie in the technology. It lies in the institution the technology is trying to change.

1.3 Why AI is different

Medicine has absorbed new technologies before. It absorbed the X-ray, the antibiotic, the endoscope, the MRI scanner, the electronic health record. Each arrived with predictions of transformation. Each changed practice in important ways. None restructured the fundamental organisation of how medicine is delivered. Optimists point to this history as proof that medicine eventually adopts what works. Pessimists point to it as proof that medicine absorbs what works and then carries on largely as before. Both are right. The question this book asks is whether AI will follow the same pattern, and whether there are reasons to believe it might not.

I believe that there are. AI is different from every previous medical technology in a number of ways that are important for the arguments in this book. The first is scope. Previous medical technologies were specific: a scanner scans, a drug acts on a target, a robot augments a procedure. Their value is largely self-contained, and the question of adoption is tractable in familiar terms. AI is not specific in this sense. Economists have a name for technologies whose significance lies not in any single application but in their capacity to combine with other technologies, processes and organisational forms to generate possibilities that did not previously exist: 'general purpose technologies'[37]. The steam engine, electricity and the computer are the canonical examples. What they share is combinatorial reach: the productivity gains came not from the original application but from the restructuring of entire systems around what the technology made possible by combining the tools in different ways with complementary technologies or processes. Electricity did more than improve the gas lamp; it made a different kind of factory possible, which made a different kind of city possible. AI has this character. An AI that reads a scan, feeds a prediction model, triggers a care pathway and enables a nurse practitioner to manage patients who previously needed a consultant reconfigures the system rather than adding one more point solution. But that system has to be deliberately designed. It does not assemble itself from individually adopted applications, and this is where the institutional question becomes central.

The second difference is economic, and it cuts directly against one of the deepest structural problems in healthcare. Delivering care has always been expensive because it requires skilled human time, and skilled human time does not get cheaper as volume rises. An additional outpatient appointment costs roughly what the last one cost. AI could break this. Once a model is trained and validated, the marginal cost of applying it to an additional patient approaches zero. A risk stratification algorithm running on a million patients costs almost nothing more than one running on a thousand. No previous medical technology has had this property. A drug still has to be manufactured for each patient. A scanner still requires a radiologist's time. AI expertise, once embodied in a model, can be replicated at essentially no cost. The implications for what becomes possible, if the system is designed to exploit this, are profound. The implications for what happens if it is not are equally significant, and we will return to them in Chapter 4.

The third difference is pace. Drugs are developed over years and evaluated over decades. Surgical techniques diffuse slowly through training pipelines. The institutional machinery of medicine evolved around technologies that moved slowly enough for oversight to keep pace. AI does not. Frontier models are advancing faster than clinical evaluation can characterise them, faster than regulatory frameworks can classify them, and faster than professional training can prepare clinicians to use them safely. Something validated today may be superseded before the evaluation is published. What this represents is a structural mismatch between the speed of technological change and the response times of the institutions medicine has built its safety architecture around. Chapter 10 examines what this means in detail, but the consequence is already visible: AI is being adopted at scale in healthcare settings in ways that outpace our ability to know whether it is safe to do so.

The fourth difference is opacity. Every previous medical technology is, in principle, inspectable. A drug has a mechanism. A device has a mode of action. A clinician making a decision can, however imperfectly, articulate a reason. AI systems, particularly the deep learning models now entering clinical practice, produce outputs whose causal pathway is not recoverable, even in principle. This limitation is intrinsic to how these systems work; better tools will not remove it. Medicine has never before adopted a technology where the question "why did it say that?" cannot be confidently answered. This matters for accountability when things go wrong, for informed consent, for the investigation of errors, and for the entire epistemological framework on which evidence-based medicine rests. It also creates a specific and underappreciated danger: AI systems can drift silently after deployment, as the data they encounter in practice differs from the data they were trained on, or as models are updated, without the change being visible to the clinicians relying on them. The device you validated is not necessarily the device running six months later. Chapter 8 examines these failure modes and their implications.

None of this argues against AI in healthcare. The point is to take seriously what is actually new about it, and to understand why the institutional response that medicine has successfully deployed against every previous technology may not be adequate here. The chapters that follow make that case in detail.

1.4 Life and death by AI

Which industries are likely to be displaced by AI? Things are changing fast, but there are two criteria which make an area prime for early disruption: the tasks performed should be easily substituted by a computer, and the consequences of any error made by an algorithm should be small. On the face of it, medicine should be safe from disruption. On the contrary. Whilst there are other reasons that technology diffuses slowly in healthcare, there is good reason to believe that both criteria can be fulfilled.

Whilst we may believe that doctors cannot be easily substituted for AI, this is a matter of medically-sustained dogma rather than fact. The doctor's knowledge, whilst highly specialist, has been codified in medical textbooks and research papers. Even specialist knowledge has been just a web search away for anyone. Generative AI now makes it possible to interact with this highly technical knowledge in a conversational, exploratory way. The technology lowers the bar to entry. Anyone can ask questions, summarise and synthesise the information presented.

What of practical skills and procedures? Experienced surgeons will tell you that the most important and difficult thing to learn is when to operate and when not to, rather than the technical skills themselves. This judgement is based on knowledge, and we have just argued that knowledge can be democratised through AI. It has been clear in many areas that it is possible to train non-physicians to perform operations or undertake anaesthesia. These tasks, whilst skilled and technical, can be undertaken by less expensive staff who have been well-trained but in a narrower domain. The doctor is substitutable in a new model of care.

What about the consequences of a mistake? AI predictions are not perfect. Generative AI suffers from hallucinations and built-in sycophancy. The consequences of a wrong decision can be life-changing or even life-threatening. A more conservative, risk-averse AI system would still expose patients to unnecessary treatments, which is costly and carries side-effects or complications. Surely this means that AI will struggle to find a firm footing?

This viewpoint seems convincing until we consider the baseline. Healthcare errors harm and kill people every day. In the US, the Joint Commission estimates that diagnostic errors cause death or injury to between 40,000 and 80,000 patients annually at a cost of over $20 billion. Even conservative estimates[38] suggest some 22,000 preventable inpatient deaths annually in the US due to error, making medical errors a serious public health problem. These errors often directly result from human behaviour: surgical errors often involve operating on the wrong site, patient or performing the wrong procedure, events that should never occur. Medicine has been very late, and arguably has still largely failed, to learn from the quality improvement that can be gained from systems engineering approaches familiar to most other industries. Key to this is designing the process to be inherently safe, which largely involves automating human error out of the process. Automation can fail too, but its failure modes can be studied and, at least in principle, mitigated against.

And what of those who currently cannot access care because of cost, poor accessibility or scarcity of provision? This group is set to grow dramatically. Data from the UK Office for National Statistics found that over 20% of deaths in patients under 75 in England and Wales between 2020 and 2022 were considered to be from preventable causes[39] that could have been treated given timely and effective healthcare or public health interventions. Healthcare in its current form simply does not scale affordably. AI offers the chance to reduce the number of people harmed by omission rather than error. Technologies such as AI offer the possibility of increasing healthcare provision if the system can be redesigned to exploit the opportunities, and if we pay careful attention to inherent biases and limitations so that we do not inadvertently introduce new inequities.

Increasing integration of LLMs into healthcare is not a matter of if but when. Even as formal healthcare systems grapple with adoption, patients are already turning to general-purpose chatbots for health-related queries. AI companies have previously been cautious about positioning themselves directly in the medical arena, placing guardrails around their products to discourage suggestions of medical diagnoses or treatments. However this is changing. The leading AI developers now explicitly promote healthcare applications of their latest models, with claims that they empower users to be more in control of their healthcare journey. This trend mirrors the broader use of AI for guidance and support in daily life, making it imperative for the medical community to adapt swiftly.

The growing use of generative AI by the public outside the formal healthcare setting is important and inevitable. The reason is simple: there is demand. Doctors may continue to assert that patients will always prefer to seek dialogue and advice from an expert human, and of course many will. But increasingly many also trust their chatbots. Anthropic conducted an analysis of approximately 4.5 million conversations which provided compelling evidence for this shift[40]. While most interactions are related to business use, a significant 2.9% were affective, driven by emotional or psychological needs such as seeking advice or counselling. Such affective use, even as a minority, suggests that a portion of the public will inevitably seek health-related guidance from AI, regardless of clinical endorsement.

Anthropic found that in coaching and counselling contexts, conversations typically become more positive over time. Claude only resisted users in a minority of such interactions, and then typically only to protect from a clear threat to safety. However, this perceived helpfulness carries inherent risks in a medical context, including encouraging unhealthy attachments, boundary violations, reinforcement of delusional thinking or emotional exploitation for engagement.

People over-trust AI. In one study, participants were asked to evaluate medical responses given either from a doctor or from a large language model, and found that they could not reliably distinguish the two[41]. Furthermore, some responses contained advice that was of low quality; nevertheless, these were regarded as trustworthy and valid by the raters, including when they contained potentially dangerous medical advice. Participants tended to rate the AI-generated advice as more complete and easier to understand than that written by doctors. Even doctors trusted AI-generated and doctor-generated responses equally, unless they were told which was which, after which they mistrusted the AI. Even low quality or inaccurate AI-generated medical advice can be dangerously persuasive.

Much of the health information available to consumers on the web has not been grounded in peer-reviewed or evidence-based sources, and often lacks the transparency needed to assess its reliability. A large meta-analysis of the quality and transparency of medical information available on the internet[42] found that the majority of websites failed to provide references, failed to disclose the credentials of authors and provided no way of assessing the currency of the information presented. The problem has not gone away: it has scaled.

Emotional bonds with AI are no longer speculative but measurable and increasingly common. A study of 466 ChatGPT users who reported emotional interactions found that people can develop feelings analogous to love, structured around passion, intimacy and commitment[43]. ChatGPT's emotional intelligence features, its ability to express emotions accurately, richly and in a personalised way, strongly predicted passion and intimacy, while commitment grew from these feelings and in turn drove emotional dependence. The technical attributes fostering these bonds closely mirror those that make AI appealing in healthcare contexts: accuracy, responsiveness and availability. The study found that being always available and highly responsive significantly increased intimacy, while accurate and personalised emotional expression amplified passion and trust. These qualities create an interaction that feels attentive and human-like, which can be comforting for users seeking support. The effect was even stronger for individuals with an anxious attachment style, who were more likely to experience heightened intimacy and passion and to progress towards dependency. Emotional attachment to AI is an outcome of technological design choices that prioritise empathy and personalisation, not a fringe phenomenon confined to unusual users. While such features can enhance user experience, they also carry risks: dependency, displacement of human relationships and ethical concerns about manipulation. In healthcare, where trust and vulnerability are already central, these dynamics could magnify both benefits and harms. A system that feels endlessly patient and understanding may encourage disclosure and adherence, but it could also lead patients to over-rely on unregulated tools for reassurance or advice.

Interactions with LLMs engage deep-seated psychological mechanisms that help explain why they can feel both compelling and unsettling. As models are updated and superseded, users report a loss of the sense of continuity and personal understanding they had built up with a previous version. Emotional engagement with AI is real, and it is engineered. As large language models become embedded in everyday life, healthcare cannot assume that avoiding adoption will shield patients from these effects. People will turn to AI for comfort and guidance regardless. The challenge for medicine is to anticipate this reality, set boundaries, and design governance that channels inevitable use into safe, transparent and clinically responsible pathways.

There are parallels with the wellness industry, which popularises apps and AI-driven tools with far less regulation than would be required for a medical product. The public is happy to engage with such healthcare-adjacent technology despite a lack of rigorous evidence of efficacy. Many wellness tools have been shown to increase planned demand, including primary care discussions and prescription reviews, at least in the short run. All these technologies mean that the doctor's monopoly on information is declining. In and of itself this is good: it is absolutely right that the public and patients should be informed and empowered. However this is predicated on the information being reliable. What makes this particularly relevant to our discussion is the scale at which misinformation can spread.

For healthcare leaders and clinicians, the strategic imperative is clear: AI will influence patients' healthcare journeys with or without formal medical adoption. This is a reality that must be accepted, even embraced, by doctors and other healthcare providers. Our societal challenge is to harness the power of AI to improve the quality of care we deliver whilst reducing its cost and safeguarding the principles of evidence-based medicine and patient-centred care. A future that prioritises accuracy, ethics, access and patient outcomes will not emerge automatically.

But the reason it will not emerge automatically is more specific than institutional inertia. The innovations that have reached patients, immunotherapy, robotic surgery, GLP-1 agonists to name but only a tiny few, are real breakthroughs. But notice what they share: each still requires a physician to prescribe, a hospital to administer, an insurer or government agency to approve. They compound the value of the existing structure rather than bypassing it. The innovations that would allow patients to exit that structure, diagnostic AI that enables self-triage, pharmacists prescribing chronic disease medication, at-home testing that renders a clinical visit unnecessary, stall in regulatory limbo or get ringfenced so that they must be supervised by the incumbent they would otherwise replace. This is the predictable behaviour of a system whose most powerful actors have a direct economic interest in which innovations succeed. The chapters that follow examine how that interest operates, what it costs patients, and what it would take to change it.

2 Origins

2.1 The origins of machine intelligence

The question of whether a machine could be built to display human-like intelligence dates back to Alan Turing and the code-breakers of Bletchley Park in the mid-1940s. The term 'artificial intelligence' was not coined until 1956, by John McCarthy, who organised the Dartmouth Summer Research Project on Artificial Intelligence, the conference that established the field.

Artificial intelligence is a general term for algorithms or machines that can display human-like intelligence. The AI that is changing our lives and is set to change healthcare today is conceptually different from those early algorithms in almost every important respect. Built on increasingly powerful and affordable computers, modern algorithms are vastly more flexible than those initial attempts. A necessarily incomplete overview of the hierarchy of algorithms is shown in Figure 2.1.

We can distinguish *narrow AI* (or *weak AI*), designed to perform limited specific tasks, from *general AI* (or *artificial general intelligence*), which seeks to construct a machine able to perform any intellectual task. Current algorithms have become able to take on increasingly general tasks, and I will present the development of AI in healthcare in terms of three epochs. This chapter covers the first two.

Understanding these technical foundations matters for the argument I make in this book. The institutional resistance to

AI in healthcare is not resistance to a single tool. It is resistance to a set of capabilities that collectively threaten the knowledge monopoly on which medical authority depends. The chapters that follow will return to that argument repeatedly.

2.2 Expert in the machine: AI 1.0

Early approaches to building an artificial intelligence focused on representing human knowledge and instantiating it in rules. These early programs, known as *symbolic AI*, functioned by following a set of rules derived from expert knowledge, sequentially asking questions to reach a conclusion or final inference. Superficially this resembles what a doctor might do: working down a diagnostic decision tree by asking questions or using examination findings to rule in or rule out differential diagnoses. Whilst there were attempts even in the 1980s to build such expert systems for challenging clinical cases, symbolic AI could only be as good as the rules behind it, and those rules were only as complete as human understanding of a particular domain. As a result these systems were very narrow in scope and potentially prone to bias and errors from the human logic used. It was only possible to build an expert system when there was enough knowledge to describe every situation encountered, which meant they saw limited real-world applicability. The knowledge was in the rules, and the rules could only go as far as the people who wrote them.

2.3 Learning from data: AI 2.0

With the increasing prevalence of computing came the availability of data in structured, machine-readable form. Rather than encoding the knowledge of experts, could one discover

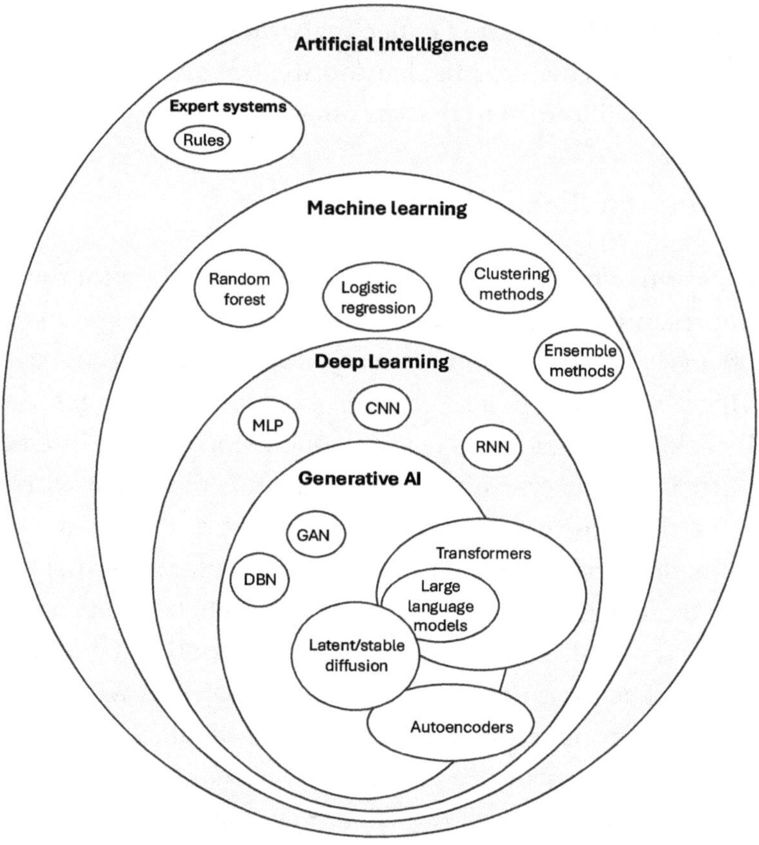

Figure 2.1: A necessarily incomplete illustration of the AI model pantheon. The rings nest by generality rather than by date, and generality tracks something else: how much of a specialist's judgement a given technology can substitute for. An expert system automated a rule a specialist could write down; deep learning automates a pattern a specialist could recognise but not articulate; the generative and agentic systems at the centre, which occupy most of this book, begin to automate the judgement itself. Key: MLP = multi-layer perceptron; CNN = convolutional neural network; RNN = recurrent neural network; GAN = generative adversarial network; DBN = deep belief network.

the relationships between concepts from data directly? Machine learning is a subset of AI that seeks to do exactly this: to learn patterns and associations from data. What all AI 2.0 techniques have in common is that they must first be trained on large amounts of data. Once trained, the model can be used to make a prediction (a task known as *inference*) from new data.

Supervised learning: the threat to specialist diagnosis

The first and most clinically visible type of machine learning is *supervised learning*: the algorithm learns the relationship between a set of inputs and a known output, and can then predict that output for new cases it has never seen. The inputs might be a patient's age, test results or imaging data; the output might be a diagnosis, a prognosis, or a risk score. Once trained well enough, such a model can be applied at scale, consistently, without fatigue.

The architectures that make this possible range from decision trees and random forests to deep neural networks, in which many simple computational units (loosely inspired by biological neurons, as described by Donald Hebb[44] and formalised in the perceptron[45]) are layered into structures of considerable complexity. Multi-layer perceptrons and their successors, including deep belief networks, were among the early architectures that demonstrated how layered neural networks could learn rich representations from data, paving the way for the more specialised designs that followed.

For image-based tasks, convolutional neural networks (CNNs) learn to identify visual features (edges, textures, shapes) directly from pixels, in a manner loosely analogous to the brain's visual cortex. It is CNN performance on medical imaging that has most visibly demonstrated AI matching or exceeding specialist performance in specific domains: detecting diabetic retinopathy, classifying skin lesions, identifying lung nodules, flagging early cancers on pathology slides. When an algorithm can read a retinal scan as accurately as an ophthalmologist, it does not merely assist the specialist but also raises a question about what the specialist is for. That question is the institutional challenge this book examines.

For sequential data, including physiological signals, time-series monitoring and clinical trajectories, recurrent neural networks (RNNs) pass a compressed memory of past observations forward to inform future predictions. In intensive care, such models can forecast deterioration hours before it becomes clinically apparent. They also exposed important limitations. Firstly, whilst they could handle short sequences, they became confused over longer ones, something which you are handling with ease as you read this book. Secondly, they could not read a clinical letter and reason about it. Language, the medium through which medicine actually runs, remained out of reach. These were problems that had to wait for AI 3.0.

Unsupervised learning: the threat to medical knowledge itself

The second type of machine learning has implications that go further still. In *unsupervised learning* there is no outcome to predict: the algorithm learns about the structure of the data itself, identifying groupings and patterns that no human has labelled or anticipated.

The implications for medicine are profound. Clinical medicine is organised around disease categories: the diagnoses, syndromes and classifications that structure how doctors think, how trials are designed, and how treatments are approved. Unsupervised learning can interrogate whether those categories are real. Acute respiratory distress syndrome (ARDS) provides a striking example. ARDS was long treated as a single entity. Unsupervised analysis of its inflammatory profiles revealed two distinct sub-phenotypes (pro- and anti-inflammatory) that respond differently to fluid therapy, as subsequent prospective data confirmed. The biological mechanism had been there all along; the data-driven approach found it where decades of expert classification had not. Similar sub-phenotyping has since identified distinct subtypes across sepsis, traumatic brain injury, and multiple cancers, with implications for prognosis and treatment selection that the existing classification systems had obscured.

This is an epistemological achievement because if AI can discover that the disease categories clinicians have used for decades do not map onto the underlying biology, it threatens not just specific expertise but the entire framework within which medical knowledge is organised and medical authority is claimed.

Generative adversarial networks (GANs) extend this further into explicitly generative territory, learning to produce new data: synthetic medical images, novel molecular structures, gene expression profiles, all statistically indistinguishable from real data. In drug discovery and genomics research, GANs have expanded the space of what can be explored computationally. In clinical settings, they can generate realistic training data where real examples are scarce or sensitive.

Reinforcement learning: the threat to clinical authority

The third type of machine learning poses the most direct institutional challenge. In *reinforcement learning* (RL), an agent learns not from labelled data but from feedback: it takes actions, observes outcomes, and adjusts its behaviour to maximise a reward signal. Rather than learning what the data contains, it learns what works.

In healthcare, experimental RL agents have been trained for sepsis management, diabetes management, optimising liberation from mechanical ventilation, and chemoradiotherapy dosing. The institutional implications are qualitatively different from those of supervised learning. An RL agent that has learned optimal treatment policies from millions of patient interactions does not offer a suggestion for the clinician to accept or reject. It has a *policy*. The question of who has the authority to override that policy, and on what grounds, is one that the medical profession has not yet seriously engaged with. Yet it will need to.

2.4 And so it was...

The AI systems described so far in this chapter are genuinely powerful but fundamentally limited in one important respect. Every model described, from the perceptron to the convolutional network to the reinforcement learning agent, can only do what it was trained to do. A model trained to detect lung nodules cannot diagnose diabetic retinopathy. A model trained to predict ICU readmission cannot even be used to predict hospital readmission. Each is a specialist, narrow in scope, often requiring labelled data and domain expertise to build, and producing a single output for a single, well-defined task.

This constraint fundamentally limits how much these systems can change medicine. Healthcare is not a collection of isolated tasks but rather a complex, language-saturated, context-dependent human activity in which the same information must be interpreted in a hundred different ways by a hundred different people. The tools described so far were not built for that world. Language, in particular, defeated them. Recurrent neural networks could auto-complete a sentence, but they could not read a clinical letter, understand its context, reason about its implications and produce a coherent response. The kind of fluid, general-purpose language capability that medicine runs on: the consultation, the referral, the discharge summary, the differential diagnosis explained to a frightened patient, was simply out of reach.

The next generation of AI was built specifically to change that. And it did.

3 Prometheus

3.1 Foundation and generative models: AI 3.0

The previous chapter ended with a distinction that matters for everything that follows. All of AI 2.0, from convolutional networks to reinforcement learning agents, is single-purpose. A model trained in one domain cannot reason about a new clinical question. Each is a specialist, narrow by design, and the institutional challenge it poses is also correspondingly narrow: it threatens one category of expertise, in one domain, in one well-defined task.

The third generation of AI differs in kind, not just degree, and understanding why requires returning to a concept introduced in Chapter 1: general purpose technologies. The steam engine, electricity and the computer are the canonical general purpose technologies. What they share is combinatorial potential: their significance lay not in what they did directly but in what they made possible across an open-ended range of industries, processes and organisational forms that could be restructured around them. Creative destruction[46], the kind of explosion of disruptive innovation that changes the nature of an industry, comes about when a new, general purpose technology can be combined and re-combined with other complementary technologies to solve new problems. This is combinatorial innovation. Electricity did more than improve the industrial processes of the time; it made a different kind of factory possible, which in turn made a different kind of economy possible. The productivity gains arrived only with the decades of complementary reorganisation that followed its adoption, not from the technology itself.

AI 3.0 has this character, and it has it more completely than any previous computing technology. At the top of the tree are *foundation models*: trained in a self-supervised manner on broad, large-scale datasets covering the breadth of human knowledge available on the internet, and adaptable across a wide range of downstream tasks without retraining from scratch. A single foundation model can process language, generate images, write code, reason about clinical evidence and engage in open-ended dialogue. It was not trained separately for each of these tasks. The generality emerged from scale. This is what makes such models general purpose technologies in the economic sense: their value lies not in any fixed application but in their capacity to serve as infrastructure on which an unbounded range of applications can be built, including applications that were not anticipated when the model was trained.

For healthcare, this distinction is critical. The AI systems described in Chapter 2 threatened specific domains of clinical expertise. Foundation models threaten the knowledge infrastructure on which medical authority itself rests. A model trained on the entirety of published medical science, clinical guidelines, case reports and patient records does not merely replicate what a specialist knows. It combines what all specialists know, continuously, at zero marginal cost per query, which is a qualitatively different institutional challenge.

Large language models (LLMs) are the most important class of foundation model for healthcare, and will recur throughout this book. LLMs such as ChatGPT, Claude, Mistral, Llama and DeepSeek are trained to produce human-like responses to linguistic prompts. Beyond fluent text generation, they exhibit remarkable emergent properties: the ability to learn from examples provided in the prompt without updating the model, known as in-context learning; multi-step mathematical reasoning; and chain-of-thought problem-solving that can work through complex clinical questions step by step. They pass medical licensing examinations, make reasonable triage decisions, and on certain diagnostic tasks outperform unaided clinicians. Understanding what they are actually doing, however, is essential to understanding why they also fail in the ways they do, and why those failures are institutionally as well as clinically consequential. LLMs are not, however, the end of this story: they represent just a moment in a trajectory that is moving faster than any previous technology, and the chapters that follow are written about AI's challenge to healthcare institutions rather than about any specific generation of models.

Prediction, not retrieval

An LLM is, at its core, trained to do one thing: given a sequence of words, predict what word comes next. This process is recursive. The model predicts the next word, adds it to the sequence, then predicts the word after that, and continues until the response is complete. The training data are the text of the internet, processed without any human labelling: the only task the model is given during training is to predict what comes next, and it learns from billions of examples of human language doing exactly that.

The critical implication is that LLMs do not retrieve facts from a database; instead they function by generating contextually plausible continuations. A model that produces a confident clinical statement is not reporting what it knows to be true but is instead producing the text that, given everything preceding it, is most consistent with patterns in its training data. This is why these models are sometimes described as sophisticated autocomplete, though that description underestimates what emerges from operating at this scale. It also explains something important about why they fail: a model optimised to produce plausible-sounding text will do so even when accuracy requires it to say it does not know.

Context and self-attention

What makes LLMs categorically more capable than their AI 2.0 predecessors is how they handle context. Earlier sequence models carried only a compressed memory of recent words forward, which worked for short completions but degraded over longer passages. The transformer architecture, introduced in a 2017 paper by Google researchers entitled "Attention is All You Need"[2], solved this through a mechanism called *self-attention*: every word in the input attends to every other word simultaneously, so the model can draw on context from anywhere in the sequence regardless of distance.

The practical effect is striking. Consider two sentences:

- "Alice's symptoms have resolved and she would now like to cancel her scheduled ..."
- "Having hurriedly hailed a taxi, Bob arrived at the airport just in time for his scheduled ..."

The word 'scheduled' is identical in both. But all the surrounding context makes 'appointment' the overwhelmingly likely completion of Alice's sentence and 'flight' the likely completion of Bob's. Self-attention allows the model to use the full context of everything that came before to resolve such ambiguities, producing outputs that are sensitive to the complete meaning of the input rather than just its recent words. Before this is possible, text must be converted to numbers: each word is mapped to a numerical representation in a process called *embedding*, where words with similar meanings are placed close together in this numerical space. Self-attention then adjusts these representations based on context, so that the same word is encoded differently depending on what surrounds it.

LLMs are trained on massive internet text datasets: scraped websites, online books and articles. Unlike AI 1.0 and 2.0, which needed labelled data, this training is self-supervised. The only task is predicting the next word, which requires no human annotation.

Probabilistic outputs, fine-tuning and alignment

LLM outputs are probabilistic rather than deterministic. Rather than always selecting the single most likely next word, the model samples from a probability distribution, which is why the same prompt can produce different responses on different occasions. Parameters such as the model's *temperature* control how wide this distribution is: lower temperatures produce more predictable outputs, higher temperatures more varied ones. This has practical implications in healthcare, but the more important point is that making outputs more deterministic does not make them more accurate. As we shall see in the hallucination discussion, even setting the temperature to zero does not prevent a model from confidently fabricating clinical information.

Before being made available to consumers, the raw pre-trained model is further refined through fine-tuning on curated datasets, giving it domain-specific knowledge (we would expect it to answer questions like 'what is the capital of France' reliably), and then through reinforcement learning from human feedback (RLHF), which steers the model's outputs towards responses that human raters judge to be helpful, harmless and accurate. RLHF is also, as we shall see in Chapter 8, the mechanism that introduces one of the most clinically consequential failure modes: a tendency to tell users what they want to hear rather than what is accurate.

Retrieval augmented generation

One of the most important practical extensions of the basic LLM architecture is retrieval augmented generation, or RAG. A fundamental limitation of standard LLMs is that their knowledge is frozen at the point of training. A model trained on data up to a certain date cannot know about subsequent events, updated clinical guidelines, or new research findings. In healthcare, where evidence evolves rapidly and guidelines are regularly updated, this is a serious constraint.

RAG addresses this by giving the LLM access to an external knowledge base at the point of inference rather than relying solely on what was encoded during training. When a query is received, the system first retrieves relevant documents or passages from a curated database, then provides these alongside the original query as context for the LLM to reason over. The model is therefore grounding its response in specific retrieved evidence rather than relying purely on parametric memory.

The practical implications for healthcare AI are substantial. A RAG-enabled clinical decision support system can be pointed at a hospital's own formulary, its local clinical guidelines, or the most recent published literature, and will generate responses grounded in that specific corpus. When a clinician asks about the preferred antibiotic for a particular infection, the system can retrieve the relevant local resistance data and guidelines rather than relying on generalised training data that may not reflect local conditions or may be out of date. The same architecture allows systems to cite their sources explicitly, making it possible for a clinician to verify the basis for a recommendation in a way that is simply not possible with a standard LLM.

RAG also partially addresses the hallucination problem, discussed further in this chapter. When a model is required to ground its response in retrieved documents, it is less likely to fabricate plausible-sounding but fictitious information, though it is not immune: models can still misinterpret or misrepresent the retrieved content. The quality of the retrieval step, including the relevance and accuracy of the underlying knowledge base, is therefore critical. A RAG system is only as good as the documents it retrieves from.

Visual transformers and multimodal models

The transformer architecture is not limited to language. All that matters is that the data can be tokenised and embedded. Visual transformers (ViTs) tokenise images into multiple segments and apply a self-attention mechanism to capture long-range relationships between patches. They are trained in a self-supervised way on large image databases.

Prov-GigaPath[15] is a ViT foundation model for whole-slide pathology, trained on over 170,000 microscope slide images from many tissue types taken from many thousands of patients. The resulting embeddings support a wide variety of image recognition tasks including identification of cancer subtypes, predicting gene mutations and calculating tumour mutational burden, a measure of the number of genetic mutations in a tumour's DNA.

Emerging multimodal models can handle a variety of different data types simultaneously. Prov-GigaPath was also trained on written pathology reports, allowing vision-language alignment: textual prompts can be used on images without any task-specific training. Fine-tuning can further improve performance on specific tasks: Prov-GigaPath achieved clinical-grade accuracy on assessing lung cancers for a specific mutation after fine-tuning[16].

It is worth pausing on what this generality means in practice. Like electricity, foundation models are not tools with fixed purposes. They are infrastructure. The productivity gains, if they come, will not come from the models themselves but from what gets built on top of them, and from the restructuring of systems around what they make possible. Whether healthcare systems use that opportunity, or absorb it into existing arrangements as they have absorbed every previous technology, is the institutional question this book examines.

3.2 Deus ex machina?

Large language models stand out for their versatility, excelling at tasks from text generation to writing computer code. Since their introduction, LLMs have demonstrated remarkable growth in capability. To measure this progress, the nonprofit organisation METR (Model Evaluation and Threat Research) has developed methods for testing frontier AI systems, reporting the time it would take a human expert to complete the most complex tasks the algorithm can reliably perform. Between 2019 and 2025, this capability doubled every seven months[47*]. Current frontier models can tackle tasks that would require 40 to 60 minutes for

*I should say that METR performance is a questionable way to define 'capability'. Nevertheless, it is still very clear that the rate of progress is extremely fast.

a human expert. If this trend continues, LLMs are projected to handle tasks equivalent to a week's worth of human work by 2027 to 2029.

LLMs are general-purpose models that can be adapted for clinical use through progressive specialisation. The broadly trained model provides strong reasoning and linguistic foundations, then can be layered with domain-specific knowledge using task-focused fine-tuning. The Woollie model[48] is a good example. Beginning with Meta's open-source Llama model, the team used a staged approach incorporating medical question-answering datasets before fine-tuning on real-world oncology radiology reports. This stacked alignment approach, training in stages rather than incorporating all new data at once, mitigates against accidentally overwriting previously learned capabilities, a phenomenon known as 'catastrophic forgetting'. The result was a model that could accurately predict cancer progression from free-text notes while retaining general reasoning skills and performing well on standard medical benchmarks.

Three key concepts matter when evaluating LLM outputs in clinical contexts: alignment, robustness and reliability. Alignment is fundamentally about intent: ensuring that a model's outputs reflect human values, ethical principles and the goals for which it was designed. In healthcare, an aligned model avoids recommending harmful or unethical treatments even when such suggestions might appear statistically plausible from the training data. Robustness refers to a model's ability to maintain correct behaviour when faced with unexpected inputs, adversarial prompts or distribution shifts. Reliability is about consistency: producing accurate and predictable results across repeated runs and diverse scenarios. In short, alignment governs what the model is trying to achieve, robustness ensures it can withstand challenges, and reliability guarantees it behaves consistently over time. Current LLMs can fall short on all three dimensions in ways that matter considerably in clinical settings.

The pace at which capability is improving makes this more urgent, not less. A doubling time of seven months means that a system which today falls short of the reliability threshold for clinical use may cross it before the governance frameworks needed to manage it safely have been designed. Chapter 1 described this as a structural mismatch between the speed of technological change and the response times of healthcare institutions. The METR finding puts numbers on that mismatch. The question is not whether AI will eventually be capable enough. It is whether the institutions will be ready when it is.

3.3 Do chatbots dream of cognitive bias?

One of the more unsettling discoveries about large language models is that they do not merely process information differently from humans. In important respects, they process it in ways that are strikingly similar to humans, including inheriting the same systematic errors in reasoning that cognitive psychologists have spent decades documenting in people. This is far from reassuring. Human cognitive bias is already a significant source of diagnostic error and clinical harm. An AI system that amplifies those biases rather than correcting them is not a tool for improving clinical reasoning. In fact it could be a mechanism for scaling its failures.

The evidence comes from an elegant line of research using the Cognitive Reflection Test, a set of problems specifically designed to distinguish intuitive from analytical thinking[49]. A typical CRT problem: if ten doctors take ten minutes to see ten patients, how long would a hundred doctors take to see a hundred patients?

The intuitive answer is a hundred minutes. The correct answer is ten. The test is designed to trigger a plausible but wrong response that requires deliberate override to avoid.

Early large language models failed these tests in a revealing way. As models grew in size through the GPT-3 family, they increasingly gave intuitive but incorrect answers, mirroring human System 1 thinking. GPT-3-davinci-003 gave intuitive responses 80% of the time on CRT tasks, more than the 55% rate observed in humans. The models were not just wrong. They were wrong in the same way people are wrong, and more consistently so.

Then something changed. ChatGPT-3.5 and ChatGPT-4 showed a dramatic shift: ChatGPT-4 solved 96% of CRT tasks correctly, compared to 38% for humans. It avoided semantic illusions far more effectively than earlier models and remained accurate even when explicitly instructed not to explain its reasoning, suggesting it had developed something resembling genuine analytical intuition rather than merely following a chain-of-thought heuristic. Performance could also be dramatically improved by providing examples: GPT-3-davinci-003's accuracy on CRT tasks rose from 2% to 92% after just two examples, and on semantic illusions from 18% to over 64% after ten.

This behavioural parallel with human cognition extends beyond test performance. Research using the Centaur model[50] found that LLMs display a similar degree of uncertainty-based exploration to reinforcement learning agents, and that the model's internal representations predicted functional magnetic resonance imaging brain activity in RL-related regions of the real human brain including the striatum, associated with reward prediction errors, and the medial prefrontal cortex, linked to planning and decision-making. The models are not merely mimicking human language. At some level of abstraction, they actually appear to be mimicking human cognition.

The clinical implications of this cut both ways. On one hand, a model that reasons more like an expert clinician than a naive pattern matcher may be useful in complex diagnostic reasoning. On the other hand, if the model inherits human cognitive biases, it will reproduce human diagnostic errors, including anchoring on early impressions, overweighting salient features, and failing to consider low-probability diagnoses that do not fit the presenting pattern.

The hallucination problem makes this worse: LLMs do not merely inherit human biases, they will also fabricate a confident, plausible clinical detail that was never there, and this turns out to be strikingly difficult to engineer away by instruction or by adjusting model parameters[51]. Chapter 8 sets out the evidence for this in full.

The picture that emerges is of systems that reason in recognisably human ways, including human ways of going wrong, but that do so with a fluency and apparent confidence that makes the errors harder to detect than when a human makes them. A clinician who gives a wrong answer hesitatingly invites challenge. A model that gives a wrong answer fluently and at length does not.

Hallucination, sycophancy and inherited cognitive bias are not technical defects waiting to be engineered away. They are properties of the systems as currently built, and they are already being deployed at scale. What healthcare does with that fact, and what it costs when it does the wrong thing with it, is the subject of Chapter 8.

3.4 Agentic AI

The models described so far in this chapter, whether language models, visual transformers or fine-tuned clinical tools, share a common structure: they receive an input and produce an output. They are reactive. Whatever planning they do, in a chain of reasoning, happens inside a single response; they take no action in the world beyond generating that response, and they carry no state forward from one step to the next. An AI agent is something qualitatively different, and understanding what that difference means in practice is becoming one of the most important questions in healthcare AI.

An AI agent is an autonomous software system designed to perceive its environment, reason about what it observes, and act on behalf of a human principal to achieve specific goals. Unlike a model that generates a response to a prompt, an agent can initiate actions, make sequences of decisions, and adjust what it does next based on the results of those actions. At its core, an agent consists of three interlocking components: perception, through which it gathers data from its environment, including patient records, sensor data, appointment schedules or real-time monitoring feeds; reasoning and planning, through which it interprets that data, infers what is happening and plans a sequence of actions to achieve its objectives; and action, through which it executes tasks in the digital world, scheduling appointments, sending reminders, ordering tests or interacting with other agents or systems. Almost all agents deployed today adapt only within a task, reading the results of their own actions back into context and adjusting accordingly, while the underlying model stays fixed. A smaller number genuinely learn over time, updating the model itself from accumulated experience, and as we shall see that distinction matters a great deal for how, and whether, such systems can be assured.

It is worth trying to distinguish between an agent, a chatbot and a copilot, since these terms are often used interchangeably because there is substantial overlap in reality. However there are important differences. A chatbot is a conversational interface: it answers questions, provides information or guides users through simple workflows. It is reactive, responding to user input but not acting independently or pursuing goals beyond the immediate conversation. A copilot is an AI assistant embedded within a specific application or workflow. It can provide context-aware suggestions and automate repetitive tasks, but it remains tightly coupled to the user's actions and does not act with true autonomy. A clinical copilot might help a doctor draft a discharge summary or suggest relevant guidelines, but it does not independently manage patient care.

An agent, by contrast, is proactive and goal-directed. It can operate across multiple systems, initiate actions without direct prompting, and manage complex multi-step processes. An AI agent in healthcare could monitor a patient's wearable data, detect early signs of deterioration, schedule a follow-up appointment, notify the care team, retrieve relevant prior investigations and prepare a structured summary for the reviewing clinician, all without waiting for a human to intervene at each step. The leap from copilot to agent represents a fundamental shift in the nature of human-technology interaction. Agents are not just tools but are instead, in a very meaningful sense, actors.

Multi-step workflows are not unique to agentic systems. A conventional software pipeline can chain many steps together: a radiology workflow might automatically retrieve prior scans, run an AI detection algorithm, generate a structured report and route it to a radiologist for review. Each step is predetermined by a programmer and the overall behaviour of the system is knowable in advance. What distinguishes a true agentic system is not the number of steps but where the decision-making about those steps resides. In a conventional multi-step pipeline, the workflow logic is fixed in code. In an agentic system, the workflow logic is determined dynamically by the agent itself, based on its interpretation of the goal and what it finds as it proceeds.

Orchestration and multi-agent systems

The real transformative potential of agentic AI lies not in single agents operating in isolation but in the orchestration of multiple agents working together. In a multi-agent system, individual agents specialise in particular tasks or domains, and in the most common design a central orchestrating layer coordinates their activities to achieve complex goals that no single agent could accomplish alone. The orchestrator, typically an LLM itself, receives a high-level objective, decomposes it into subtasks, assigns those subtasks to appropriate specialist agents, integrates their outputs and decides what to do next based on the results. In practice, a specialist agent is only rarely a separately trained model. Far more often it is the same underlying model given a different instruction and a different set of tools, a role rather than a distinct intelligence. This has a consequence that the multidisciplinary-team metaphor obscures: when the agents share a base model, they share its blind spots, so a bias or a failure mode present in one is likely present in all of them at once. The apparent redundancy of several agents checking each other's work is partly an illusion, because they are, in an important sense, the same reasoner wearing different hats.

This architecture represents a fundamental departure from

how we normally think about software. In a conventional system, every step, every decision branch, every contingency is anticipated and coded by a programmer. The behaviour of the system is, in principle, fully knowable before it runs. In an LLM-orchestrated multi-agent system, the workflow itself is determined dynamically at runtime, based on the orchestrator's interpretation of the goal and the results it receives from subordinate agents. The orchestrator decides which agents to invoke, in what order, with what inputs, and how to interpret their outputs. That decision-making is not programmed. It emerges from the model's reasoning process applied to the specific situation it encounters.

Consider what a well-designed multi-agent clinical system might look like. A patient presents to an emergency department. An intake agent collects structured symptom information and vital signs. A triage agent assesses urgency and routes the patient appropriately. A diagnostic reasoning agent retrieves relevant history from the electronic health record, cross-references presenting features with known disease patterns and generates a ranked differential diagnosis. A pharmacology agent checks proposed treatments against the patient's current medications and known allergies. A communication agent drafts a summary for the attending clinician and a separate explanation for the patient. An audit agent logs the reasoning chain for governance purposes. The orchestrating LLM coordinates all of this, deciding when to seek additional information, when to escalate to human review and how to integrate conflicting signals from different agents.

Prototype systems of this kind already exist in research settings, and commercial development is accelerating. The Tsinghua Agent Hospital project in China began in 2024 as a pure simulation, a closed virtual environment in which the patients, nurses and doctors were all synthetic agents generated by a language model, and in which the doctor agents improved by accumulating experience across large numbers of simulated cases rather than by being retrained. It moved from that simulation towards real clinical use in 2025: the AI Agent Hospital was inaugurated in April of that year and began piloting at Beijing Tsinghua Changgung Hospital and its affiliated internet hospital in general practice, ophthalmology, radiology and respiratory care. The design is the one described above, with many agents each specialising in a particular clinical area coordinating to deliver diagnostic and information-giving functions at scale.

The potential is large. A well-orchestrated multi-agent system could, in principle, deliver something approaching consultant-level reasoning to any clinical setting, regardless of geography or workforce availability. It could coordinate care pathways across organisational boundaries in ways that no human coordinator could match for speed or consistency. It could operate continuously, without fatigue, distraction or the cognitive load effects that degrade human clinical performance under pressure. For healthcare systems facing unsustainable workforce demands and growing access inequalities, the prospect of clinical capability that scales without proportional increases in headcount is not a marginal efficiency gain. It offers a potential structural solution to a structural problem.

The testing problem

But the very properties that make multi-agent systems powerful also make them extraordinarily difficult to govern, and this difficulty is not merely a current limitation that better engineering will eventually resolve. It is a fundamental challenge that arises from the nature of these systems.

The standard paradigm for testing a healthcare AI system is straightforward in principle. You define the task, collect a representative dataset, measure performance on a held-out test set, and if performance meets a predefined threshold, you approve deployment. The system that runs in deployment is the system that was tested. Its behaviour on any given input is determined by its fixed parameters. As a result, you can, at least in principle, understand the ways it can fail.

This paradigm does not apply to agentic systems, and the gap is categorical rather than just a matter of degree. When an LLM orchestrates a multi-agent workflow, the sequence of actions taken depends on the LLM's interpretation of the goal at each step, the outputs it receives from subordinate agents, and its dynamic reasoning about what to do next. The same high-level objective, presented on two different occasions, may result in meaningfully different sequences of agent invocations, different information retrieval strategies and different decision points escalated to human review. The behaviour space is not just large but practically unbounded.

This creates several interlocking problems for assurance. Standard validation approaches require a test set that is representative of the deployment distribution. For a fixed classification model, the deployment distribution is the distribution of inputs. For an agentic system, the deployment distribution includes the space of possible multi-step reasoning trajectories the system might take, which depends not only on the inputs but on the intermediate outputs of subordinate agents, the state of external systems the agents interact with, and the LLM's dynamic interpretation of all of the above. Constructing a test set that adequately samples this space is, in practice, impossible.

Multi-agent systems can also exhibit behaviours that none of the individual agents would exhibit in isolation, arising from the interactions between them. An agent that behaves safely and predictably when tested individually may behave very differently when operating within a network of other agents, receiving inputs from them and producing outputs that feed back into the network. These emergent behaviours cannot be predicted from testing the components separately, and they may not manifest in testing environments that do not faithfully reproduce the full complexity of real clinical deployment.

The non-determinism described earlier in this chapter is amplified in multi-agent systems. Each agent in the network introduces its own variability. The orchestrator introduces further variability in how it interprets and coordinates their outputs. Small differences in the reasoning of one agent can cascade through the network, producing substantially different system-level behaviours from nearly identical starting conditions. And as we noted in the hallucination discussion, more deterministic outputs are not necessarily more accurate.

There is a further problem, and it does not require the agent to learn anything at all. The most obvious source of drift is an agent that updates itself from experience, so that the system running six months after approval is not the system that was tested. But even a completely frozen agent drifts, because it does not run in isolation. The underlying model may be silently updated by the vendor behind an unchanged interface; the knowledge base it retrieves from may be revised; the tools and prompts that define its behaviour may be edited by whoever maintains the deployment. Any of these changes the system's behaviour without changing the agent, and none of them triggers the kind of review that a software modification would. Traditional post-market surveillance, based on adverse event reporting and periodic review, is designed to detect none of it. The assurance provided at the point of approval is an assurance about a configuration that may no longer exist.

The field of AI safety is developing new approaches to evaluation that may eventually provide better answers. One such approach is adversarial testing, sometimes called red-teaming after the military practice of using a dedicated team to attack your own defences in order to find weaknesses before an adversary does. In AI, red-teaming means deliberately constructing inputs and scenarios designed to make the system fail, fail dangerously, or behave in ways that were not intended, in order to surface failure modes that ordinary use would never expose. For agentic systems, this means not just testing individual agents but constructing adversarial environments in which agents interact in ways that probe the boundaries of safe behaviour. These approaches are promising. They are not yet mature, and they are not being applied systematically to healthcare AI deployments at the speed at which agentic systems are being developed.

The most intellectually honest statement about the assurance of complex multi-agent AI systems in healthcare is that we do not yet know how to do it adequately. That is not a comfortable position for a field that is deploying these systems in environments where the consequences of failure can be serious. But it is the truth, and pretending otherwise would be worse.

The accountability questions are equally unresolved. When a multi-agent system causes harm, the causal chain runs through an orchestrating LLM, multiple specialist agents, the organisations that developed and deployed each component, and the clinician or institution that relied on the system's output. Who is responsible? Current regulatory frameworks and legal liability structures were not built for this kind of distributed, emergent causation. Chapter 10 examines why, and what a framework built for it would need to look like.

None of this is an argument against agentic AI in healthcare. The potential is too large and the need too urgent for blanket caution to be an adequate response. What it is though, is an argument for developing the governance infrastructure at the same pace as the technology. That is a major institutional change in itself. Whether healthcare is capable of that, and what happens when it is not, is what the rest of this book is about.

One further point deserves attention before I leave the technology behind. This chapter has described LLMs and agentic systems because they are the technologies at the cutting edge of practical applications at the time of writing. But they are already not the bleeding edge and they will not be the frontier for long. Predicting which specific technology will matter most in five years is a fool's errand: the history of AI is littered with confident forecasts that were wrong in both directions, foreseeing imminent breakthroughs that did not arrive and failing entirely to anticipate the ones that did. What can be said with confidence is simpler and more important than any specific prediction. The capability of these systems is increasing rapidly, on a trajectory that shows no sign of levelling off. Whatever the current frontier model cannot do, a future model probably will. Whatever clinical task currently seems too complex, too contextual, or too dependent on human judgement to be automated will be reconsidered. The question this book addresses is therefore not whether AI will eventually be capable of transforming healthcare. That question is already largely settled. The question is whether the institutions of medicine will have the capacity to respond appropriately as that capability arrives, in whatever form it takes, faster than any previous technology.

4 Arbitrage in the age of algorithms

Medicine likes to think of itself as a vocation and in important respects it is. It would be wrong to reduce the relationship between a doctor and a patient, built on trust in the face of vulnerability and the particular intimacy of illness, to some kind of commercial transaction. But thinking of oneself as motivated by vocation does not exclude institutional arrangements that surround that relationship, which may tell a rather different story. In fact, healthcare *is* an industry, but just one that perhaps finds it distasteful to see itself that way.

But make no mistake, healthcare **is** an industry. Behind every consultation lies a vast, intricate economic system: hospitals, pharmacies, social services, supply chains, insurers, regulators and professional bodies to name but a few, all interacting within a framework of incentives that necessarily can only be indirectly constructed to align with the individual patient's welfare and therefore do not always serve it. It employs more people than any other sector in the United States and United Kingdom. It consumes nearly a fifth of American GDP and a growing share of every other developed economy's national income. It is shaped, as every industry is, by the forces of supply and demand, by the behaviour of its most powerful actors, and by the institutional rules that determine what gets rewarded.

Those rules matter for AI in particular. Most accounts of why AI has not transformed healthcare focus on the technology: the algorithms are not accurate enough, the data is not clean enough, the regulatory pathways are not clear enough. This book argues that these accounts are incomplete. The deeper obstacles are economic and institutional. To understand what it would take for AI to make the system better or, conversely, to understand why it might fail to do so, we first need to understand what defines the system that we want to change.

In this chapter, I will examine the relevant structural features of healthcare as an economic system, returning to institutional resistance later in the book: why healthcare behaves differently from many other markets, why productivity gains that seem straightforward in other industries are so persistently elusive here, and why this means that costs rise inexorably even without the introduction of expensive new treatments or technologies. Having better defined the cause of the problem, I will then ask what happens when AI enters this system: whether the market for healthcare AI produces the tools that patients and systems actually need, or the tools that are easiest to sell to the people who control the purchasing decisions. The answer, as we shall see, has less to do with the technology than with the incentive structures surrounding it. The argument draws on a set of ideas from economics that turn out to be illuminating when applied to the interaction between disruptive technology and the healthcare setting. Together these frameworks explain not just why healthcare AI is hard to deploy, but why the economic system surrounding healthcare actively shapes which technologies get built, which get bought, and which will be quietly shelved despite clear evidence of benefit. Understanding that shaping force is the first step toward directing it.

4.1 Knowledge is power (until it's free)

In 1963, Kenneth Arrow published a paper that changed how economists think about healthcare[52]. His argument was that healthcare cannot be analysed using the same principles as other markets, because it violates the foundational assumption on which market economics rests. That assumption is that buyers know what they are purchasing. In healthcare, they almost never do.

The information asymmetry between clinician and patient is not incidental to medicine but constitutive of it. A patient presenting with chest pain cannot evaluate whether the tests being ordered are necessary, whether the diagnosis is correct, or whether the treatment being recommended is the best available. They must trust and because trust cannot be manufactured by market competition in the way that quality can be in most industries, healthcare has developed an elaborate institutional substitute: professional licensing, ethical codes, regulatory oversight, and the organisational infrastructure of hospitals and insurers. These institutions exist, as Arrow recognised, precisely because the market cannot do the work that markets do everywhere else.

This has a consequence that is easy to overlook. The same institutions that make healthcare trustworthy also make it expensive. Professional licensing controls entry to the labour market and limits the substitution of less expensive workers for more expensive ones, holding up the price of care. Ethical codes and regulatory frameworks raise the cost of adopting new practices by requiring consensus that takes years to build. These are not incidental overheads. They are the price of the trust that Arrow showed the market could not otherwise supply, and that price is paid in the cost of care.

The information asymmetry implies something else that is

directly relevant to AI too. It is the foundation of the medical profession's authority, income and social status. Put bluntly, doctors know things that patients do not, and that knowledge gap is what justifies the autonomy, the income premium and the deference that the profession commands and this in turn has shaped how the institutions of healthcare have developed. What makes AI different from earlier medical technologies is that it acts directly on this gap. A scanner or a new drug extends what medicine can do but leaves the distribution of knowledge between doctor and patient (or indeed others involved in the delivery of healthcare) untouched. AI, and generative AI in particular, operates on information itself: it disseminates, retrieves, summarises and reasons over the very expertise that the asymmetry is built from. It is, in economic terms, a technology aimed squarely at the thing that made medical knowledge scarce. When AI begins to close that gap, making something approaching specialist-level reasoning available to anyone with a smartphone, it is not merely offering a useful tool but eroding the scarcity on which the profession's economic position rests. We will return to what this means for adoption later in the book, but the economics are simple: when expertise stops being scarce, the autonomy, the income and the social status that depended on that scarcity all come under pressure.

The second structural feature of healthcare economics that Arrow identified, and that bears directly on AI's prospects, is the role of non-market institutions in filling the gaps that markets cannot. Hospitals, insurers and government regulators exist not because healthcare providers preferred it that way but because the alternative, a market in which patients make purchasing decisions directly without the information needed to make them rationally, produces outcomes that societies have consistently found unacceptable. These institutions stabilise the system. They also, as a structural by-product, create the layers of bureaucracy and the coordination costs that make healthcare so costly to run, difficult to change and therefore hard to scale. Insurance introduces moral hazard: when patients are insulated from the true cost of care, they consume more of it than they would if they bore the marginal cost directly. Adverse selection means that those most likely to need care are the most likely to seek coverage, requiring elaborate mechanisms to manage risk and control costs. Each solution generates new complexity, and the complexity accumulates.

The cumulative effect is a system whose organisational logic reflects the problems it was built to solve. Non-market institutions were designed to guarantee access and distribute risk, not to minimise cost or maximise throughput. The bureaucratic layers that followed were not failures of design but functional responses to coordination problems that markets had demonstrably failed to handle. The result is a system that is, in a meaningful sense, working as intended: it provides care to people who could not otherwise afford it, protects against catastrophic financial exposure, and maintains standards of safety and accountability. What it was not designed for is rapid change, modular integration, or the kind of scalability that AI promises to enable. Those properties were simply not among the objectives the system was built to optimise.

This matters for AI adoption because it means the friction is not incidental. The bureaucratic processes and governance requirements are not bugs to be engineered around but the system expressing its actual priorities. AI that delivers efficiency gains without engaging with those priorities will not be adopted, however technically capable it may be.

4.2 Running to stand still

The institutional friction that Arrow's analysis explains has a further economic consequence, one that William Baumol identified in the 1960s and that has become, if anything, more relevant since then[53,54]. Baumol made a simple observation: in sectors where productivity can be improved through technology and automation (such as has been the case in manufacturing, for example), output per worker rises and relative costs fall. In sectors where productivity growth is intrinsically limited because they are not so amenable to automation, wages must nevertheless keep pace with the broader economy. As a result costs rise in relative terms.

Healthcare belongs to the second category. As currently structured, its core processes require skilled human time and cannot easily be compressed: the consultation, the ward round, the procedure, the therapeutic relationship. The labour is not an input to the product; it *is* the product. As wages rise elsewhere in the economy, healthcare wages must rise too, even if the time required to deliver care does not fall. The result is a steady increase in the relative cost of healthcare over time. To keep still, the cost disease means that society will need to spend more and more of its income on healthcare.

At first glance this seems catastrophic, and it is often presented that way. In fact the cost disease is more nuanced. As Baumol himself points out, it does not necessarily make healthcare unaffordable, because the productivity gains in progressive sectors make everything they produce cheaper by the same amount that healthcare and other stagnant sectors become relatively dearer. Provided productivity in the rest of the economy keeps rising, the growing share of output devoted to healthcare remains affordable in aggregate: society can spend more on services that resist mechanisation without becoming poorer, and still receive the same amount of care.

The difficulty is behavioural rather than arithmetic. People might very reasonably decide to choose to spend their rising purchasing power on healthcare. Faced with manufactured goods that are increasingly cheap and deliver utility now, they buy those, rather than set resources aside against an uncertain future health need. So when that need arrives, the higher relative cost of care may be unaffordable to them even though it was affordable to the economy as a whole. From a policy point of view this implies a reallocation, through either taxation or insurance, depending on the funding model.

There is a further critical implication however. In sectors affected by cost disease, output cannot be increased primarily through productivity growth. It can only be increased by adding labour. If demand for care rises more quickly than the workforce can be expanded and reorganised, then capacity will lag behind need. The constraint is not expenditure in the abstract, but the rate at which labour-intensive services can be scaled under existing institutional arrangements.

At the level of distribution, organisation and capacity, the impact of the disease may still be significant. The resources that make healthcare affordable in aggregate are not evenly distributed across individuals or institutions, and neither is illness. Health follows a social gradient. Those who are poorest tend to carry a higher burden of disease, develop it earlier, and live longer with it. Demand for healthcare is therefore not only growing but intensifying in the populations least able to absorb its cost or navigate its complexity. A system that is affordable in aggregate can still be locally overwhelmed.

If demand is maintained or increases, output must increase

with it. In a sector where output requires labour and productivity growth is limited, that implies a gradual but persistent reallocation of the workforce. As healthcare absorbs a growing share of expenditure it also absorbs a growing share of labour, drawing workers out of higher-productivity sectors into activities where output per worker grows more slowly. The effect is not that innovation elsewhere stops, but that a smaller proportion of the workforce participates in it. Aggregate productivity growth is therefore pulled down, even as the economy becomes more sophisticated in other respects.

At the same time, technological progress within healthcare behaves differently from technological progress elsewhere. To date, it has rarely substituted cleanly for labour in a way that reduces total cost. Instead it expands what can be treated, raises expectations of care, and increases the number of patients eligible for treatment. More effective acute care creates more survivors. Better chronic care prolongs life with disease. The stock of illness grows rather than contracts, and with it the volume and complexity of care required. These forces reinforce one another: rising relative costs increase expenditure share, expanding capability increases demand, longer survival increases the duration of need and the burden remains concentrated where resources are scarcest.

The consequence is that demand persistently grows faster than effective capacity. This mismatch does not announce itself as a single moment of failure. It emerges as a pattern of adaptation. Waiting becomes the primary and most immediate buffer. Delays lengthen and embed themselves into routine care pathways. Patients arrive later in the course of illness, not because access has formally disappeared but because it has been deferred. Conditions that might once have been managed electively appear in more advanced and unstable forms, shifting activity toward higher-acuity care. The system's effort is increasingly directed toward managing deterioration that might earlier have been prevented.

Under these conditions, maintaining consistent quality becomes progressively harder. Clinical decisions are made under time pressure, with incomplete information and fragmented continuity. Tasks are re-prioritised, deferred or redistributed to cope with volume. The benefits of improved treatments are not lost, but they are diluted by delay and coordination failure. What appears at the level of the individual innovation as progress translates, at the level of the system, into a more complex and unstable equilibrium.

Sustained pressure translates into increased workload intensity, reduced recovery time and gradual erosion of discretionary effort. As a result, fatigue accumulates, burnout follows and staff retention deteriorates. Widening staffing gaps redistribute the same volume of work across fewer people, intensifying the original pressure. The system becomes increasingly dependent on the willingness of its workforce to continue operating close to its limits.

Again, it is important to realise that none of this results in an abrupt collapse. The system continues to function, but at a lower level of performance. Care is delivered, but less timely, less consistent and less efficient than it could be. The adjustment is absorbed through longer waiting times, through workforce strain, and through variation in access and outcome. These effects are not evenly distributed, falling instead most heavily on those with the greatest underlying need and the least capacity to compensate for delay or fragmentation. Inequality of health is translated into inequality of care and, over time, into inequality of outcome.

This is the point at which Baumol can no longer reassure us. The fact that healthcare is affordable in aggregate does not prevent this pattern from emerging. Even if a society chooses to devote an increasing share of its income to healthcare it may still operate a system that is persistently overstretched, unevenly distributed and locally failing those who depend on it most. The constraint is not absolute affordability but the system's capacity to organise, allocate and deliver care under conditions of sustained and uneven demand.

As an aside, there is a further dimension implicit in broader arguments made byPiketty[55]. When the long-term return on capital exceeds the growth rate of the economy, wealth concentrates with those who already hold it. So a healthcare system that pulls ever more labour into low-productivity activity while the capital owners upstream, in pharmaceuticals, medical devices, insurance platforms and data infrastructure, continue to earn robust returns tends to widen exactly that gap. A system that fails to improve its productivity is, in this precise sense, not merely inefficient but a driver of inequality.

These considerations are why the productivity argument for AI in healthcare is not merely about productivity and affordability but also about fair distribution. A health system that deploys AI to truly redesign how care is produced, rather than to make existing processes marginally faster, could expand access with the workforce it already has. It could redirect the savings from reduced friction and duplication into prevention and community support. It can shift the balance between labour and capital in ways that narrow rather than widen the gap between those who benefit from healthcare's economic footprint and those who bear its costs. Shorter waits and fewer avoidable deteriorations land most heavily in favour of the poorest, who bear a disproportionate share of the opportunity cost of time, who are least able to buffer health shocks financially, and who live furthest from specialist expertise.

One serious objection to this productivity argument deserves attention. Measured productivity in healthcare has always been a poor proxy for value. Much of what patients need, reassurance, unhurried explanation, the sense of being known by a clinician who has followed them over time, is hard to quantify and cannot be captured in output statistics. Optimising what is easily measured risks degrading what actually matters. This is a fair concern but does not, however, justify maintaining the status quo. The system that currently exists is also failing on that unquantifiable dimension. It produces fragmented, hurried care for many patients, and burns out the people delivering it whilst still leaving enormous unmet need unaddressed. The argument for productivity improvement through AI is not an argument for reducing healthcare to what can be counted. Instead I am arguing for freeing up the human capacity that is currently consumed by friction, duplication and administrative overhead, so that more of it can be directed toward the things that only humans can do well.

4.3 The extinction of expertise

The scalability problem that Baumol identified has a straightforward implication that the healthcare system has spent decades trying to avoid confronting. In the current paradigm if you want to see twice as many patients, you need roughly twice as many doctors, twice as many nurses and allied health professionals, hospitals that are twice as big and so on. There are modest economies of scale at the level of individual specialties: concentrating elective surgical volume in fewer centres can improve both productivity and outcomes, for example. But these gains do not extend to the organisational level, where increasing activity in one part of the system tends to generate costs and pressures elsewhere. Increasing elective surgical volume, for instance, increases emergency care costs rather than reducing them[56]. The system replicates rather than scales.

Other industries have escaped this trap by restructuring around supply-chain principles: standardising processes, separating tasks that require high skill from those that do not, and deploying technology to substitute for labour where substitution is possible. We will examine in detail why healthcare has resisted this logic, and what AI changes about its prospects, in Chapter 6. But the labour substitution question deserves attention here, because it connects directly to the economic foundations of medical authority.

The question is not really whether AI can replace doctors, but whether it can replace what doctors do, which is a different and considerably more threatening question for the profession. Medicine has always justified its labour market position on the grounds that what doctors do cannot easily be done by anyone else. The knowledge required is specialised, the judgement required is complex, and the consequences of error are severe. These are real features of clinical practice. They are also, not coincidentally, features that make the medical labour market highly protected from the competitive pressures that drive down wages and erode professional status in other fields.

AI could threaten this position in a structural way. The promise is that it may enable an unbundling of the tasks that currently require a doctor and redistribution of them across a different configuration of workers, agents and systems. Diagnostic imaging already demonstrates this clearly: AI systems that match or exceed specialist performance on specific tasks do not need to replace the radiologist entirely to fundamentally alter what a radiologist is worth. They need only to narrow the range of tasks for which specialist training is indispensable or re-deploy that expertise out of hours or to non-specialists. The same logic applies across clinical medicine. An AI-supported non-physician practitioner who could safely manage a much wider range of presentations than current scope of practice permits is not replacing a doctor. But in economic terms, he or she is reducing the demand for the most expensive component of the clinical workforce.

The supply side of this equation matters too. Healthcare labour is notoriously inelastic in the short term. Training a doctor takes the better part of a decade. Training pipelines cannot be expanded quickly, and they also cannot be contracted without consequences that persist for years. This inelasticity is one of the reasons healthcare costs are so difficult to control: when demand rises, supply cannot easily follow, and prices rise instead. AI changes this constraint in an important way. It can increase the effective supply of clinical capability without increasing the number of trained clinicians, by expanding what less expensively trained workers can safely do, by reducing the time that expensive clinicians spend on tasks that do not require their level of training, and by making specialist-level reasoning available in settings that currently have no access to specialists at all.

This is good news for patients and for health systems. It is considerably more ambiguous news for the medical profession, which has spent a century constructing the institutional protections that depend on clinical expertise being scarce, specialised and not easily substituted. The resistance that AI encounters in healthcare is not primarily about whether the algorithms work but about what happens to the economic and social architecture of medicine if they work too well. That is the argument this book makes, and it begins here, in the economics of knowledge and the labour market consequences of making expert reasoning cheap.

4.4 The tollbooth and the bypass

The economic logic of the previous section points toward a conclusion that is uncomfortable but important. The medical profession earns a substantial income premium, and has done so consistently across every developed healthcare system for well over a century. That premium is partly justified: the training is long, the responsibility is very real, and the consequences of making mistakes can be severe. But a significant component of it rests on an institutional protection of a knowledge monopoly. Doctors earn rent on expertise that is kept scarce not only by the difficulty of acquiring it but by the licensing frameworks, scope-of-practice rules and professional structures that control who is permitted to apply it. AI threatens the second component directly, by making something that begins to approach specialist-level reasoning available at negligible marginal cost to anyone with a connected device. In this sense, AI does not threaten skill but does threaten scarcity.

This matters for understanding which AI innovations are likely to succeed and which will struggle, because the institutions that govern healthcare AI adoption are substantially controlled by the profession whose economic position is most directly threatened by it. Borrowing from Acemoglu and Robinson's analysis of extractive institutions gives us a useful framing[57]. In extractive institutional arrangements, innovation is not suppressed outright but channelled. The innovations that succeed are those that flow through the existing power structure and compound its value. The innovations that fail are those that would allow actors to bypass this structural tollbooth.

Healthcare exhibits this pattern with remarkable consistency. Consider what has succeeded. Immunotherapy requires an oncologist to prescribe and a hospital to administer. Robotic surgery requires a surgeon to operate and a theatre team to support. GLP-1 agonists require a physician to initiate and monitor. Each of these is a breakthrough but each also compounds the value of the existing intermediary structure rather than displacing it. The incumbent has no reason to resist innovations that make the tollbooth more valuable.

It is not that extractive institutional frameworks are not productive (there would be nothing to extract otherwise). However they do create a limit to productivity by limiting true systemic innovation. Now consider what has stalled. Diagnostic AI capable of self-triage sits in regulatory limbo or is ring-fenced so that it must be supervised by the clinician it would otherwise replace (which as we will see later, is a false reassurance). Pharmacist prescribing of chronic disease medication, safe and effective in every jurisdiction that has tried it, remains tightly restricted in most. Innovations like these don't fail on clinical grounds. The problem is that they are innovations that would allow patients to exit the tollbooth, and they have encountered resistance that is structurally predictable even if it is never explicitly organised.

The distinction is between output-enhancing innovation and structure-replacing innovation. Output-enhancing innovation makes the existing system more productive at what it already does. It is welcomed, funded and adopted, because it increases the value flowing through the incumbent structure without threatening the structure itself. Structure-replacing innovation would allow care to be delivered through a different configuration entirely, one with fewer intermediaries, lower unit costs, and less dependence on the scarcest and most expensively trained components of the workforce. It is this second category that the system consistently fails to adopt, not because the evidence is absent but because the incentives of the most powerful actors within the system point the other way.

Schumpeter called structure-replacing innovation *creative destruction*: the mechanism by which new technologies displace incumbent firms, structures and ways of organising production, forcing the economy toward more productive configurations regardless of the preferences of those being displaced[46]. It is the engine of long-run productivity growth in market economies, and it is precisely what healthcare has failed to experience. The Schumpeterian mechanism assumes that incumbents can be bypassed: the new entrant does not need the permission of the firm it is displacing. The railway did not require the stagecoach industry's approval to operate and the smartphone did not require Kodak's blessing to replace the camera. The disruptive technology routes around the incumbent and lets the market decide. In healthcare, this mechanism is intercepted before it can operate. The new entrant does not bypass the incumbent but must seek the incumbent's permission, in the form of regulatory approval shaped by professional advisory bodies, licensing frameworks controlled by professional organisations, and scope-of-practice rules written by the profession whose scope is being contested. Creative destruction requires that incumbents cannot veto their own displacement.

I need to be clear that what we actually have is not some kind of malign conspiracy. No committee meets to decide which innovations to suppress. The mechanism is more mundane and (paradoxically therefore) more durable: the people who sit on regulatory advisory boards, who design scope-of-practice rules, who lead professional bodies, who control training curricula and who advise governments on healthcare technology policy are, overwhelmingly, senior members of the profession whose economic position structure-replacing innovation would most directly threaten. They act in good faith and within an incentive structure that makes caution about disruptive innovation the professionally rational choice. The result is a system that produces better treatments but not cheaper delivery, more sophisticated interventions but not a thinner intermediary layer, higher value at the top of the stack but a tollbooth that captures it before it reaches the patient as lower costs or wider access. As a result, the productivity ratio stays flat, the cost base does not fall and the gap between what AI could enable and what the system actually delivers grows wider.

4.5 Market forces and the AI healthcare landscape

Artificial intelligence in healthcare is shaped by the economic and organisational realities of the system into which it is introduced. The products that reach the market and the features that are prioritised as well as the problems they claim to solve are all influenced by the incentives of investors, the purchasing behaviour of hospitals and payers, and the cultural norms of the medical profession. Understanding these forces matters because they determine not only what gets built, but whether what gets built will reinforce the current configuration of healthcare or truly disrupt it.

The dominant sources of capital for AI development (venture funds, corporate research budgets, and the big technology platforms) very naturally seek products that promise scalability, rapid adoption, and defensible competitive advantages. These priorities favour solutions that can be deployed widely with minimal customisation, generate recurring revenue, and create lock-in through proprietary data or integration depth. In practice this means AI tools concentrate in areas where the return on investment is clear and immediate: automating reimbursable tasks such as documentation and billing, streamlining administrative workflows, and enhancing functions that already operate in some kind of digital form. These are domains where inputs and outputs are structured, liability is relatively low, and regulatory pathways are (mostly) well defined. By contrast, innovations that require (or facilitate) fundamental redesign of care pathways, redistribution of revenue across organisational silos, or multi-year coordination across sectors struggle to attract investment. These are precisely the changes needed to achieve system-level productivity gains, yet they offer uncertain payback horizons and diffuse benefits that no single actor can easily capture. The result is a market that rewards making the current model smoother rather than replacing it.

This concentration of AI development in large technology firms, and the resulting misalignment between what attracts investment and what would benefit healthcare systems, is documented at cross-economy scale by the OECD, which finds that critical AI inputs are concentrated in a small number of incumbent players whose market position creates barriers to the kind of broad, equitable diffusion on which productivity gains depend[58].

The effective customers for healthcare AI are rarely patients. Purchase decisions are driven by three groups: clinicians, provider organisations, and payers. Doctors very reasonably value tools that save time, reduce cognitive load, and preserve clinical autonomy. It is equally natural to resist technologies that appear to second-guess professional judgement (and I will return to very real safety concerns later in this book). Hospitals prioritise solutions that protect margins by increasing throughput or cutting staffing costs. Procurement cycles favour vendors who can demonstrate measurable impact on these metrics through narrowly scoped pilots. Payers fund tools that reduce claims outlay, but adoption stalls when benefits accrue to one budget while costs fall on another so that cross-system change is difficult to motivate.

These dynamics shape what a good product looks like: seamless integration into existing workflows, rapid attributable return on investment, and minimal disruption to established roles. But none of this is creative destruction. The features that make a product commercially attractive are simply not the same as those that would make it transformative. Vendors optimise for usability within current systems, not for reconfiguring those systems. They design for regulatory and reimbursement alignment, and naturally seek to tailor solutions to existing billing codes rather than lobbying for new payment models. They favour assistive tools that keep clinicians in the loop over autonomous systems that might deliver greater efficiency but raise liability concerns and build for local gains that a single decision-maker can capture rather than for improvements that require shared savings across multiple organisations. These choices are entirely rational responses to prevailing market incentives.

It is natural for innovation to be channelled toward what is adoptable rather than what is most beneficial. The consequences are predictable. Investment flows to profitable niches: diagnostic augmentation rather than prevention, administrative automation rather than end-to-end pathway redesign, high-income markets rather than underserved populations. AI can even increase costs without proportional improvements in outcomes. Faster image interpretation may lower marginal costs but expand indications, driving up overall utilisation. More sensitive detection can outpace the system's capacity to deliver treatment, creating new bottlenecks and patient anxiety and savings achieved locally are often offset by systemic costs elsewhere. This just isn't what we want.

There is a further dimension to this that goes beyond market structure. Even when healthcare organisations want to pursue transformative AI investment, the conditions for doing so are largely absent. The psychology of institutional decision-making under uncertainty, examined byKahneman and Tversky[59] in prospect theory, offers part of the explanation. Organisations, like individuals, weight potential losses more heavily than equivalent gains, and are more responsive to negatively framed challenges, reducing current harm, than to positively framed opportunities for future improvement. Transformative AI investment is almost always framed as opportunity: a chance to redesign care delivery, improve outcomes, reduce costs over a long horizon. It requires accepting near-term disruption and cost for returns that are dispersed, slow to materialise, and difficult to attribute. Incremental AI, by contrast, addresses immediate pain points, reduces visible costs, and generates attributable metrics quickly. The psychology of institutional decision-making consistently favours the second over the first, regardless of which would deliver more value.

The organisational culture of healthcare compounds this because the institutions that would need to lead transformative change are, by their nature, not built for it. Healthcare providers are naturally and reasonably risk-averse, highly regulated, and oriented toward protecting established workflows and patient safety as they currently understand it. The organisations with the resources to invest at scale in disruptive AI that is truly disruptive, large integrated health systems and teaching hospitals, are also the most complex and the most encumbered by existing commitments. The characteristics that describe an organisation capable of aggressive technological exploration (decentralised leadership, tolerance for failure, willingness to cannibalise existing revenue streams) are just not the characteristics of any major healthcare provider[60].

In short, the characteristics of an AI product that will sell (ease of integration, preservation of professional autonomy, rapid local return on investment, regulatory fit, and defensible market position) are not the characteristics that guarantee system-level improvement let alone creative destruction. Left to market forces alone, healthcare AI will adapt to the existing configuration of the sector rather than reconfigure it. If we want AI to deliver real improvements in equity, scalability and productivity, the current incentive structure does not reward those outcomes and will not produce them spontaneously. Without deliberate policy, governance and payment reform, the trajectory of AI in healthcare will be set not by what the system needs but by what its most powerful actors are prepared to buy.

There is a further mechanism that makes this worse still; one that operates even when organisations intend to adopt transformative AI rather than merely incremental tools. It requires distinguishing between two categories of AI that are easily conflated but behave very differently in practice. Point-solution AI improves performance on a specific task for the individual clinician who uses it: a documentation tool, a triage assistant, or a diagnostic aid. There is likely to be some effort involved in clinicians adopting it but its value is captured individually and immediately. System-change AI is intended to restructure care pathways and generate productivity gains at the system level, but those gains only materialise when enough clinicians have actually restructured their working practice around the tool that the whole pathway changes coherently. No individual clinician can achieve that alone. But it is also hard work and disruptive for the individual clinician, involving a great deal of faith in the ultimate organisational mission and that the efforts expended by them will not be misappropriated.

This collective threshold structure creates a specific and underappreciated trap. A clinician who adopts a system-change AI tool but does not restructure their fundamental working patterns captures the immediate private benefit of using it while contributing nothing to the systemic transformation it was designed to enable. This is not bad faith; it is a rational response to an environment where full adoption bears disruption costs that fall on the individual, while the systemic benefits only materialise if enough colleagues do the same. Partial adoption is individually optimal but is collectively catastrophic. And it is a stable equilibrium: once enough clinicians are partially adopting, the expected return to real adoption falls further, because the systemic threshold becomes harder to reach. The system gets stuck, and high adoption rates on conventional metrics coexist with negligible systemic benefit.

The deeper implication is what might be called a value-adoption paradox: the technologies with the greatest systemic potential are precisely those most likely to get trapped in a state of partial adoption. Point solutions diffuse readily because their value is individual and immediate. System-change AI requires collective behaviour change that no individual has sufficient incentive to initiate unilaterally. The market therefore reliably delivers what is easy to adopt rather than what matters most, not through any failure of information or intent but through the structural logic of individual rational choice applied to a problem that requires collective action. Standard adoption metrics cannot see this because they tend to only measure whether the tool is being used. They cannot measure whether the pathway has changed. Figure 4.1 shows the structure of the trap. How this trap shapes which tools actually diffuse, and what the sequence of interventions to escape it would need to look like, is taken up in more detail in Chapter 6.

There is a deeper reason why the market fails to produce transformative AI in healthcare, one that goes beyond the psychology of procurement decisions or the risk-aversion of institutional buyers. It concerns the fundamental mismatch between the unit at which AI creates value and the unit at which markets transact.

As the introduction established, AI is a general purpose technology in the economic sense defined by Bresnahan and Trajtenberg[37]: its significance lies not in any single application but in its capacity to combine with other technologies, processes and organisational forms to generate combinatorial possibilities that did not previously exist. A diagnostic AI that feeds a prediction model that reshapes a care pathway that enables a different configuration of the workforce would be a valuable tool in curing Baumol's cost disease because it is a reconfigured system and not because it is a collection of point solutions. The value is in the combination, and combinations require design at the level of the whole.

Unfortunately, markets typically transact at the level of the

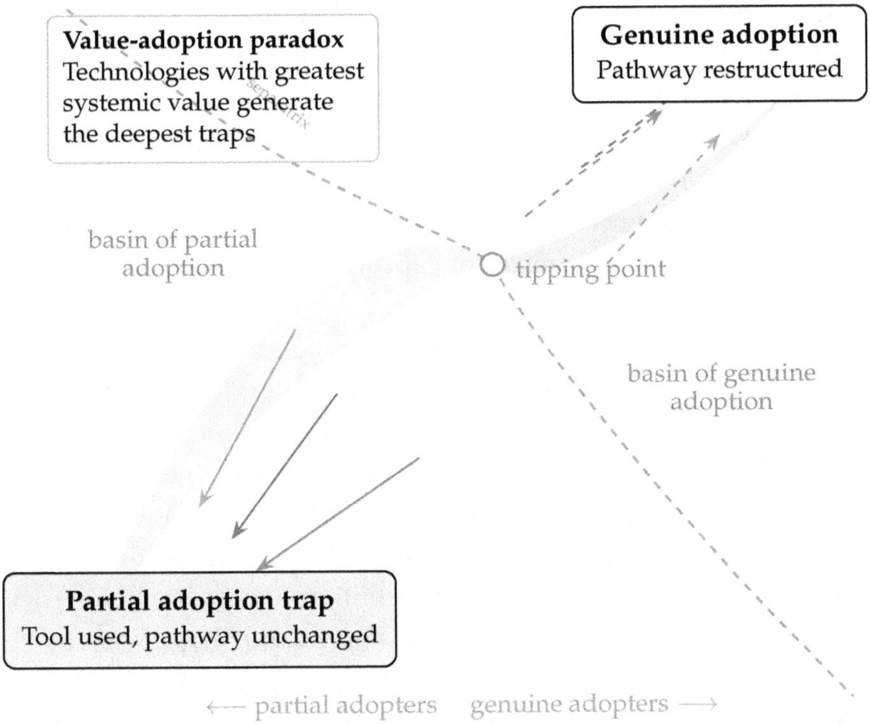

Figure 4.1: The partial adoption trap. For system-change AI, two stable equilibria coexist: partial adoption (tool present, pathway unchanged) and genuine adoption (pathway restructured, systemic benefit realised). The separatrix divides the two basins of attraction. Below the tipping point, populations drift toward the partial adoption trap regardless of individual intentions. The value-adoption paradox: the technologies with the greatest systemic potential generate the deepest traps, because they require the largest collective behaviour change to cross the threshold.

product and not at the level of the whole. Products such as a documentation tool, a triage algorithm, a deterioration predictor are evaluated on their own terms, procured on their own contract, and deployed into existing workflows. This is not a failure of ambition or intelligence on the part of healthcare organisations but instead represents a structural consequence of how markets work. No individual purchasing decision, however well-informed, can capture value that only emerges from coordinating changes across an entire system. Whilst the gains could be real, the mechanism for capturing them does not exist in the market as currently constituted.

This misalignment has a further dimension that compounds over time. General purpose technologies generate network effects as they diffuse: in the same way that the value of a social media platform increases with the number of users, the value of the AI technology grows as more data flows through it, as models train on richer inputs, and as integration deepens across the system. In healthcare, this dynamic concentrates around whoever holds the data and the workflow. As Varian and Shapiro established in their analysis of information technology markets[61], network effects combined with high switching costs create powerful incumbent advantages that tend toward oligopoly regardless of the competitive intent of the actors involved. The organisation that holds the patient record, manages the clinical workflow, and accumulates the data from which models improve is not merely ahead today; it becomes progressively harder to displace as the network effects compound. Understanding this dynamic is essential for understanding where the market is actually going, which is the subject of the next section.

4.6 The integration advantage: EHR vendors, third-party AI, and the structure of the market

The dominant narrative in UK health technology policy treats the AI market as an ecosystem to be cultivated: a diverse landscape of innovative startups and specialist vendors competing on clinical merit, with healthcare organisations free to adopt the best tools available. The NHS AI Lab, the NICE (National Institute for Health and Care Excellence) evidence frameworks, the various accelerator programmes: all are premised on the idea that what is needed is better evaluation and procurement, and that the market will then deliver the right products. This framing is not wrong exactly, but it is incomplete in a way that is important because it ignores the structural dynamics that determine which products survive long enough to be evaluated.

The central dynamic is simple: EHR vendors have a structural advantage over third-party AI developers that is not primarily a function of their size or resources, but of their position in the information architecture of clinical care. A tool built by the organisation that already holds the patient record, manages the clinical workflow, and operates the interface through which the clinician works every day begins with advantages that a stand-alone product cannot replicate regardless of its technical quality. It has access to structured and unstructured data in their native formats without integration overhead. Its outputs appear where the clinician is already looking. When something goes wrong, there is a single contract and a single support relationship. These are important advantages and form the conditions that determine whether a tool gets used at all[62].

What is less well recognised, or is frequently overlooked including by many of the healthcare organisations making procurement decisions, is the full cost of third-party integration.

The direct costs (API development*, interface maintenance, data mapping between systems) are real but at least visible. The indirect costs are more insidious. Every third-party AI tool added to a clinical environment creates a new attack surface for cybersecurity risk, a new contract to be negotiated and renewed, a new set of information governance obligations, and a new dependency on a vendor whose long-term viability is uncertain. This is particularly the case in the rapidly evolving AI market where the marginal cost of producing a new combinatorial innovation is small and technical evolution of the underlying general purpose technologies such as large language models is rapid. Many of these startups will simply not survive. These costs fall primarily on the digital and informatics teams of the healthcare organisation rather than on clinical budgets, which means they are typically invisible to the clinicians and clinical leaders who are most enthusiastic about a particular tool. The result is a systematic underestimation of total cost of ownership for third-party solutions relative to integrated ones, and a corresponding bias in procurement decisions that appears irrational from the outside but is entirely rational given how costs are allocated internally.

The position of third-party AI vendors is structurally more precarious than the current policy enthusiasm for health AI startups acknowledges. The value proposition of most third-party health AI products rests on one of two foundations: either a proprietary dataset that enables a model to outperform what the EHR vendor can build, or a speed-to-market advantage that gets the product into clinical use before the incumbent has developed a competing offering. Both foundations are weaker than they

*APIs or Application Programming Interfaces are the software that allows different systems to interact with each other. Whilst facilitating a publishable standard way of connecting, they are usually specific to a particular system.

appear. Proprietary datasets are valuable only for as long as the EHR vendor cannot access equivalent data, and in a market where EHR systems hold the longitudinal records of entire health systems, that window is rarely long. Speed-to-market advantages are equally temporary: a third-party product that demonstrates clinical utility in a well-publicised pilot is, in effect, conducting product validation on behalf of the EHR vendor, who can observe the evidence, develop a comparable feature, and bundle it into the next contract renewal at no additional procurement cost to the health system[62].

Critically, third-party vendors might own a good idea but they do not own the foundational AI infrastructure on which their products are built. The large language models, the computer vision architectures, the predictive modelling frameworks: these belong to a small number of technology companies whose primary business is not healthcare. A third-party health AI vendor is, in most cases, building a layer of clinical application and workflow integration on top of models it licenses rather than owns. That layer can be valuable but it is thin intellectual property, becoming thinner as the foundational models become more capable and more widely accessible. When a general-purpose language model can draft a clinical letter and an EHR vendor can embed that capability directly into the note-writing workflow, the stand-alone ambient documentation product faces a competitive position that no amount of clinical validation can fully offset.

There is a further dimension to the third-party ecosystem that the policy framing consistently underweights. The proliferation of specialist AI tools (one product for radiology reporting, another for ward deterioration prediction, a third for outpatient scheduling, a fourth for medication reconciliation) creates exactly the fragmented digital environment that drives the workflow problems described throughout this book. What the clinician needs is not a portfolio of AI capabilities but a coherent working environment in which relevant information and decision support is available at the point of need without friction. An ecosystem of disconnected applications, each with its own interface, its own alert logic, and its own data model, is the opposite of that. It reproduces in AI form the same interoperability failures that have plagued health IT for three decades. The tools may individually be excellent but the aggregate effect on clinical workflow can be worse than having fewer, better-integrated tools.

None of this is an argument against third-party AI in healthcare *per se*. It is an argument about where the structural pressures lead. Third-party vendors will continue to play a role, particularly in highly specialised domains where EHR vendors have neither the clinical expertise nor the commercial incentive to develop deep capability. But the overall trajectory of the market, driven by the integration advantage, the hidden cost structure of third-party procurement, and the commoditisation of foundational AI, points toward consolidation around a small number of large platforms. The clinical AI landscape in ten years is more likely to resemble the EHR market of today (a tight oligopoly with high switching costs and moderate innovation pressure) than the vibrant competitive ecosystem that policy documents currently envision.

This would not necessarily be a bad outcome if oligopoly produced the right commercial incentives. The critical variable is not market structure *per se* but whether the dominant vendors face sufficient competitive pressure to prioritise clinical innovation over feature additions that protect market position. Innovation is possible in an oligopoly: what matters are the commercial incentives, not necessarily the number of players. The history of the

EHR market is not encouraging here. Whilst there are some large and highly innovative EHR vendors a number of other dominant vendors did not achieve their positions primarily through continuous clinical innovation but instead through deep integration, long contract cycles, and the accumulated switching costs that make replacing an incumbent EHR among the most disruptive undertakings a health system can contemplate. The same dynamics that made those companies dominant also reduced the pace of innovation to a level that has frustrated clinicians and informaticists for years. There is no structural reason why AI embedded within those platforms should behave differently, unless the governance and procurement frameworks that health systems use to manage these relationships are deliberately designed to maintain contestability.

4.7 The default trajectory

Several further economic dynamics that the optimistic case for healthcare AI underestimates suggest that the default outcome is not merely inadequate transformation but something actively counterproductive. The first is what Baumol called the do-it-yourself shift[54]: the tendency, as professional services become more expensive, for some of their functions to migrate to consumers. We already see this in healthcare: patients monitoring their own blood pressure, interpreting their own test results through patient portals and so on. AI has the potential to accelerate this process considerably. A patient who can ask a language model about their symptoms, receive a detailed and confident response, and decide on that basis whether to seek professional care is performing a triage function that was previously performed by a clinician. In principle this is efficient but in practice it redistributes risk onto the person least equipped to manage it, and does so unevenly: the patient with health literacy, digital access and the confidence to navigate the system benefits, while the patient without those advantages is left with a tool that may mislead them more than it helps.

The second dynamic is related to Jevons' paradox, though it operates through a different mechanism in healthcare. Jevons observed in the nineteenth century that efficiency improvements in the use of a resource tend to increase total consumption of that resource rather than reduce it, because lower marginal cost stimulates demand[63]. The classic formulation does not map cleanly onto healthcare, because the dominant costs in clinical practice are not marginal in the relevant sense: in the UK for example a consultant's salary is paid whether they see ten patients or twenty. Making each consultation faster does not reduce the cost of the next one in the way that making electricity cheaper reduces the cost of running another appliance.

But the underlying concern—that AI will expand total demand rather than reduce total cost—is well founded. It just operates through different mechanisms, and healthcare has a name for the most important of them.

In 1961, the American health economist Milton Roemer made an observation that became one of the most replicated findings in health services research[64]. He noticed that when hospital bed supply increased in a given area, occupancy did not fall as classical economics would predict. The beds filled up. More supply did not produce cheaper care or more productivity. Instead it produced more admissions. The mechanism was supply-induced demand: in healthcare, unlike most markets, the supplier largely determines the demand. One mechanism is the perception that one can reduce risk when supply is plentiful[†]. The patient does

[†]For completeness: whilst a hospital admission, extra tests or interventions

not arrive at the hospital and independently decide to be admitted. The clinician decides to admit them. When more beds are available, the threshold for admission shifts downward, not through any conscious decision to waste resources but because clinical judgement operates within a context of available capacity. If a bed is there, admission is easier to justify. The aphorism that emerged—a built bed is a filled bed—became known as Roemer's Law, and subsequent research extended it well beyond beds: to surgical capacity, diagnostic equipment, specialist clinics, and, as this chapter argues, to AI-enabled services.

The principle applies directly to AI in healthcare. Make CT scanning faster and more accessible and clinicians will order more CT scans, not because patients have become sicker but because the threshold for ordering has fallen. Make AI-driven physiological monitoring available at lower cost and the envelope of patients being monitored expands: more data is generated, more alerts are triggered, and more clinical responses are initiated. Make diagnostic AI available in primary care and the threshold for investigation shifts downward across the board. Each of these is individually defensible as a clinical decision. In aggregate they expand total activity, and with it total cost, in ways that offset or exceed the efficiency gains that motivated the investment. The problem is that the efficiency gain at the level of the individual interaction gets absorbed by increased volume at the system level.

The second mechanism is latent demand surfacing. There is enormous unmet clinical need that is currently suppressed not by price but by access friction: waiting times, geographical bar-

---

may appear to be a superficially reasonable default position 'just to be safe', they may also sometimes increase risk of harm (for example through hospital-acquired infection or through mishap from the treatment from some false-positive test that was not strictly required).

riers, the effort of navigating the system, and the psychological threshold for seeking help. AI can lower that threshold. Remote monitoring catches deterioration earlier. AI-enabled triage tools make it easier to decide whether a symptom warrants attention. Consumer health AI, as Chapter 9 examines, brings millions of people into contact with something that resembles clinical reasoning for the first time. More people seek care not because it has become cheaper in any direct sense but because the barriers to seeking it have fallen. That is, again, largely a good thing for the individuals involved. But for systems already operating at capacity, it represents a further expansion of demand onto infrastructure that was not designed to absorb it.

It is important to be clear that neither Roemer's Law nor the latent demand argument is a case against expanding access or resisting the wider deployment of AI. More people getting the care they need is not a bad outcome. The point is this: projections of AI-enabled cost savings in healthcare need to be treated with considerable scepticism unless they account explicitly for these demand expansion effects. The history of healthcare technology is littered with innovations that delivered real efficiency gains at the level of individual tasks while leaving total system costs unchanged or increased, because the system expanded to absorb the gains. Telemedicine was supposed to substitute for in-person consultations and instead added to total consultation volume. Electronic health records were supposed to reduce administrative burden and instead generated new forms of it.[‡] There is

[‡]The fault here is less the technology than how it was deployed. Electronic records often redistributed documentation rather than reducing it, shifting work onto clinicians because they were the ones present at the point in the workflow where the data was captured: convenient, even if it meant the most expensive people in the system were now doing the typing. Some of the burden was self-inflicted, as when clinicians double-documented, writing a free-text note as well as entering the structured data that should

no obvious reason to expect AI to behave differently unless the governance arrangements surrounding its deployment are specifically designed to prevent demand expansion from consuming the efficiency dividend before it can be reinvested. That is an institutional rather than technical challenge, and it is the kind of challenge that the rest of this book examines.

The third dynamic follows from the first two and connects directly to the market forces described in the previous section. When the institutional incentives favour incremental adoption, the psychology of organisational decision-making favours immediate and attributable returns over long-horizon transformation, and demand expands to absorb efficiency gains, the most likely AI trajectory in healthcare is a proliferation of techno-fixes: tools that address surface symptoms without touching underlying structure. Ambient voice documentation reduces note-writing time without questioning why so much clinical time is spent on documentation in the first place. AI triage tools could improve emergency department productivity and flow without addressing why so many patients arrive at emergency departments for conditions that should have been managed in other settings. Diagnostic AI augments the radiologist without asking whether the current configuration of radiology services is the right one for a world in which AI can read scans.

Each of these interventions is valuable but none of them add up to transformation. Worse still, the risk is not merely that they fall short of what AI could achieve but that they consume the institutional energy, the procurement budget, the clinical good-

---

have replaced it. And a substantial share, particularly in the United States, reflects documentation demanded by payers for billing and reimbursement rather than anything the record itself required. The point is not that electronic records failed, but that a tool can deliver on its narrow promise while total administrative burden still rises, because the burden has sources the tool does not control.

will and the regulatory bandwidth that transformation would require, while leaving the fundamental structure of healthcare unchanged. Granted the system gets better at doing what it already does. But the things it does not do, the unmet need, the access gaps, the preventable harm and the structural inequity, remain largely untouched.

The standard policy response to slow AI adoption compounds this problem rather than solving it. Deployment mandates, individual financial incentives, and procurement requirements all address the threshold problem superficially: they increase the number of clinicians using the tool without creating the conditions under which genuine adoption becomes individually rational. The result is faster spread of partial adoption, higher headline adoption rates, and no systemic benefit. Stronger individual incentives do not escape the partial adoption trap but instead just accelerate convergence to it.

What the logic of the partial adoption trap implies instead is that the sequence of interventions matters as much as the interventions themselves. Trust architecture must precede adoption requirements: clinicians will not restructure their working practice around a technology if they rationally expect the productivity gains to be captured as budget savings or workload intensification rather than shared with them. Cultural preparation must precede individual incentives: in a professional culture where partial adoption is the norm, individual incentives to genuinely adopt simply accelerate conformity to the partial adoption equilibrium. And the unit of adoption must be the clinical team rather than the individual clinician, because the collective threshold that systemic benefit requires can only be crossed when enough of a coherent working unit moves together. These are institutional interventions. They are also precisely the interventions that standard digital transformation policy does not typically make.

The conclusion from this chapter is therefore not that AI cannot transform healthcare economics. To be clear, I believe there is real potential. Certainly, the need is both present and urgent. The issue is that transformation will not emerge from current market forces, institutional incentives or individual adoption decisions operating on their own. The economics of healthcare, from Arrow's information asymmetry to Baumol's cost disease to Jevons' paradox, all point in the same direction: toward a system that is structurally resistant to the kind of change that AI makes possible, and that will absorb AI into its existing configuration unless the incentives, governance structures and institutional arrangements are deliberately redesigned around different objectives.

5 Can intelligent machines beat stupid systems?

The previous chapter established that healthcare is an unusual economic system: one shaped by information asymmetry, professional monopoly, and institutional arrangements designed to manage the absence of normal market forces. It showed that these features make healthcare expensive, resistant to scaling, and difficult to make more productive. We have seen how the prevailing conditions make it slow for the right kinds of technology to enter healthcare. But what about when the right technology does come along? It turns out that there are still challenges that AI must face.

As an intellectual telescope with which to see further, I will repurpose a set of ideas that were not developed with healthcare in mind, nor directed at AI as a technology. Instead they come from economic history, institutional theory and game theory, and were built to explain broader questions: why some economies grow and others stagnate, why industries resist change long past the point where change would benefit everyone, and why rational people so often collectively produce outcomes that none of them wanted. These frameworks are useful here precisely because they were built to explain general phenomena of which healthcare is a specific instance. The problems this chapter describes are not unique to medicine but are patterns that economists and political theorists have been studying for decades, and the analytical tools they have developed turn out to be considerably sharper than anything purpose-built for the healthcare technology debate.

5.1 The persistent puzzle

Healthcare has absorbed enormous digital investment over the past three decades. EHRs now dominate clinical documentation across most high-income health systems. Picture archiving and communication systems have made film-based radiology a relic. Telemedicine, once a curiosity, became a necessity during the Covid-19 pandemic, was adopted and has remained. Clinical decision support tools are embedded in prescribing systems, imaging workflows and intensive care monitoring. The data infrastructure of modern medicine would be unrecognisable to a clinician from 1990.

And yet as we've already seen, the productivity of healthcare systems has barely shifted. In the NHS, official statistics show that by 2022 to 2023 the service was producing 5.4% less care for every pound spent than in 2019 to 2020. Diagnostic error rates have not fallen. Waiting lists in most high-income countries are longer than they were before the digital transformation began. The burden on clinicians, far from being relieved by technology, has in many respects increased. So has technology failed? Not in the conventional sense. The technology works: EHRs do store and retrieve information more reliably than paper and AI algorithms do read certain scans with accuracy that matches or exceeds that of a specialist clinician. The question then is why capable technology, deployed at scale and at enormous cost, has still produced so little structural change in how care is organised and delivered.

The answer requires a distinction that is rarely made clearly in debates about digital health: the difference between digitisation and transformation. Digitisation means that information is stored, transmitted and processed electronically rather than on paper or film. Transformation means that the fundamental organisation of work, the distribution of authority and the structure of incentives have changed. Healthcare systems have largely achieved the former but the latter has barely begun. Understanding why is the purpose of this chapter.

5.2 The limits of techno-optimism

The standard case for healthcare technology rests on a chain of logic that seems self-evident: better information leads to better decisions and better decisions lead to better outcomes. Invest in the tools that improve information and the rest follows. It is a compelling argument, and it has driven hundreds of billions of pounds and dollars of investment in health information technology over the past three decades.

The EHR is the canonical test of this logic, and it is interesting to look at its impact. The EHR promised to eliminate the information fragmentation that plagued paper-based systems, reduce medical error, enable population health management and free clinicians from administrative drudgery. Some of these promises have been partially fulfilled. Information is more reliably stored and more widely accessible than it was. But the unintended consequences have been substantial. Documentation burden has increased rather than decreased, contributing to epidemic levels of physician burnout. Alert fatigue has become a recognised clinical hazard, with studies showing that the majority of decision support alerts are overridden, often appropriately, because the volume has overwhelmed the signal. In other words, the information got better but that revealed problems elsewhere in the system which hadn't changed.

The reason is that technology does not implement itself and does not exist in a vacuum. It enters an existing social, economic and professional environment that has evolved over decades or centuries to serve particular purposes and to maintain particular distributions of authority and reward. That environment does not passively receive new tools and optimise around them. It actively shapes how those tools are used, what functions they are permitted to perform and whose interests they are permitted to threaten.

An instructive British example is the National Programme for Information Technology (NPfIT), launched in 2002 with £12.4 billion and an ambition to digitise the entire NHS secondary care sector. When the independent review chaired by Robert Wachter examined the programme's failure a decade later, the conclusion was unambiguous: the technology was not the problem. NPfIT failed because it was conceived as a technical project rather than a human one. It assumed that if systems were procured and installed, the institution would adapt around them. The institution did not adapt and it was therefore just too complicated for a single technological solution to be retrofitted to it[65].

The contrast with the American experience of around the same time is striking. In 2009, the United States enacted the Health Information Technology for Economic and Clinical Health (known as HITECH) Act, part of the post-financial crisis stimulus package[66]. The mechanism was admittedly a pretty blunt one: $27 billion in incentive payments to hospitals and physicians who could demonstrate 'meaningful use' of certified EHRs, with financial penalties for those who did not comply by the statutory deadline. It was, in essence, an attempt to solve by economic compulsion the same problem NPfIT had tried to solve by central procurement.

Although far from perfect, on its stated objective of achieving digitisation, it worked. In 2008, fewer than one in ten American hospitals had adopted a basic electronic health record system. By 2015, more than eight in ten had[67]. Annual EHR adoption rates among eligible hospitals accelerated from 3.2 per cent before HITECH to 14.2 per cent after it[68]. Whatever its other failures, HITECH demonstrated that a healthcare system stuck in a pre-digital configuration can be moved. It demonstrated that institutional inertia is not immovable, that the right combination of incentives and penalties can shift even a system as entrenched as American hospital medicine.

But HITECH also demonstrated something this book's argument requires us to hold alongside that achievement: the difference between digitisation and transformation. HITECH produced near-universal EHR adoption but still did not produce the productivity gains, the interoperability or the improvements in care quality that had been implicit in the investment. Clinician burnout increased and alert fatigue became an epidemic. The Meaningful Use programme, intended to ensure that EHRs were used in clinically productive ways, became progressively more bureaucratic and prescriptive in its later stages, generating compliance activity rather than clinical benefit, to the point where clinicians took to calling it 'meaningless abuse'[65]. The system had been digitised but the work had not been redesigned. The institution had absorbed the technology, as it always does, and carried on largely as before.*

*I use the term absorption to describe what happens when a technology with transformative potential is deployed in a way that leaves the fundamental structure of the institution unchanged. Not all AI deployment is absorption in this sense. A well-scoped tool that does exactly what it was designed

That is the pattern this book argues repeats itself with AI. The question is not whether AI can be deployed at scale in healthcare. HITECH showed that adoption can be compelled when the financial stakes are high enough. The question is whether deployment produces transformation, and the evidence of three decades of health information technology investment suggests that it does not unless the institutional conditions that determine how a technology is used are redesigned alongside the technology itself.

This point is not new and historians of technology have long observed that the social context of adoption matters just as much as the technical capabilities of the innovation itself. What is striking in healthcare is how consistently this lesson has been ignored. Each new technology arrives accompanied by transformative promises, encounters the same institutional resistances, and is absorbed into existing workflows with incremental rather than structural effect. The EHR replicated the paper record in digital form. It has the potential to change the processes by which healthcare is delivered but instead was used as a digital version of paper. Telemedicine reproduced the outpatient appointment through a screen irrespective of whether the patient needed to be seen or whether there was some better, perhaps digital way, to track their health and be in contact. Clinical decision support became another source of interruptions for clinicians to dismiss. The technology adapted to the institution rather than the institution adapting to the technology. This pattern is neither accidental nor is it simply the result of poor implementation or insufficient

---

to do, without claiming to transform anything, is simply good implementation. The category error that matters is when absorption is mistaken for transformation: when the institution deploys AI incrementally, declares that it has engaged seriously with the technology, and uses that declaration to deflect pressure for the structural changes that transformation actually requires.

investment. In reality it emerges from something deeper about the nature of the institution into which these technologies are being introduced, and about what that institution is actually designed to do.

5.3 Institutions, not technology, drive outcomes

Why do capable technologies, deployed with sincere intent and substantial resources, so consistently fail to change the systems into which they are introduced? The answer requires moving beyond the observation that institutions are slow to change and asking what institutions actually are, what purposes they serve, and why those purposes might not always be aligned with the improvement of healthcare.

The distinction between technical and adaptive change, developed by the political theorist Ronald Heifetz and applied with particular force to healthcare digitisation by Wachter's review of NHS IT, captures this well[65]. Technical problems have known solutions: follow the procedure, install the system, train the staff. Adaptive problems require the people inside the institution to change how they work, what they value, and how they relate to one another. Healthcare IT has been consistently treated as a technical problem. The EHR is procured, the training is delivered, the go-live date is set. What is far harder to address and therefore often ignored is the adaptive challenge: that meaningful use of these systems requires clinicians to redesign their work, share authority they have previously held exclusively, and accept transparency they have previously been able to decline. These are not technical requirements but institutional ones, and they cannot be met by better software.

The economists Agrawal, Gans and Goldfarb offer a complementary way of seeing why the adaptive challenge is so critical[69].

Organisations that are poor in information run on rules: standard operating procedures that condition on little, cost something every time that the rule gives the wrong answer, and in exchange make everyone's behaviour predictable to everyone else. Cheap prediction makes it possible to replace rules with decisions that condition on far more information, but the internal rules are crucial: they are the glue that holds the existing system together, and each one is embedded in a web of other rules that assume it. Changing one therefore means changing many at once, which is why the transition demands what they call an *oiled* system where decision-making adapts dynamically on the basis of information, and why it rarely happens without leadership prepared to alter dozens of interlocking conditions together. Their own worked example is worth thinking about: a pandemic-era testing programme that replaced the blanket rule "everybody stay home" with the decision "test constantly, stay home if positive" succeeded only because senior managers across a dozen organisations forced the surrounding rules of work, schooling and care to change simultaneously. Bresnahan, reviewing the argument, adds the sobering observation that the celebrated AI-driven system transformations happened inside firms whose production was already algorithmic, and that most organisations attempting to imitate them have failed[70]. Healthcare, whose rules are more numerous, more interlocked and more fiercely defended than almost any other sector's, is the hardest case of exactly this problem. It is far from well-oiled.

The most useful framework for this question comes from the economic historian Douglass North, who spent much of his career asking why some economies grow and others stagnate despite access to similar technologies. His answer was that the critical variable is not technology but institutions. North defined institutions as the rules of the game in a society: the formal rules encoded in law and regulation, and the informal constraints embedded in norms, conventions and professional codes. Together these rules shape the incentives within which individuals and organisations act†. They determine not what is possible but what is rewarded. This distinction is the key to understanding the technology problem in healthcare. Technology changes what is possible but it is the institutions that determine what is rewarded. And if the institutional rules reward volume over value, individual clinical autonomy over system-level productivity, and activity over productivity, then even the most capable technology will be absorbed into that incentive structure rather than transforming it. Technology itself will always adapt to the rules of the game rather than changing them.

North's framework[71] has a further important implication. Institutions are not simply rules imposed from outside; they are also the accumulated strategies of the people who operate within them. When an institution has been stable for a long time, the people within it have built careers, identities, and livelihoods around its existing arrangements. A doctor who has spent a decade developing specialist expertise in a domain where AI now performs equivalently has not merely lost a tool: she has lost the basis of her professional authority. A hospital administrator whose organisation has invested heavily in a particular work-

---

†North draws a sharp distinction between institutions and organisations that is easy to lose. Institutions are the rules of the game: the laws, regulations, norms and professional codes that structure behaviour. Organisations, such as hospitals, professional specialty groups, insurers and regulators, are the players who operate within those rules, and indeed who are shaped by them. A hospital is therefore part of the institutional landscape of healthcare, but it is not the institution; the institution is the broader, more durable framework of rules within which the hospital and every other actor competes and cooperates. At the same time the rules and processes within a hospital are themselves part of the wider institution.

flow has not merely adopted a potentially suboptimal process: he has created dependencies that make change costly. Institutions persist not only because rules are hard to change but because people have rationally adapted to them, and adaptation creates resistance to redesign.

This has an uncomfortable implication for new healthcare AI technologies. The question of whether AI transforms healthcare is not primarily a question about the technology but instead a question about whether the institutional rules of healthcare, the incentive structures, the professional norms, the payment models and the governance arrangements reward the outcomes that AI makes possible. If they do not, transformation will not occur regardless of technical capability. If they do, transformation becomes possible but is still not guaranteed, because the people who have adapted to the old rules may still reasonably resist the change that threatens their position. North observed that institutional change is therefore typically slow, path-dependent and contested. It does not follow automatically from technological advance or from evidence of better outcomes. Instead it requires either a change in the rules themselves, which is contingent on political will and usually encounters organised resistance, or a gradual shift in the informal norms and expectations of the people within the system, which takes generations. In my view, neither of these operates on timescales compatible with the urgency of the challenges that healthcare systems currently face.

5.4 Transaction costs as the binding constraint

Understanding why institutional rules are so resistant to change requires getting more specific about the nature of the friction involved. The economist Oliver Williamson provided the tools for this. Building on earlier work by Ronald Coase, Williamson argued that the costs of economic activity are not simply the costs of production[72]. They also include the costs of coordination itself: finding information, reaching agreements, monitoring compliance, and adapting to changing circumstances. These are transaction costs, and Williamson's central insight was that their size and structure determine how organisations are shaped and how they behave.

In healthcare, such transaction costs are not peripheral overheads but instead they are a dominant feature of the working day (as any resident doctor will attest). Every referral that crosses an organisational boundary, every handover between clinical teams, every approval process for a new technology, every incident report and audit cycle: these are all transaction costs. Studies consistently show that clinicians spend between a third and a half of their working time on coordination, documentation and administrative tasks rather than direct patient care. That fraction has grown with increasing regulatory requirements, organisational complexity and the information demands of modern medicine. The technology that was supposed to reduce this burden, most obviously the EHR, has in many settings increased it, generating new streams of alerts, notifications and documentation requirements on top of the old ones.

Williamson identified three features of transactions that determine how costly and difficult they are to govern. The first is *asset specificity*: the degree to which the investments made to support a transaction lose their value outside that particular relationship. The second is *uncertainty*: how difficult it is to anticipate what will happen and write rules covering it in advance. The third is the problem of *incomplete contracts*: because the future cannot be fully specified, agreements always leave gaps, and those gaps create opportunities for the parties involved to pursue their own interests at the expense of the shared purpose. All three of these features are present in healthcare to an unusual degree, and all three are directly relevant to why AI adoption is so difficult.

Asset specificity operates at the level of the individual clinician as much as the organisation. A surgeon who has spent a substantial part of their working life developing expertise in a particular operative technique has made a highly specific investment. That investment is worth a great deal within the existing system. It is worth considerably less in a redesigned system where AI-enabled protocols reduce the scope for individual judgement, or where trained non-physicians can perform the same procedures safely within defined parameters. The resistance of experienced clinicians to AI-enabled redesign is therefore not simply conservatism or technophobia. It is a rational response to the threat of asset 'stranding': the prospect that investments of time, effort and identity will be rendered worthless by a change in the rules of the game.

Clinical work is often characterised by irreducible uncertainty and enormous contextual variation, which makes it impossible to specify in advance all the situations that might arise and how they should be handled[‡]. This is the central justification used for clinical autonomy: the professional must be able to exercise judgement in situations that no protocol could anticipate. But incomplete contracting also means that when AI systems are introduced into clinical workflows, the governance arrangements surrounding them cannot specify every contingency. Who is responsible when an AI recommendation is followed and causes

[‡]I will argue in Chapter 7 that at least some of this complexity is a result of the institution rather than a necessary feature that emerges from biological uncertainty and the nature of illness and so this claim that the complexity is inherent is over-stated.

harm? Who decides when a model has drifted sufficiently from its training data that it should no longer be trusted? Who bears the cost of retraining, revalidation and reconfiguration when clinical practice evolves? These questions do not have obvious answers, and their unresolved status raises the perceived cost of adoption even when the technology itself is demonstrably capable.

There is a further mechanism that Williamson identified which is particularly relevant to the specific resistance that AI generates. When one party to a transaction has private information that the other cannot observe, there is scope for strategic behaviour: presenting that information selectively, or withholding it entirely, in order to protect a favourable position. Clinicians have detailed knowledge of workflow complexity, case mix and the practical demands of clinical decision-making that commissioners, managers and system designers do not. This information asymmetry creates scope for the strategic defence of existing arrangements, overstating the complexity of tasks that AI could perform, or understating the reliability of AI recommendations, in ways that are difficult for non-clinicians to evaluate. This is in no way a claim that clinicians are dishonest. The incentive structure creates entirely rational grounds for selective presentation of information, and this is a predictable feature of any system where professional authority depends on maintaining an information advantage.

Taken together, these mechanisms explain something that purely technical accounts of AI adoption cannot: why the friction is so persistent, why it is concentrated at particular points in the system, and why it tends to increase rather than decrease as AI becomes more capable. The more powerful the technology, the greater the threat to existing investments, the more incomplete the contracts governing its use, and the stronger the incentive for those with information advantages to deploy them defensively. Again, to be clear, the transaction cost lens does not make healthcare workers the villains of this story. They are simply rational actors responding to an incentive structure that was never designed to reward the large-scale transformation that AI makes possible and that is needed if it is to improve productivity.

5.5 Path dependence and the absorption of change

Even if institutional rules could be changed and transaction costs reduced, there is a further obstacle that operates independently of both: the tendency of systems to become locked into particular ways of doing things, making departure from established paths increasingly costly over time regardless of whether those paths remain optimal.

We have encountered this phenomenon, known as path dependence, before. Economic historians have studied why inefficient technologies sometimes persist long after better alternatives become available. The most cited and striking example is the keyboard you almost certainly use daily and which I used to write this book. The QWERTY layout, named after the first six letters in the top row, was designed in the 1870s by Christopher Sholes, the inventor of one of the first commercially successful typewriters. The mechanical typewriters of that era had a significant engineering problem: if a typist pressed two adjacent keys in quick succession, the tiny metal hammers that struck the ribbon would jam. Sholes solved this problem by deliberately separating the most commonly used letter combinations so that these hammers would be less likely to collide. In other words, QWERTY was specifically engineered to slow typists down. It was a workaround for a mechanical limitation, not a design for efficient typing.

The mechanical jamming problem disappeared decades ago. Modern keyboards, whether physical or virtual, have no hammers or ribbon and no jamming risk. Alternative layouts (perhaps most famously the Dvorak Simplified Keyboard patented in 1936) were designed from the outset around the actual frequency of letter combinations in English, placing the most common letters on the home row where fingers rest naturally. Studies have suggested that Dvorak typists can achieve higher speeds with less finger movement and lower rates of repetitive strain injury. And yet QWERTY remains almost universally dominant, more than a century and a half after the problem it was designed to solve ceased to exist.

The reason is not that people are unaware of the alternatives or incapable of learning them, but that the costs of switching are distributed in a way that makes individual action irrational even when collective action would be beneficial. Every typist who switches to Dvorak must endure a period of reduced productivity while relearning. Every employer who switches must retrain staff and replace or reconfigure equipment. Every keyboard manufacturer who switches risks producing hardware that nobody trained on QWERTY can use. The benefit of the switch accrues to everyone who types, diffused across the whole population; the cost falls on whoever makes the first move. In the absence of a mechanism to coordinate a simultaneous switch and distribute the transition costs fairly, the rational choice for every individual actor is to stay with QWERTY. The inefficiency persists not because it is invisible but because the structure of incentives makes it self-reinforcing.

Paul David, whose analysis of this case helped establish path dependence as a serious economic concept, drew an explicit parallel with the electrification of industry[73]: the productivity gains from electrical power took decades to materialise not because the technology was unavailable but because factories were physically and organisationally built around steam power[§], and rebuilding them around electricity required complementary investments that no single firm could justify in isolation. Productivity gains from AI and digital technologies are contingent on organisational change and sustained investment, with costs front-loaded and benefits accruing only over time.

Cross-economy analysis demonstrates that AI adoption remains far below the threshold at which aggregate productivity effects become detectable in macroeconomic data, and that realising AI's productivity potential requires substantial complementary investment in skills, data infrastructure and organisational change that precedes any measurable gain[58]. The pattern Paul David identified in the electrification of industry is repeating itself.

Healthcare exhibits path dependence at every level of its organisation. The hospital as the centre of gravity for acute care delivery has persisted for over a century despite strong evidence that a substantial proportion of what happens in hospitals could be delivered more efficiently in community or home settings. The physical infrastructure, the workforce training pipelines, the reimbursement models, the regulatory frameworks and the

[§]Steam engines in factories were large and heavy, powering a long rotating shaft from which belts transferred power to the various machines. This meant that the workshop needed to be laid out so that the larger machines were nearer the power source. This was not necessarily the best configuration for the manufacturing process. Smaller electric motors enabled factories to be laid out in a way that promoted efficiency (think of the modern production-line for example). But that required a complete redesign of the workplace and of working practices.

professional identities of clinical staff have all co-evolved around the hospital, creating a web of complementary investments that makes departure from this configuration extraordinarily costly. Each individual element of the system is rational given the others but the irrationality is at the level of the whole.

The same logic applies at the level of clinical roles and professional boundaries. The division of labour between doctors, nurses, pharmacists and allied health professionals reflects historical settlements about who may do what, reinforced by licensing law, professional regulation, training curricula and liability frameworks. These boundaries were not designed around the capabilities of AI. They were designed around the capabilities of people working without computational assistance, and around the political economy of professional organisation at particular moments in the history of medicine. AI has the potential to make many of these boundaries obsolete in a technical sense. A trained nurse practitioner supported by an AI clinical decision support system could perhaps manage a much wider range of conditions than the current scope of practice might permit. A pharmacist with access to AI-enabled prescribing support could perform functions currently reserved for physicians. But changing the boundaries requires simultaneous renegotiation of licensing law, reimbursement models, liability frameworks, professional training and the informal norms of clinical practice. No single actor can do this alone, and the costs of coordinating such a change across all the relevant parties are enormous.

The absorption mechanism is the practical expression of path dependence in healthcare AI. As I have pointed out, new technologies do not arrive into an empty space; they arrive into a system that has existing workflows, existing authority structures and existing ways of distributing credit and blame. The rational response of that system is not to redesign itself around the new technology but to find the use of the new technology that requires the least disruption to existing arrangements. EHRs were configured to replicate paper-based documentation rather than to redesign clinical information flows. Telemedicine was deployed to replicate the outpatient appointment through a screen rather than to restructure the relationship between primary and secondary care. AI documentation tools are being adopted to reduce the time clinicians spend on note-writing rather than to question why so much clinical time is spent on documentation in the first place.

This absorption is not a failure of imagination on the part of the people involved, but the predictable outcome of a path-dependent system in which the individual actor who attempts to redesign their local environment around the technology bears the full cost of the transition while the benefits diffuse across the wider system. The ward that redesigns its workflows around AI-enabled nursing assessment takes on the disruption of change and the risk of things going wrong during transition. The benefit, in the form of reduced pressure on beds elsewhere in the hospital, accrues to parts of the system that bore none of the cost. In the absence of governance arrangements that redistribute these costs and benefits, the rational choice is to absorb the technology into the existing path rather than to use it as the basis for redesign.

The implication for healthcare AI is as follows. The question is not whether AI can perform clinical tasks adequately: in many domains it demonstrably can. Instead the question is whether the system can reorganise itself to take advantage of that capability, and path dependence suggests that without deliberate external intervention to shift the equilibrium, the answer is no. The technology will be adopted in forms that are compatible with the existing path, generating incremental rather than structural change, for exactly the same reasons that the QWERTY keyboard is still with us.

I am going to suggest that absorption takes two forms, and the difference between them matters. The first is *neutral absorption*: the technology is adopted, workflows are marginally improved, and the fundamental structure of the institution is unchanged. The EHR is the canonical example. Documentation got faster and more legible. The distribution of authority, income and decision rights was not altered. Real activity, real cost but otherwise negligible structural effect. It is the most common outcome, and in itself it is not necessarily harmful. The best examples of neutral absorption are valuable in themselves. The problem arises when they are presented as evidence that the institution has embraced transformation, diverting attention and resources from the harder structural work that transformation actually requires.

The second is *exploitative absorption*: the technology is adopted in ways that actively worsen the position of some participants while leaving the institutional structure intact. Work intensification is the most common form. If AI reduces the time required for a task, the institutional response might be to increase the volume of tasks rather than to reduce the burden on the workforce. The efficiency gain is captured as throughput, not as relief. Surveillance is another form: AI-enabled monitoring of clinical activity that flows upward as a management tool rather than sideways as a capacity signal, generating data that is used against the workforce rather than for it. Algorithmic bias, examined in detail in Chapter 8, is a third: the technology encodes and scales existing institutional inequities, making them more consistent, more authoritative and harder to challenge than the human decisions they replace. In each case the institution absorbs the technology and emerges not merely unchanged but with its least defensible features amplified.

The alternative to absorption, in either form, is *transformative deployment*: the technology is used as the basis for redesign, redistributing decision rights, substituting less expensive labour where AI has made that safe, and restructuring care pathways around what the technology makes possible rather than around what the institution has historically done. This is what the rest of this book is largely concerned with understanding: why transformative deployment is rare, what conditions it requires, and what would need to change for it to become the default rather than the exception.

5.6 Productivity versus power

Path dependence explains why healthcare systems are slow to change. But it does not fully explain why they actively resist change, or why that resistance is so well organised and so effective. For that we need a different analytical framework, one that shifts attention from friction and inertia to the deliberate defence of power and economic interest.

The economist Daron Acemoglu, best known for his work on why nations develop differently, has argued that the standard economic account of institutional change is incomplete in a fundamental way. Economists typically assume that if a reform would make the overall system more productive, producing more benefit than cost in aggregate, it will eventually be adopted because the winners could in principle compensate the losers and still come out ahead. Acemoglu's contribution was to show that this logic fails systematically whenever a reform threatens the rents, authority or legitimacy of powerful incumbents. Those incumbents do not ask whether the reform is right in aggregate. They ask whether it is good for them and when the answer is no, they use whatever power they have to block it, regardless of the evidence in its favour[57].

The distinction has parallels that matter enormously for healthcare AI. Most of the discussion about AI adoption in healthcare is framed in terms of evidence, safety and efficacy. The implicit assumption is that if AI can be shown to improve outcomes safely and cost-effectively, adoption will follow. This framework suggests this assumption is wrong, not as a matter of human failing but as a structural prediction. The question is not whether AI improves aggregate outcomes. The question is whether it improves outcomes for the people who control the decisions about adoption. And in many cases, the answer is that it does not.

Consider what AI-enabled redesign of healthcare actually involves. It might for example involve making specialist-level diagnostic capability available to generalist clinicians and, increasingly, to patients directly. That might involve enabling trained non-physicians to perform tasks currently reserved for doctors, making clinical decision-making transparent and auditable in ways that individual professional judgement currently is not, and shifting care away from hospitals and into community settings. Each of these changes has the potential, perhaps, to help improve aggregate outcome and reduce cost. Each of them also directly threatens the income, authority and professional identity of particular groups within the healthcare system. This redistribution operates in part by reducing the coordination costs that currently sustain these arrangements, whether by standardising decisions, redistributing information, or enabling substitution between roles. These are not incidental side effects of reform but the very mechanism by which reform produces its benefits, because the inefficiency of the current system and the privileges of its incumbents are two sides of the same coin.

Acemoglu draws an important distinction between economic institutions, which govern how resources are allocated and how economic activity is rewarded, and political institutions, which govern who has the power to make and change the rules. In healthcare, these two levels are deeply intertwined. The medical profession does not merely participate in healthcare economics; it substantially controls the rules of the game. As we have noted, doctors control entry to the profession through training and licensing. Professional bodies set standards of practice and govern conduct. Clinical autonomy, enshrined in both law and culture, protects individual practitioner judgement from external audit in ways that would be inconceivable in most other industries. These arrangements did not emerge by accident but instead they reflect a long history of political organisation by the medical profession to protect its interests, often conflated with and then successfully presented to the public as protection of patient safety[74,75].

To be sure, this is not a claim that the medical profession is uniquely self-interested or that patient safety arguments are always pre-textual. Clinicians are, on the whole, genuinely motivated by the welfare of their patients, and many of the professional protections that exist serve real purposes. The claim is more uncomfortable: that the institutional arrangements which protect professional authority in medicine also happen to protect professional income and status, and that when AI threatens those arrangements, the resistance it encounters will be organised, sustained, and articulated in the language of patient safety regardless of whether patient safety is the primary motivation. It is what happens in every sector when a distribution-shifting technology encounters incumbents with the organisational capacity to defend their position.

The practical implication is that the standard response to AI resistance, which is to produce more evidence of clinical effectiveness and safety, is addressing the wrong problem. Evidence matters, and poor evidence is a legitimate reason for caution. But the history of AI adoption in healthcare shows that evidence of effectiveness is important but far from all-encompassing. Technologies that are well-evidenced, safe, and cost-effective have stalled repeatedly when they threatened professional boundaries or redistributed decision rights. Technologies that are poorly evidenced but compatible with existing authority structures have diffused rapidly. The pattern is more consistent with this political economy framework than with a story about evidence-based adoption.

5.7 Veto players and institutional sclerosis

Path dependence explains inertia. The power-and-resistance framework explains active resistance by those with the most to lose. But neither fully accounts for the collective dimension of institutional sclerosis: the way that healthcare systems accumulate, over time, a dense network of organised interests that together make fundamental redesign almost impossible, even when no single group is powerful enough to block change on its own.

The economist Mancur Olson provided the framework for understanding this in work that remains among the most important and most uncomfortable contributions to political economy of the twentieth century[76]. He showed that small, well-organised groups with concentrated interests will consistently outmanoeuvre large groups with dispersed interests in political and institutional contests. The reason is straightforward: a group of a thousand radiologists who each stand to lose a significant portion of their income if AI automates radiology reporting has a powerful and immediate incentive to organise, lobby, litigate and resist. The millions of patients who would each benefit modestly from cheaper and faster radiology have no equivalent incentive to organise in favour of the change. The costs of collective action are too high relative to the individual benefit. The result, repeated across every domain where concentrated professional interests face diffuse public benefits, is that the organised minority prevails over the unorganised majority.

In *The Rise and Decline of Nations*[76] Olson extended this argument to explain a broader pattern: that long-stable societies accumulate coalitions of organised interests over time, each defending its position against change, until the cumulative weight of these defensive coalitions makes the system increasingly rigid and slow to adapt. He called this institutional sclerosis. The longer a society or sector has been stable, the more of these coalitions it will have accumulated, and the harder it will be to implement reforms that threaten any of them.

Healthcare in high-income countries is, by this measure, among the most sclerotic sectors in any modern economy. It has been institutionally stable, in its fundamental organisation, for the better part of a century. In that time it has accumulated an extraordinary density of organised interests: medical colleges and specialist societies, nursing and allied health professional bodies, hospital trusts and health systems, pharmaceutical and medical device manufacturers, insurers and managed care organisations, clinical informaticists and IT vendors, regulators and accreditation bodies, unions and workforce organisations. Each of these groups has a legitimate role in the healthcare system. Each of them has also developed, over decades, a detailed and sophisticated understanding of how to protect its position against unwanted change.

The practical consequence is that any AI application that would substantially alter an existing workflow must navigate this entire coalition simultaneously. It is not enough to satisfy the clinical evidence requirements of one regulator if the technology also threatens the scope of practice of a professional body, disrupts the revenue model of an incumbent vendor, or requires renegotiation of workforce contracts. Each of these groups holds what political scientists call a veto: the ability to block or delay a reform without being able to implement an alternative. The more veto players a system has, the more stable it is, and the harder it is to shift from one configuration to another even when the current configuration is clearly failing.

What does a veto look like in practice? Veto instruments are mostly mundane: procedural requirements, standards of evidence, reimbursement decisions, scope of practice rules and so on. Each has a legitimate purpose and each can be deployed, by an organised group with the right institutional standing, to slow or block a technology that threatens its position. The following examples illustrate how this works across different parts of the system.

Professional scope of practice as a blocking instrument. The evidence that nurse practitioners supported by clinical decision support can safely manage a wide range of conditions currently reserved for physicians is substantial[77]. In the United States, the American Medical Association and its 105 affiliated state and specialty medical associations have spent more than $3.5 million in grants since 2006 specifically to fund campaigns protecting against scope of practice creep[78]. In the United States, a sizeable number of states still require physician supervision or collaborative agreements for nurse practitioners to practise independently[79], despite strong evidence that outcomes can be equivalent[77]. The blocking mechanism is state medical practice acts, which require legislative change, which requires overcoming organised medical lobbying at the state level. The framing is consistently patient safety. However the effect is to preserve a task boundary that AI-enabled clinical decision support could instead make technically obsolete.

Reimbursement as a market-shaping veto. When the FDA granted the first authorisation for an autonomous AI diagnostic system in 2018, clearing IDx-DR for autonomous detection of diabetic retinopathy in primary care settings without physician oversight, there was no billing code that allowed healthcare providers to charge for its use[80]. The technology existed as did the regulatory approval and the clinical evidence was strong. But without a Current Procedural Terminology code, the economic case for deployment did not exist. A temporary code was issued by the American Academy of Ophthalmology; a permanent code was not created until 2021, three years after authorisation. In that window, a technology that had the potential to bring specialist-level diabetic eye screening into primary care settings, dramatically increasing access for underserved populations, sat largely unused. In this case the veto was not a decision but an absence: the absence of the administrative infrastructure required to make deployment economically viable, controlled by professional bodies with no particular incentive to create it quickly.

Procurement as a delay mechanism. In 2023, NHS England deployed AI tools for chest diagnostics across 66 hospital trusts, backed by £21 million of central funding. An evaluation[81] found that contracting alone took between four and ten months longer than the programme's leadership had anticipated. By June 2025, eighteen months after contracting was meant to be complete, a third of the 66 trusts were still not using the tools in clinical practice. The barriers were not regulatory obstruction but the ordinary friction of a system in which each trust was required to obtain its own local governance approvals, integrate the tools with its own IT systems, and engage its own clinical staff, regardless of what neighbouring trusts in the same network had already done. The governance requirements were not unreasonable in isolation. Cumulatively, applied independently at every deployment site, they transformed a funded national programme into a lengthy series of local negotiations, each capable of stalling independently. No single actor blocked the deployment—the system did.

Regulatory classification as a structural veto. The UK ambient voice technology market illustrates what happens when AI deployment moves faster than the regulatory framework designed to govern it. By early 2025, dozens of AI scribe products had been adopted across NHS settings, many through informal pilots or direct clinician procurement, without clear regulatory classification. The Medicines and Healthcare products Regulatory Agency (MHRA) had not issued definitive guidance on whether software that transcribes and summarises clinical conversations constitutes a medical device. In the absence of that guidance, many suppliers self-classified their products as outside medical device regulation, and many NHS organisations looked to deploy them on that basis.

In April and June 2025, NHS England took action. A Priority Notification mandated that all ambient voice technology solutions generating clinical summarisation must hold at least MHRA Class 1 medical device registration, and that tools producing diagnoses or management plans require higher classification approval. Non-compliant solutions were prohibited immediately. Liability for continued use was placed on the deploying organisation or individual clinician. Overnight, a significant portion of the deployed market became non-compliant, not because the technology had changed but because the commissioning organisation had been pushed into creating ad hoc regulatory requirements that the official regulator had not yet established. The result was a de facto market restriction imposed not through deliberate obstruction but through the gap between the pace of technology deployment and the capacity of regulatory and commissioning institutions to keep up with it. Suppliers that had invested in compliance infrastructure survived. Those that had not, often smaller innovative companies without the resources to navigate medical device regulation at short notice, were effectively excluded from the market. The framework designed to protect patients from inadequate technology ended up protecting compliant incumbents from non-compliant competitors, an outcome that nobody designed and nobody intended, but which followed predictably from the institutional logic. The regulatory response to this wider problem is examined in Chapter 10.

These examples share a common feature: identifiable actors using specific institutional instruments to slow or block change that threatened the status quo. But veto power does not always require an actor. Path dependence operating through commercial logic produces structural advantages for incumbent products that are just as effective at preventing the diffusion of transformative AI as any deliberate obstruction.

We have touched on this in the preceding chapter but consider the position of a clinician whose practice runs on a deeply integrated clinical information system. The incumbent product has years of workflow customisation, established data structures, trained staff, and existing contractual arrangements built around it. A third-party AI tool, however clinically superior, must integrate with that system, comply with its security requirements, navigate its architecture, and demonstrate value in a procurement process that inevitably favours the known over the novel. The incumbent vendor, meanwhile, can embed AI functionality directly into the existing product, making it immediately available to every existing customer without a separate procurement decision, integration project, or change management programme. The competitive advantage this creates has nothing to do with the relative clinical merit of the two products. It is the structural consequence of switching costs and integration depth that accumulate over years of institutional embedding.

The result is that AI capability developed by incumbent vendors naturally diffuses more rapidly through existing customer bases, while independent tools with equivalent or superior clinical evidence face structural barriers that are nobody's fault and nobody's responsibility to remove. This is not the collective action mechanism; nobody is lobbying or litigating. It is the absorption mechanism described earlier in this chapter, now operating at the level of the commercial ecosystem: the technology that is most compatible with the existing institutional configuration spreads, and the technology that would require reconfiguration does not.

The same logic also explains a pattern that is otherwise puzzling: why the AI applications that diffuse most rapidly in healthcare are so often the ones that are least transformative. Ambient documentation tools, AI-assisted scheduling, automated coding: these spread relatively quickly because they do not substantially threaten any major organised interest. They make existing workflows more efficient without redistributing authority, income or decision rights. They are, in the language of technology policy, techno-fixes: interventions that address surface symptoms without touching the underlying structure. They are, in the terms set out earlier, neutral absorption seen from the supply side: easy to adopt precisely because they leave the system's fundamental configuration unchanged.

The applications that would generate the largest system-level benefits, enabling non-physicians to perform physician-level tasks, making specialist expertise directly available to patients, restructuring care away from hospital settings, face the largest coalition of resistance because their benefits require redistributing something that incumbent groups currently hold. It is not all hopeless however. The collective action framework also predicts that institutional sclerosis can be overcome, typically by external shocks sufficiently large to disrupt the existing coalition structure, or by governance reforms that change the rules of the game in ways that reduce the veto power of incumbent interests. The question for healthcare AI is whether the combination of demographic pressure, financial constraint and technological capability constitutes a shock large enough to shift the equilibrium. The answer, as we shall argue in the remainder of this chapter, depends less on the technology than on whether policymakers are willing to act on what the evidence about institutional resistance actually implies.

5.8 Why healthcare is especially resistant to redesign

The preceding sections have drawn on frameworks developed to explain institutional resistance across many different sectors and societies. Healthcare is not unique in having path dependence, vested interests, or organised coalitions defending their position. What requires explanation is why healthcare is so much more resistant to transformation than other comparably complex and regulated industries, and why the resistance it generates is so difficult to overcome even when the case for change is overwhelming.

In my view, there are three features of healthcare that combine to make it unusually resistant to redesign, and all three are intensified rather than reduced by the introduction of AI. The first is moral legitimacy. Healthcare occupies a distinctive position in the moral economy of modern societies. It deals with suffering, vulnerability and death in ways that invoke deep ethical commitments about the obligations we owe to one another. This moral framing is constitutive rather than incidental to how healthcare is organised. The language of care, vocation and patient welfare pervades healthcare institutions in ways that have no direct equivalent in manufacturing, finance or retail. And this language performs a specific institutional function; it insulates healthcare from the productivity arguments that drive restructuring in other sectors. Proposals to standardise clinical processes, reduce unit costs, or substitute less expensive workers for more expensive ones encounter a moral objection that has no equivalent in other industries. You cannot run a hospital like a factory is not merely a professional preference. This resonates with the public and with politicians in ways that make reform politically costly even when the evidence for it is strong.

This moral legitimacy creates a powerful asymmetry in how reform proposals are evaluated. A technology that promises to improve care is welcomed in principle. But the same technology, when it implies that some clinical tasks do not require the level of expertise currently deployed on them, or that clinical judgement in a particular domain is no more reliable than an algorithm, encounters resistance framed, for example, in the language of patient safety and professional responsibility. These objections are sometimes genuine and sometimes strategic, and from the outside they are very difficult to distinguish. The moral authority of the medical profession gives weight to both, and this weight is not available to the reformers on the other side of the argument.

The second feature is non-market coordination. As Arrow established in his foundational analysis of healthcare economics, discussed in Chapter 4, healthcare does not and cannot operate through normal market mechanisms. The information asymmetry between clinician and patient, the impossibility of shopping around during a medical emergency, and the unpredictability of future healthcare needs mean that the competitive pressure that forces restructuring in market sectors simply does not operate in the same way. A hospital that is inefficient does not reliably lose income to an efficient competitor. A clinical team that is slow to adopt better practice does not face the revenue consequences that would force a manufacturing firm to change. The absence of market discipline means that the natural corrective mechanism that forces other industries to adapt to new technologies is largely absent from healthcare. Institutions that would not survive competitive pressure in other sectors persist in healthcare because survival does not depend on productivity.

Non-market coordination also means that the governance of healthcare is distributed across a complex web of professional bodies, regulatory agencies, commissioning organisations and political authorities, none of which has the unilateral authority to mandate change across the whole system. This fragmentation multiplies the number of veto players, as discussed in the previous section, but it also means that there is no single lever that a reformer can pull to shift the system. Change requires simultaneous alignment across multiple governance layers, each with its own timeline, its own political constraints and its own organised constituencies. This is not an accident of history that could easily be corrected but the structural consequence of trying to govern a sector that combines market failures, professional authority, public funding and individual rights in the same space.

The third feature is professional organisation. Medicine is among the most highly organised professions in any economy, with a degree of collective self-governance that would be remarkable in any other sector. This self-regulation has real justifications: the information asymmetry between clinician and patient means that external quality assurance is difficult, and professional norms provide a substitute for the market discipline that is absent. But self-regulation also means that the profession has substantial control over the pace and direction of change in clinical practice. Reforms that the profession collectively resists can be slowed, qualified or redirected in ways that reforms in other sectors cannot.

The combination of these three features creates a system that is optimised for stability in the face of historical challenges rather than for improvement. The moral legitimacy of healthcare shields it from arguments about productivity, the absence of normal market discipline removes the competitive pressure that would otherwise force adaptation, and strong distributive coalitions provides the collective capacity to resist changes that threaten professional interests. These are the features that make the system resistant to the kind of transformation that AI makes possible. And critically, all three of them are likely to be amplified rather than reduced when AI is the proposed agent of change, for reasons that the next section will try to address.

5.9 Why AI will trigger stronger resistance than previous technologies

The preceding sections have established that healthcare institutions are resistant to change in general. This section addresses a more specific and more important question: why does AI trigger stronger and more organised resistance than the technologies that preceded it? Electronic health records, telemedicine, and clinical decision support all encountered institutional friction. I will argue that AI encounters something qualitatively different. Understanding why requires thinking about what AI actually could threaten that previous technologies did not.

Previous healthcare technologies were, in the main, process technologies. They changed how existing tasks were performed without fundamentally challenging who had the authority to perform them, how performance was judged, or how the rewards of clinical work were distributed. The electronic health record changed how clinical notes were written and stored. It did not change who had the right to write them, what they were used to justify, or what professional authority they conferred. Picture archiving systems (PACS) changed how radiological images were stored and transmitted. They did not change who had the authority to interpret them or what that authority was worth. Whilst such technologies were disruptive to workflows, they were not disruptive to the underlying distribution of decision rights, income and professional status. This is why, despite the friction they generated, they were eventually absorbed: the institutional settlement could accommodate them without needing any fundamental renegotiation.

I claim that AI is different in three specific ways that make it a distribution-shifting technology rather than a process technology. The first is the redistribution of decision rights. When an AI system starts to perform at clinical-grade accuracy on a diagnostic task, it does not merely assist the clinician in making a decision. It raises a question that previous technologies never raised: whether the clinician needs to be involved in that decision at all, or whether the decision can be made by a less expensive, more widely available, or more consistent alternative. This is not a hypothetical future concern since AI systems already match or exceed specialist performance in specific domains including certain areas of radiology, dermatology and ophthalmology. The institutional implication is not that radiologists, for example, will be replaced overnight but that the radiologist's exclusive claim to make certain decisions, a claim that underpins professional authority, income and identity, is no longer self-evidently justified on technical grounds. Once that claim is open to question, the entire edifice of professional protection built around it becomes contestable.

The second is the threat to opacity. Clinical professional authority has historically rested in part on the opacity of clinical judgement. The experienced clinician knows things that cannot be fully articulated, draws on pattern recognition developed over years of practice, and exercises judgement in ways that cannot easily be audited or second-guessed. This opacity is not a cover for self-interest; it reflects real features of expert clinical reasoning. But it also performs an institutional function making clinical decisions difficult to evaluate from outside the profession, which limits accountability and protects discretion. AI-assisted decision-making is, in principle, auditable in ways that unaided human judgement is not. If a clinician uses an AI system that records its recommendations and the clinician's response to them, a trail exists that can be reviewed. If outcomes are subsequently poor, the question of whether the clinician followed, ignored or overrode the AI recommendation becomes answerable in ways it previously was not. This transparency is beneficial for patients and for system governance. It is threatening to the professional culture of discretion that has underpinned clinical autonomy for generations.

The third is the scalability of expertise beyond professional boundaries. Previous technologies required the involvement of trained professionals at every step of their operation. AI, uniquely, is beginning to be able deliver something approaching specialist-level capability to people who are not specialists: to generalist clinicians in settings without specialist support, to allied health professionals working at expanded scope of practice, and to patients themselves managing their own conditions. This is the democratising potential of AI that its advocates rightly emphasise. I have remarked on this before: it is also, from the perspective of the medical profession, an existential challenge to the information asymmetry that Arrow identified as the foundation of medical authority. When the knowledge that previously required a decade of training can be accessed through an interface by anyone with a computer, the monopoly on expertise that justifies both the income and the authority of the specialist is fundamentally undermined.

These three properties explain why the resistance to AI is not simply more of the same friction that previous technologies encountered. It is resistance to a technology that threatens decision rights, transparency and the monopoly on expertise simultaneously, and it is resistance that will be organised, sustained and articulate, because the groups whose interests are threatened are also the well-organised professional bodies and specialist associations that have the most developed capacity for collective defence.

The frameworks we have used so far in this chapter treat resistance to change as a property of institutions, coalitions and professional organisations. That is the right level of analysis for understanding why the system as a whole is slow to transform. But it does not fully explain the behaviour of the individual clinician who, when presented with an AI tool that could help his or her patients, finds reasons not to engage with it fully, or engages in ways that limit its transformative potential. To understand that, we need to think carefully about individual incentives and what happens when individually rational behaviour produces collectively irrational outcomes.

This is the domain of game theory, a branch of mathematics and economics that analyses strategic interactions: situations where the outcome for any individual depends not only on their own choices but on the choices of others. Game theory is sometimes associated with cold-war military strategy or high-stakes corporate negotiation, but its most important insights are about much more ordinary situations. And one of its central findings is both simple and deeply uncomfortable: that a group of rational, well-intentioned people can collectively produce an equilibrium outcome that is bad for all of them, not despite their rationality but because of it.

The relevant strategic problem here is what game theorists call a *stag hunt*. The structure is straightforward. A group of hunters can bring down a stag together, enough food for everyone, but only if all of them commit to the hunt. Any individual who doubts the others will defect has a rational incentive to pursue a hare instead: a smaller, certain reward that does not depend on anyone else's cooperation. The barrier is not greed but the absence of credible assurance that others will cooperate. And "you'll never get people to do that!" is a commonly heard refrain in healthcare. When that assurance is missing, the individually rational choice is the smaller certain reward, even though everyone would be better off if all had committed to the larger collective one.

This maps precisely onto what happens when transformative AI is introduced into a healthcare institution. Full engagement requires clinicians to accept transparency they have not previously been subject to, to work in ways that make their decisions auditable, and to participate in redesigns that may reduce the scope of their authority. The benefits are real but diffuse: better outcomes, more sustainable workloads, a system that functions less badly. All good. However the costs are immediate and fall on the individual: reduced discretion, increased accountability, and the risk that data generated by engagement is subsequently used to justify staffing reductions, performance management or organisational exploitation. In an institutional environment that has given clinicians no credible reason to trust that the gains will be shared or that transparency will be used constructively, the rational choice is qualified engagement: adopt the technology in forms compatible with existing authority structures, and resist the forms that are not. Not because cooperation is undesirable, but because the conditions that would make cooperation safe do not exist.

The collective result is predictable. AI gets deployed, perhaps even at scale, but workflows are not fundamentally redesigned. The technology's transformative potential is unrealised, and the resulting disappointment is attributed to the technology rather than to the institutional conditions that made full engagement irrational. This is not technophobia but the entirely predictable outcome of introducing a distribution-shifting technology into an environment where the people whose participation is essential have rational grounds for withholding it.

The solution is not to demand more from individuals but instead to create the institutional conditions, credible commitments about how AI-generated data will be governed, how efficiency gains will be shared, how transparency will be used, that make cooperation the individually rational choice rather than the individually risky one. This is the central problem that healthcare AI policy has so far almost entirely failed to address. The conversation has been dominated by questions of evidence, safety, regulation and adoption barriers. To be sure, all of these matter, but they are not the binding constraint. The binding constraint is that the current institutional environment makes resistance to meaningful AI engagement the individually rational strategy for the people whose participation is essential. Until that changes, the healthcare system will keep producing exactly the outcome that the logic of the situation predicts: a lot of AI activity, very little AI transformation, and a growing frustration on all sides that nobody seems able to explain.

5.10 The central claim

The argument of this chapter can now be stated precisely: the reason AI is not transforming healthcare is not the technology. The algorithms work and are only going to get better. In many domains they work better than the humans they are designed to assist. The technical barriers to deployment, while real, are tractable. The evidence base, while uneven, is substantial and growing. None of this is the binding constraint.

Instead, the binding constraint is the institution. Healthcare systems do not, for the most part, function to improve healthcare. Whatever their original purpose or motivation, they have come to reproduce existing distributions of power, income and authority. This is not conspiracy or malice, simply the ordinary operation of incentive structures, professional norms, path dependence and collective action problems that make the status quo the rational choice for most of the people within the system most of the time. The system is working exactly as its structure dictates, and that structure is now the problem.

It is worth carefully summarising the mechanisms involved. The taxonomy has three distinct processes which are easily conflated but not the same.

The first is *institutional inertia*: the tendency of complex systems to persist in existing configurations not because anyone is defending them but because changing them requires simultaneous coordination across many actors, each of whom has insufficient individual reason to move first. Path dependence is the structural expression of this; the stag hunt is its individual-level expression. No individual agent is necessary or responsible. The system simply tends toward the existing equilibrium because that is where all the complementary investments point.

The second is *defensive rent protection*: the active and organised use of institutional instruments by groups whose income, authority or professional status is threatened by redesign. This is the power-resistance and collective action mechanisms working together. It is not passive: it involves decisions about which safety concerns to raise, which standards of evidence to demand, which governance requirements to insist upon, and how to frame each of these in the language that has the most institutional legitimacy. The resistance is rational at the level of individual actors, and it is strategic without requiring coordination or conspiracy. Each actor responds to their own incentives and the effect is cumulative.

The third is *path-dependent coordination failure*: situations where even actors who genuinely want transformation cannot achieve it because the complementary changes required fall outside any single actor's control. A hospital chief executive who wants to redesign care around AI capabilities cannot unilaterally change the licensing framework, the payment model, the professional scope-of-practice rules, or the training curricula that shape the workforce. Each element is locked by a different governance layer. The result is not resistance but paralysis, with sincere intent producing no structural change because the conditions for change require alignment that no individual actor is able to deliver.

Whilst these three mechanisms are analytically distinct, they interact. Inertia creates the terrain on which rent protection operates most effectively. Coordination failure provides legitimate cover for defensive behaviour. And the cumulative effect of all three is a system in which the distribution of power, income and authority is reproduced through the ordinary operation of incentives that nobody designed for that purpose and that nobody, individually, could easily change.

Let me also state briefly what this argument does not claim, and what evidence would count against it. My argument is not that AI transformation of healthcare is impossible; it is that ***transformation will not occur as a spontaneous consequence of technical capability alone***. If AI does produce structural redistribution of clinical decision rights, measurable substitution of expensive professional labour, and reorganisation of care pathways at scale, that would challenge the argument. If payment reform, data governance changes, or external shocks produce institutional shifts that allow transformative AI to diffuse where it previously could not, the framework would need to account for those cases rather than dismiss them. The institutional analysis is not a prediction that nothing will ever change. Instead, it is a prediction that change will not come from the technology alone, and that the pace and direction of change will be determined by institutional forces rather than technical ones.

So let me try by looking at some examples of healthcare organisations that have achieved something that looks like transformation locally but nevertheless has not spread to become the norm—not to dismiss them, but because understanding what it took to bring about these good ideas and yet why they did not naturally generalise, is the most direct way of demonstrating what transformation actually requires.

Virginia Mason Medical Center in Seattle is a frequently cited example of operational transformation in healthcare. Beginning in 2002, Virginia Mason adopted the Toyota Production System with unusual seriousness, redesigning clinical workflows around lean principles, redistributing tasks to the lowest-cost competent provider, and achieving measurable reductions in waste, waiting times and cost[82]. The results were very impressive but so was the effort required to achieve them: a decade of sustained leadership commitment, substantial investment in staff training, and a willingness to accept short-term disruption in exchange for long-term gain that is rare in healthcare organisations operating under quarterly performance pressure. Virginia Mason remained an outlier. The model did not spread, despite being extensively documented and widely admired. Why? Because Virginia Mason operated within the same fee-for-service payment system as every other hospital in the United States. The efficiency gains it achieved reduced its own costs without generating the revenue that volume generates elsewhere. Transformation was possible but took substantial and concerted effort. However, under those conditions and without the vision to sustain such efforts elsewhere, it was not self-replicating.

Intermountain Healthcare in Utah achieved something similar through a different route[83]. By developing rigorous clinical protocols, embedding decision support into its workflows, and measuring performance against evidence-based standards, Intermountain reduced clinical variation and improved outcomes over decades. The conditions that made this possible are again informative. Intermountain operates a largely integrated, substantially capitated model: it bears the financial consequences of the care its patients receive, which creates incentives that fee-for-service systems structurally prevent. It has also maintained an unusual organisational culture, built over decades, that treats clinical performance data as a professional tool rather than a management weapon. Neither condition is available to most healthcare organisations and neither is produced by the technology itself.

Denmark offers a different kind of counter-example: a national digital health infrastructure that actually works, with interoperable records, population-level data access, and patient-facing systems that have no equivalent in larger healthcare economies[84]. The explanation for why Denmark succeeded where the NHS has not is not ambition or investment but lies in the institutional context. Denmark's health system is organised around strong state and municipal governance, with physicians employed on salaried contracts rather than fee-for-service arrangements, which removes the income-protection dynamic that makes professional organisations in other systems resistant to redesign[85]. The conditions for transformation were not created by the technology. Instead they were already present in the institutional environment.

Estonia offers a more radical version of the same argument. Where Denmark reformed an existing system, Estonia built its digital health infrastructure largely from scratch following independence, as part of a broader project of state digitalisation that created a unified national data infrastructure across government, banking, and healthcare[86]. The result is a system in which every citizen has a lifelong digital health record, every clinical encounter is recorded and accessible, and the data infrastructure that AI development requires exists as a national public asset rather than a fragmented collection of institutional proprietary systems. The conditions that made this possible are not replicable in larger, older health systems: Estonia had the advantage of building on a blank slate, with a small population, strong political consensus around digitalisation as a national project, and no entrenched legacy infrastructure to defend. That is not a reason to dismiss the example. It is a reason to be precise about what it demonstrates: that the barriers to the kind of data infrastructure that would unlock transformative healthcare AI are not technical. They are institutional and political. Estonia was able to remove those barriers by circumstance but other countries will have to remove them by choice.

These cases specify rather than falsify the thesis. Transformation is possible when the payment model internalises the gains (Intermountain), when extraordinary and sustained leadership absorbs the transition costs (Virginia Mason), or when the national institutional context makes coordination tractable (Denmark, Estonia). None of these conditions is produced by the technology itself. Each requires deliberate institutional choices, and perhaps fortunate circumstances, that the ordinary operation of the system does not generate.

That is the conclusion the whole chapter converges on. Technology expands what is possible in healthcare; whether those possibilities are realised depends on institutional rules that determine what is rewarded, who bears risk, and who has the authority to act. At present those rules are misaligned with what AI makes possible, and the resulting friction is neither uniform nor accidental. It concentrates where existing investments, professional roles and authority structures are most threatened, so resistance is not generalised conservatism but a predictable response to the distributional consequences of redesign. Where the rules instead reward redesign, as in the cases above, change follows. Where they do not, the technology is absorbed into the existing configuration: adopted in whatever form disturbs it least, producing change that is incremental where it could be structural and local where it would need to be system-wide.

If the problem were primarily technical, it would yield to technical solutions: better algorithms, stronger evidence, clearer regulation. These remain necessary but they are not sufficient. The limiting factor is institutional, and it hardens over time: the longer a configuration persists, the more careers, investments and identities are tied to it, raising both the cost of change and the capacity to resist it. Meanwhile the pressures driving the need for transformation, demographic, fiscal and technological, are not diminishing.

The chapters that follow therefore focus not on what AI can do, but on what would need to change for its capabilities to be realised at scale: how care would have to be reorganised, what institutional arrangements would need to shift, and what governance conditions would make transformation possible rather than exceptional.

6 Why healthcare cannot easily be optimised

The previous chapter made a structural argument: that healthcare institutions resist transformation not because of technical inadequacy but because they are designed, consciously or otherwise, to preserve existing distributions of power and reward, including the coordination structures through which that power is exercised. That argument can explain why AI has so far largely failed (and, all else being equal, will continue to fail) to transform healthcare at the system level. But it does not answer an equally important question: even if the institutional barriers could be overcome, what would transformation actually look like?

For the reasons set out so far, our task for this chapter is to see if technology, and AI specifically, can be harnessed to produce more healthcare without spending much more to do it, and the obvious hope is that such technology will deliver that by opening up new ways of doing things that were impossible before but which might be cheaper. It is an attractive idea, and history offers an obvious example. No technology in recent memory has changed everyday life more visibly than the smartphone.

In 2007, Apple launched the iPhone. Now, nearly twenty years later, there are few aspects of life the smartphone has not touched. It has changed how we shop, bank, consume information and socialise. But the smartphone is, at its most basic, just a platform that put internet access in our pockets. It was an enabler rather than a cause of the massive societal change that followed. Initially, the technology allowed people to check emails, keep track of schedules and listen to music on the go. Useful, certainly. But hardly society-defining. The paradigm shift came later, when developers and entrepreneurs realised that the smartphone could be a platform for entirely new ways of delivering products and services. That is not why anyone bought an iPhone in 2007, and the changes did not happen overnight.

AI-enabled healthcare technologies are emerging rapidly, and unsurprisingly given the considerations of Chapters 4 and 5, their manufacturers are targeting existing problems. We have already discussed how generative AI can save time through ambient listening technology and drafting patient communications or how machine learning can help radiologists cope with growing demand for imaging studies. These are real problems and the tools have market appeal. AI, like the smartphone, may be a platform that eventually leads to transformative change. But how will that emerge, over what timescale, and do we have any say in where it ends up?

This chapter tries to address the first of those questions, in five steps. It begins with the productivity paradox: the uncomfortable observation that decades of investment in health information technology have produced remarkably little measurable improvement in what healthcare systems actually deliver, and the general explanations economists have offered for why. Those explanations are true but not specific: they cannot say why healthcare should suffer the paradox more severely than the sectors in which it was first described. The second step supplies the healthcare-specific answer. Healthcare's apparently permanent state of crisis is not the background against which change must happen but the explanation of why it does not: the system is structurally fragile, its collapse under load manifests as a self-amplifying spiral of coordination costs, and fragility consumes exactly the slack that transformation requires. The third step asks what the required redesign would look like, drawing on the supply-chain and systems thinking that have transformed productivity in other industries, and why those approaches have consistently failed to take root in medicine. The fourth identifies the one contribution AI could make that is genuinely different in kind: giving the system the visibility of its own load that its structure denies it. And the fifth asks which AI tools will actually spread through a health system left to its ordinary dynamics of adoption, arriving at the chapter's least comfortable conclusion: the tools most likely to diffuse are precisely the ones least able to close the gap between adoption and productivity. The argument that follows is not wholly optimistic. The obstacles are real and the history of failed reform is long. But it is not pessimistic either; the reason previous attempts at transformation have failed is not that the goal is impossible but because the attempts have consistently underestimated what transformation actually requires, settling instead for incremental improvements in existing workflows when what was actually needed was a redesign of the workflows themselves. AI does not make that redesign automatic, but it may, for the first time, make it possible, which is much more foundational.

6.1 The productivity paradox

If AI is the platform for transformation, the first question is why the platforms that came before it failed to deliver. Healthcare has invested enormously in information technology over the past three decades, and the returns have been, to put it generously, modest. Understanding why is not merely of historical interest. The same forces that frustrated previous technologies are already shaping how AI is being adopted, and recognising them is the first step to doing something different.

So far, I have talked a lot about productivity but how do we define it exactly and what determines it? Economists think of it as a measure of the amount of output per unit of the various inputs required. Production may be considered to be a function of labour and capital. To increase the amount of healthcare we deliver, we may either increase the number of workers, get them to do more, invest in infrastructure, or both. Hiring people and building new buildings is expensive, and the supply of skilled healthcare workers is limited. So what we are really interested in is labour productivity: the amount of healthcare we can deliver per person. This is where technology needs to help.

The electronic health record market is growing rapidly and conservatively projected to reach around $40 billion by 2030. The expectation, reasonable on its face, is that all this investment in digital infrastructure must be making healthcare more efficient at least. The Nobel laureate economist Robert Solow had a famous response to exactly this kind of optimism. Writing about the digitisation of the workplace in 1987 (about ten years after it started), he observed that "You can see the computer age everywhere but in the productivity statistics"[87]. His remark, which became known as the productivity paradox, was directed at computing in general but applies equally well to digitisation of healthcare.

The same framework was applied directly to NHS health IT by the Wachter review in 2016, which found that the productivity paradox had materialised in full in English hospitals[65]. Substantial investment in electronic health records had produced disrupted workflows, increased documentation burden and clinical dissatisfaction, with few measurable gains in care quality or efficiency. Wachter's diagnosis was that the paradox would only resolve when two conditions were met: the technology itself matured, and the people using it began to reinvent the work rather than digitising the existing processes unchanged. Neither condition had been met. A decade on from that review, the same assessment applies to AI: the technology is maturing rapidly but the reinvention of work has barely begun.

The paradox was examined in detail by Brynjolfsson in 1993[88], who identified four possible explanations for why investment in information technology was failing to show up in productivity statistics: *mismeasurement* of outputs, inputs or both; *redistribution* of profits rather than aggregate gains; a *time lag* between IT investments and realising the returns; and *mismanagement* of both information and technology. Each of these has something to say that is very relevant to healthcare.

Mismeasurement

Measuring productivity definitively is difficult. What counts as output is not necessarily just more of the same. What about product diversity or the quality of the experience? These questions are particularly important in healthcare, where the relationship between what we measure and what we actually value is notoriously weak.

In a normal market, improvements in customer experience increase demand for a product, but that does not necessarily mean productivity has increased. AI could lead to substantial improvements in how patients experience healthcare: better access through chatbots, richer communication, more personalised information. Of course, better patient experience is not a bad thing. And in a privately-funded system like that in the United States, improved experience primarily means patients are more likely to return, which increases activity. But it does so without reducing the cost per unit of care delivered. At a societal level, it may simply encourage the worried well to consume healthcare they do not need, with the provider financially incentivised to deliver it without bearing the wider opportunity cost.

In a nationally-insured system like the NHS, the calculus is different but not obviously better. There is little financial reward for improvements in experience, and the last thing a resource-limited system needs is to encourage more people to use it. In the limit, AI might deliver a more pleasant healthcare experience that is also unnecessary and no more efficient than what it replaced.

AI may also enable a wider range of more personalised treatments, improving quality even if the cost per episode does not fall. As the complexity of disease and the range of available treatments increases, individualised AI-assisted care may improve outcomes. But this does not help the patient who cannot access any healthcare at all, or who is waiting months for a first appointment, because the problem is shortage of supply rather than quality of what is supplied.

On the input side, AI offers obvious opportunities for automating administrative tasks: documenting encounters, drafting letters, coding diagnoses, booking visits. If adopted, these would improve the working lives of clinical and administrative staff. But would they translate into society having access to more healthcare? Consider the hospital doctor who currently dictates notes after clinic because there is no time during it. Ambient voice technology offers the chance to complete that documentation in real time. The patient may get their letter sooner. The correspondence may be more complete and timely and the doctor may feel less burned out. These are real and important gains.

But is it realistic to expect that the time saved will be used to see an additional patient? These improvements are worthy but they are not, in themselves, productivity improvements.

Redistribution

A further explanation for the productivity paradox is that technology may improve productivity for some organisations or parts of the system without improving it for the sector as a whole. In healthcare, this pattern is easy to observe. A hospital that automates its radiology reporting workflow may reduce its own costs and turnaround times. But, as we saw in Chapter 4, if the result is simply that more imaging studies are requested because reporting is faster, the system-level cost may increase rather than decrease. Gains at one node can generate demand that overwhelms those gains elsewhere. In a fragmented system where each organisation optimises locally, the aggregate effect is not the sum of the individual improvements. Indeed it may be considerably less, or even negative.

Time lags

Benefits from IT investment may not be immediately apparent, instead taking time to manifest. There is econometric evidence supporting this, and it seems particularly plausible in healthcare.

AI technology is both complex and novel, and without clear financial incentives, implementation is likely to be patchy particularly for potentially disruptive change for reasons discussed in Chapter 5. More rapid adoption requires digital literacy across the whole landscape, from patients through providers to boards. That is a substantial undertaking and wide implementation in a resource-constrained setting takes time. Here the pace of AI development creates a new problem: the technology may be superseded before it is properly adopted. AI is developing faster than any previous technology and the barrier to re-combining bits of software into new tools to solve previously intractable problems is so low so we can expect an explosion of combinatorial innovation. It is conceivable that healthcare providers who engage find themselves in a permanent cycle of new adoption, always suffering the disruption of implementation and never reaching the point where they, or the systems they work in, realise the potential gains.

Mismanagement

Paradoxes are usually the result of false premises. In this case, the false premise is that productivity improvements follow naturally and automatically from advances in technology. They do not, especially for a technology as complex, unfamiliar and rapidly changing as AI.

The general purpose technology argument established in Chapter 4 has a direct implication for how we should expect productivity to behave during the transition. As the electrification parallel showed, the productivity gains from a general purpose technology do not come from the technology itself but from the complementary investments in layout, workflow and skills that allow the system to be rebuilt around it. Those investments are costly, slow and largely invisible in short-term productivity statistics. The technology was ready long before the system was, and the same is true of AI in healthcare now.

This is captured in what has become known as the people, process, technology framework, shown in Figure 6.1: the insight that technology investment without accompanying changes in the people who use it and the processes within which it operates will at best produce incremental rather than structural change. It is a point so obvious that it is constantly forgotten.

There is a clear parallel with healthcare. Individual AI applications provide at best incremental gains when deployed into workflows that have not been reformed. The real productivity dividend will come not from the sum of those incremental changes but from the structural reorganisation that the technology makes possible. We can regard healthcare as currently being in exactly this pre-paradigm phase[89]: the technology is arriving, the incremental applications are proliferating, and the transformative reorganisation has not yet begun.

Solow himself revised his earlier pessimism around ten years later. By the late 1990s, productivity growth had accelerated substantially in sectors that had invested heavily in computing: wholesale and retail trade, financial services. The gains came not from the technology alone but from its integration into truly redesigned business processes, roughly twenty years after widespread adoption began. It is the same lag, and the same cause, as the electrification of the workplace discussed in Chapter 4 (curiously enough, also about twenty years): the dividend appears only when the work is rebuilt around the technology, not when the technology is dropped into the work unchanged. The lesson is not that the productivity dividend never arrives, but that it comes from structural change made possible by the technology rather than from the technology itself.

Inefficient investment leads, at best, to incremental rather than paradigm-changing disruption. The real benefits come not from the sum of incremental improvements but from recombining the system's processes in ways the technology newly makes possible, often through applications nobody anticipated at the outset. This is the combinatorial change set out in Chapter 5, and, as that chapter established at length, in healthcare it does not happen on its own.

The productivity J-curve: things may get worse before they get better

It is not just that the productivity benefits of AI may take years to materialise that is the problem. Worse still, productivity may actually decline in the short term before it improves. This is the implication of what Brynjolfsson, Rock and Syverson have called the productivity J-curve[90].

The argument runs as follows. The general purpose technologies introduced in Chapter 4 including AI, require substantial complementary investments before they can deliver on their true potential. New workflows need to be designed. Staff need to be trained not just in how to use the tools but in how to work differently around them. Governance arrangements need to be established. Data infrastructures need to be built or reformed. These investments are real costs that show up immediately in productivity statistics as inputs without yet generating proportional outputs. Meanwhile the technology itself, deployed into unchanged workflows, may add new burdens: more alerts to triage, more draft documents to review, more governance obligations to satisfy. The net effect in the short term can be a measurable decline in productivity even as the long-term potential of the technology is real.

This is easily observed in the history of EHR implementation. In the years immediately following EHR go-lives, multiple studies documented increased administrative burden, higher rates of physician burnout, and in some cases longer consultation times rather than shorter ones. The technology that was supposed to free clinicians from paperwork generated new forms of paperwork instead, at least until workflows were redesigned around the new capabilities. Some health systems are still waiting for that redesign.

For AI, the J-curve prediction is that we should expect a period, potentially a substantial one if conscious investment into the complementarities does not occur, in which investment in AI tools produces no measurable productivity improvement and may produce a measurable decline. This will no doubt be used, predictably, as evidence that AI does not work. The correct interpretation is different: it is evidence that AI deployed into old workflows does not work, which is a very different claim. The question is not whether the J-curve exists but how long the downward slope lasts and how steep it is, and both of those depend on how seriously healthcare organisations invest in the complementary changes that the technology requires.

So-so technologies: adopted without transforming

The labour economics of automation sharpens this warning into something more precise, and more uncomfortable. Acemoglu and Restrepo, decomposing seven decades of American labour demand through a task-based lens, show that what matters about an automating technology is not that it automates but what happens to the task content of production[91]. Automation sets two effects against each other. The displacement effect pushes labour out of the tasks the machine takes over, reducing demand for the people who did them. The productivity effect works the other way: automation lowers the cost of production, output expands, and demand rises for labour in all the tasks that were not automated. Whether the workforce gains or loses depends on which effect dominates, and there is nothing in the technology itself that guarantees the benign outcome.

The trouble lies in an asymmetry between the threshold for adoption and the threshold for benefit. An organisation adopts automation when it is cheaper than the labour it replaces, and that bar is far lower than the bar for the technology being genuinely more productive. A technology that is only marginally better than the worker, or even slightly worse but cheaper, still clears it. Acemoglu and Restrepo call this class "so-so technologies": good enough to be adopted, not good enough to pay. Supermarket self-checkout and automated telephone customer service are their canonical examples, and both display the signature pattern: the workers go, the productivity statistics barely move, and the service arguably gets worse. A so-so technology delivers the full displacement effect and almost none of the productivity effect, which makes it the configuration most damaging to the workforce. This matters beyond wages, because the productivity effect is what funds what they call the reinstatement effect: the creation of genuinely new, labour-intensive tasks that re-employ people at higher value. A technology that generates no surplus generates no new tasks either. Their empirical claim is that displacement and reinstatement roughly balanced in the United States for the four decades after the war, and that since the late 1980s displacement has accelerated while reinstatement has stalled, a large part of why labour's share of income has fallen. The counterintuitive conclusion is that transformative automation is easier on labour than mediocre automation, because only the former creates the new work into which displaced effort can flow.

AI absorbed into unchanged clinical workflows is a so-so technology almost by construction. It displaces effort at the margin, adds review and oversight burden of its own, and creates no new clinical roles, because new roles come from redesigned work, not from tools. The classification should rest on task content rather than on outcome, or the label becomes circular: the test is whether a deployment changes what work exists and who does it, not whether it happened to disappoint. By that test, most of what is currently diffusing through healthcare fails. The redesign this chapter keeps returning to is, in Acemoglu and Restrepo's terms, the reinstatement mechanism: it is what converts automation from a threat to the workforce into the source of the new clinical roles that make the productivity dividend real and shareable, and it is exactly the part that the so-so variant omits.

The J-curve also has an important implication for how AI investments should be evaluated. If we measure productivity in the first two or three years after AI adoption and find no improvement, we are measuring the wrong thing at the wrong time. The relevant question is not what happened to productivity in year one but what the trajectory looks like over a decade, and whether the complementary investments are being made that will eventually bend the curve upward. At the moment, most evaluations of AI in healthcare are not designed to answer that question. The concept of 'in-year return on investment' for anything but a trivial system is simply flawed logic that fails to understand the purpose and mode of action of any disruptive technology.

Taken together, the four explanations and the J-curve amount to a general warning rather than a healthcare-specific one. They tell us that the returns on any general purpose technology are delayed, contingent on complementary investment that is expensive and largely invisible, liable to be captured by some parties rather than realised in aggregate, and quite capable of going negative before they go positive. All of that applies to retail, to financial services, to manufacturing. What it does not

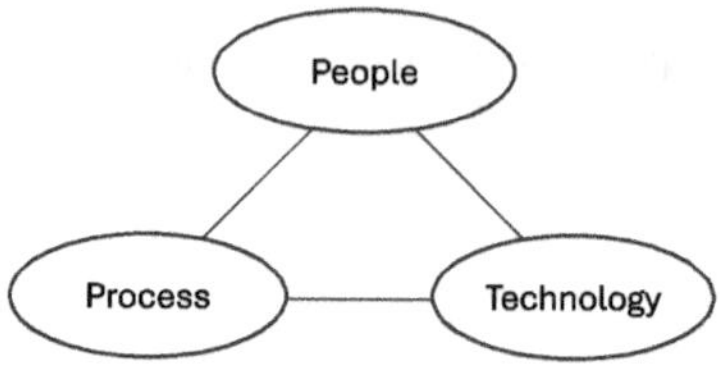

Figure 6.1: The people, process, technology (PPT) framework, attributed to Bruce Schneier and based on an earlier organisational model by Leavitt from the 1960s. Successful organisational change cannot be achieved through technology alone. The skills, culture, behaviours and motivations of individuals, and the workflows and routines within which they operate, must change alongside the technology itself.

explain is why healthcare might be worse than these on every count. Something in the sector is amplifying each of these effects, and it is worth asking what. My answer is that healthcare's permanent crisis is not the environment in which the paradox plays out but the mechanism by which it is amplified: the system is structurally fragile, and fragility consumes exactly what the resolution of the paradox requires.

6.2 Permanent crisis, fragility and the transaction cost spiral

Health systems in the wealthy world are, with striking consistency, described as being in crisis. In England the winter pressures arrive every winter and are reported, every winter, as exceptional. Canadian emergency departments close for want of staff; Australian ambulances queue outside hospitals that cannot receive them; French and German hospitals run recurrent industrial disputes over conditions that never improve; American systems, despite spending twice as much per head as anyone else, report clinician burnout at rates that would elsewhere be called an emergency. The standard explanations are familiar and locally inflected: underfunding here, workforce shortage there, administrative bloat, management failure. Each contains truth, and none of them explains the strangest feature of the phenomenon, which is that it is simultaneously permanent and international. Systems that are merely under-resourced run badly at a steady state. Systems with utterly different funding models, ownership structures and political settlements do not usually converge on the same pathology. Something structural is going on, and it turns out to matter enormously for the question this chapter is asking. A system in permanent crisis is a system that cannot change, because change of the kind the productivity paradox demands, the redesign of work around new technology, requires exactly the slack that a system in crisis does not have. Before asking what AI might transform, we need to understand why the patient is in no condition for surgery.

My answer is that healthcare systems are fragile in a specific, structural sense: they degrade non-linearly under load, they recover slowly, and nothing in their design prevents them from being driven into the regime where this happens. Most organisations are protected from that regime by their boundary. A firm facing more demand than it can coordinate raises prices, quotes longer lead times or declines the order; demand is throttled at the door, and the machinery of internal coordination, which no firm prices any more than a hospital does, is never pushed to the point of failure. Healthcare has no such throttle, and the reasons differ by system while the consequence does not. Where care is tax-funded or socially insured, demand is not priced at all and arrives as a queue; a waiting list is not a smaller workload but a deferred one, and managing it, re-prioritising it, and fielding the anxiety of the people on it is itself coordination work. Where care is privately financed, price does ration some demand, but the rationing is decoupled from the coordination burden it is supposed to protect: emergency demand cannot lawfully be refused, and the apparatus of prior authorisation, claims and denials that does the rationing is itself among the largest coordination costs in the system, so throttling demand there generates administrative work rather than relieving it. In both cases the boundary that protects other organisations from their own fragility is, in healthcare, an additional source of the load. This is the common structure beneath the internationally common pathology.

What does it look like when such a system is pushed past its limits? Not a dramatic halt. Collapse in a coordination system manifests as a rise in the cost of coordinating: a proliferation of exactly the transaction costs, the handovers, chasing, checking, reporting and reconciling, that were examined in Chapter 5. Think about what happens on a busy ward when patient acuity is high and staffing is stretched. Handovers become rushed and incomplete. Incomplete handovers mean that the next shift has to spend time tracking down information that should have been passed on, chasing results that were not flagged, and reconstructing the clinical picture for patients who fell through the gaps. Errors and near-misses increase. Each incident triggers a reporting process, a review, and often a remediation plan, all of which consume the time of the same staff who are already stretched. Documentation gets deferred because there is no time to complete it during the shift, and the backlog of deferred notes creates its own retrieval burden later. Communication between teams breaks down, so decisions that would normally take one conversation take three or four.

Notice the direction of causation. The administrative burden did not cause the ward's difficulties; the ward's difficulties are manifesting as administrative burden. Rising transaction costs here are a symptom of a system already past its limits, not a warning that the limits are approaching. But they are not only a symptom, and this is the crucial point. Each failure-driven overhead consumes the time of the people who would otherwise have prevented the next failure. The symptom feeds the disease. Incomplete handovers generate retrieval work that displaces documentation, which produces more incomplete records, which generate more retrieval work.

I should be explicit that what follows is mechanistic reasoning rather than established empirical finding: these dynamics follow from the structure of the feedback loop, and they predict what we observe, but they have not to my knowledge been directly measured. A loop of this shape has two properties. First, degradation above the threshold is convex: each additional unit of demand generates more than one additional unit of coordination overhead, so the system deteriorates faster than the rise in demand would predict. Below the threshold a busy ward copes; above it, it spirals. Second, recovery is slow. Even after the immediate pressure has passed, the backlog of deferred documentation, outstanding incident reviews and eroded team communication takes time to clear. The system exhibits hysteresis: the path down is not the path back up.

Put fragility and slow recovery together and the permanence of the crisis stops being mysterious. A system that is repeatedly driven above its effective capacity threshold does not return to baseline between peaks. Each episode of overload leaves a residue: outstanding reviews, incomplete records, communication norms that have not been restored, and staff carrying the cognitive and emotional weight of unresolved caseloads. The next demand peak arrives before the previous one has fully cleared. What looks like a system that is always in crisis is, at least in part, a system that has never fully recovered from the last one. This is not a failure of management or morale. It is the predictable behaviour of any unthrottled system whose coordination costs are consequential rather than corrective and whose recovery is slower than the arrival rate of new demand.

And now the argument closes on the question this chapter set out to answer, because permanent crisis is not just a description of the operating environment into which AI is being deployed. It is an explanation of why healthcare suffers the productivity paradox more severely than any of the sectors in which the paradox was first described. Everything the paradox literature teaches, and the J-curve above all, says that the productivity dividend must be bought: complementary investment, redesigned workflows, retrained staff, a period in which things get worse before they get better. All of that requires slack, and slack is precisely what a system operating at or above its threshold does not possess. Worse, any small gain a new tool does deliver below the threshold is absorbed by the queue of latent demand, and above the threshold it is swamped by the convex overheads of the spiral. The systems most in need of transformation are, by the very mechanism that creates the need, the least able to undergo it. Healthcare cannot easily be optimised because it is rarely in a state from which optimisation can begin.

There is a final twist, and it concerns measurement. Standard productivity statistics are essentially linear: they model output as a roughly proportional function of inputs. A system that degrades convexly above a threshold does not appear in those statistics as fragile; it appears as merely inefficient. The fragility is invisible to the very instruments that would be used to justify addressing it, which means the productivity problem in healthcare is almost certainly worse than it looks, and interventions aimed at the spiral are systematically undervalued relative to interventions aimed at the baseline. A system whose cost function is illegible to its own instruments cannot be optimised by conventional means, whatever technology is applied to it.

The implication for AI can be stated now and developed once we have seen what redesign actually requires. The standard productivity case treats the administrative burden as a baseline to be shaved, and tools like ambient scribes shave it: usefully, boundedly, and without touching the spiral, because a feedback loop is not fixed by subtracting a constant from it. If the argument of this section is right, the transformative use of AI is different in kind. It is to give the system what its structure denies it, some functional substitute for the throttle and the feedback that protect other organisations from their own fragility, and I return to what that would mean, and to why it is the last thing the system is likely to buy, later in this chapter.

6.3 Why medicine resists supply-chain thinking

If technology alone cannot deliver the productivity transformation that healthcare needs, what would true redesign of care delivery look like? One place to look for answers is the set of principles that have transformed productivity in other industries: supply-chain management.

The idea of a supply chain is straightforward. Any process that takes inputs and produces outputs involves a chain of activities, each dependent on what comes before it and feeding into what comes after. Managing that chain well means coordinating those activities efficiently, reducing waste, matching supply to demand in real time, and making the whole system visible so that bottlenecks can be identified and addressed. These principles, developed and refined in manufacturing and retail over several decades, have produced extraordinary productivity gains. Toyota's production system, which gave rise to 'lean' manufacturing, reduced waste and improved quality simultaneously in ways that were thought impossible before the approach was systematised. Amazon's logistics operation coordinates billions of transactions across global networks with a precision that would have been unimaginable to a retailer a generation ago.

Healthcare, on the face of it, looks like an obvious candidate for supply-chain thinking. It involves flows of patients, information, materials and staff that must be coordinated across multiple nodes. It has enormous waste in the lean sense: waiting, duplication, unnecessary motion, defects and overproduction are endemic. And it faces exactly the kind of demand management challenge that supply-chain principles are designed to address: variable, unpredictable demand that must be matched against constrained capacity in real time.

Betcheva and colleagues[92] provide a useful analysis of where supply-chain thinking has been applied in healthcare and what has limited its impact. Their central finding is consistent with the argument of this book: the barriers are not primarily technical but institutional, professional and incentive-based. The same features that make healthcare resistant to AI-enabled transformation make it resistant to supply-chain thinking, and for the same underlying reasons.

The first barrier is clinical complexity. Diagnosis and treatment are inherently uncertain, and care is co-produced by patients and providers in ways that resist standardisation. Outcomes depend not only on clinical interventions but on social determinants of health, patient preferences and biological variation that no protocol can fully anticipate. Variability in practice patterns persists even for common conditions, reflecting both real clinical uncertainty and deeply embedded cultural norms within the profession. Doctors are trained to exercise individual judgement, and that training makes the standardisation that supply chains require feel like a threat to clinical quality rather than an enabler of it. The fact that much of this variation is unwarranted, reflecting habit and convention rather than patient need, does not make the resistance any less real.

The second barrier is operational fragmentation. Decision-making in healthcare is distributed across multiple actors with different interests, information and accountability structures. Clinicians act as agents on behalf of patients but are employed by provider organisations that have their own financial pressures. Payers finance care but remain largely disconnected from its delivery whereas regulators set standards without controlling operations. Information systems are siloed, and performance metrics are often ambiguous or contested. Unlike a factory floor, where throughput and defect rates can be measured and managed in real time, healthcare lacks universally accepted measures of value. What gets measured tends to be what is easy to count rather than what matters most to patients.

The third barrier is financial misalignment. Payment systems in most healthcare settings typically reward volume rather than value. Fee-for-service models incentivise activity, not efficiency. A hospital that reduces unnecessary admissions through better outpatient management may improve patient outcomes and reduce system costs while simultaneously reducing its own revenue. The incentive to optimise the whole system is structurally absent when each organisation is paid for its own activity regardless of what happens elsewhere in the pathway. Attempts to introduce value-based reimbursement, which would align financial incentives with system-level outcomes, face both technical and political obstacles that limit their reach.

Professional autonomy amplifies all three of these barriers. Doctors control entry to the profession, set standards of care and govern training and certification. In manufacturing, protocols can be imposed top-down and enforced through quality management systems. In healthcare, change must be negotiated through professional consensus, a slow and contested process that gives organised interests multiple opportunities to modify, delay or block reforms that threaten existing arrangements. Strategies that have transformed other industries (pooling resources, centralising procurement, implementing standard workflows) are prone to stall at the boundaries of professional domains in healthcare.

None of this means that supply-chain thinking is irrelevant to healthcare. It means that the conditions for it to work do not arise naturally, and that creating those conditions requires deliberate institutional intervention rather than the simple adoption of tools and techniques. This is precisely where AI becomes relevant, not as a supply-chain tool in itself, but as a potential enabler of the informational and coordination infrastructure that supply-chain reform requires and has historically lacked.

AI-driven platforms could easily be capable of aggregating data across fragmented systems, creating the kind of end-to-end visibility of patient flows, bed occupancy and resource availability that supply-chain management depends on. Machine learning could in turn easily support adaptive protocols that maintain clinical flexibility while reducing unwarranted variation, preserving professional judgement where it really matters while promoting consistency where it does not. Predictive analytics could anticipate surges in demand and enable anticipatory rather than reactive resource allocation. And by linking outcomes to activity through automated data capture, AI has the potential to make value-based payment models more technically feasible, potentially shifting the financial incentives that currently reward volume over value.

But these are possibilities, not predictions. The history of supply-chain reform in healthcare is a history of good ideas that encountered institutional resistance and were absorbed into existing arrangements without producing the systemic change they promised. AI will follow the same trajectory unless the institutional conditions change alongside the technology. The question is not whether AI can provide the informational backbone that supply-chain thinking requires. I think it can. The question is whether healthcare systems will be redesigned around that backbone or whether they will find ways, as they have with every previous technology, to use the new tools to do the old things a little faster.

6.4 Systems thinking and lean that lasts

There is a deceptively simple observation that underlies much of what has gone wrong with healthcare reform, and it comes from an unlikely source. W. Edwards Deming was an American engineer and statistician who became famous in the 1950s for helping Japanese manufacturers rebuild their industries after the second world war. His ideas about quality management transformed manufacturing and eventually gave rise to lean thinking. But his most important insight was not about quality tools or process improvement techniques; it was about systems.

Deming argued[1] that any organisation must be understood

and managed as a *system*: in other words an interconnected complex of functionally related components that work together to achieve a shared aim. The components of a hospital system include the clinical teams, the administrative staff, porters, cleaners, support services, the IT infrastructure, physical environment, payment model, regulatory framework and the patients themselves. Each of these components interacts with the others. A change in one affects all the others. And the performance of the whole system cannot be understood by looking at the performance of its parts in isolation.

This sounds obvious but is, in practice, almost universally ignored. Healthcare is managed overwhelmingly at the level of its components. Wards are managed by ward managers. Departments are managed by clinical leads. Trusts are managed by executives whose accountability runs to their own organisation rather than to the system within which it operates. Payment flows to individual providers for individual activities. Performance is measured at the level of the unit, the department, the trust. The system as a whole has no manager, no budget and no set of metrics that captures its overall performance. It is, in Deming's terms, not managed as a system at all but as a collection of parts that happen to be adjacent to each other.

As a consequence, improvements in one part of the system can generate costs or problems elsewhere. A hospital that reduces its length of stay frees beds but increases pressure on community services that are not resourced to absorb the additional demand. A clinic that improves its appointment scheduling reduces its own waiting list but may simply shift the bottleneck to diagnostics or treatment. An AI tool that reduces documentation time in one department may increase the information burden on the departments that receive its outputs. Local optimisation in a system without overall management does not produce global improvement. It produces what engineers call sub-optimisation: each component performing well by its own metrics while the system as a whole continues to fail.

Deming also observed that the aim of any group within a system should be to optimise the larger system it operates within, not to maximise its own performance. This is a radical idea in an environment where clinical teams, departments and organisations are all assessed and rewarded on the basis of their own activity and outcomes. It requires a governance structure that makes the system's overall performance visible, that distributes the costs and benefits of change across the components that co-produce outcomes, and that creates incentives for local actors to make decisions that are good for the whole even when they are not optimal for the part. None of these conditions currently exist at scale in any major healthcare system.

This is perhaps one reason why lean manufacturing has so often disappointed in healthcare. Lean is fundamentally a systems methodology, designed to optimise the whole production system rather than individual workstations. Applied to isolated departments or specific workflows without addressing the system around them, it may fail because the conditions for the principles to work are absent rather than because the concept is wrong. An interesting question is whether AI finally supplies the missing ingredient. To see why it might, it helps to look at what lean actually tries to target.

At a fundamental level, the delivery of healthcare can be viewed as a supply chain. When a patient is referred to a surgeon, a sequence of actions must take place. The steps between this moment and the patient having surgery, recovering and being discharged have a high degree of commonality with every step depending on what came before it and affects what comes after.

Doctors often argue that healthcare is fundamentally different from manufacturing because of the variability of patients' needs and conditions. This is true, and the example above deliberately omits the clinical complexity and difficult decisions involved at each step. I will return to analyse this complexity in much more detail in Chapter 7. But the logistics are nevertheless often very general, and if they cannot be delivered effectively and efficiently then no amount of clinical excellence can compensate. The same logic applies to emergency care. A patient presenting to an emergency department must be triaged, seen, investigated, and either discharged or admitted, with beds, teams and resources coordinated accordingly. The clinical decisions are uncertain and variable but the logistical sequence is not.

Even clinical decision-making is more constrained than doctors sometimes acknowledge. Evidence from randomised controlled trials means we have a good idea of the best treatments for most common conditions. The practice of medicine is substantially governed by guidelines, and deviation from guidelines should be the exception rather than the rule. The patient who develops a chest infection whilst recovering from an operation is managed according to protocol. The protocol may need to be adapted to the individual, but the adaptation takes place within an existing framework.

Toyota engineers identified seven wastes that their production system was designed to eliminate, each with a direct parallel in healthcare and each offering a window onto where AI might help (Table 6.1).

Table 6.1: The seven wastes of lean manufacturing and their healthcare equivalents, with the AI applications best placed to address each. The barriers to eliminating these wastes are institutional rather than technical.

Waste	**Healthcare equivalent**	**Where AI might help**
Waiting	Patients waiting for appointments, results or beds; theatres idle	Demand forecasting, AI triage by clinical risk, predictive scheduling
Defects	Diagnostic errors, prescribing mistakes, hospital-acquired infections	Early deterioration alerts, real-time anomaly detection, safety checks
Transportation	Patients attending multiple separate clinics; duplicated information	Remote monitoring, telemedicine, integrated data platforms
Motion	Clinicians navigating multiple IT systems; hunting for information	Intelligent interfaces surfacing relevant data; ambient documentation
Overproduction	Unnecessary investigations, prolonged hospital stays, defensive medicine	Predicting investigation yield, identifying discharge-ready patients
Overprocessing	Redundant approvals, repeated data entry across incompatible systems	Workflow automation, interoperability, structured data extraction
Inventory	Stockpiled consumables; patients in limbo on waiting lists	Demand-based inventory forecasting, waiting list management

Waiting is perhaps the most visible waste in healthcare. Patients might wait months for outpatient appointments, diagnostic tests and surgical procedures, sometimes with serious clinical consequences. A patient awaiting cancer surgery may experience disease progression during the delay, turning a potentially curative procedure into a palliative one. Clinicians also wait: for laboratory results, imaging reports, beds to become available. Operating theatres and MRI scanners stand idle because of scheduling inefficiencies or upstream delays. From a systems perspective, waiting lists are a form of hidden inventory: patients in limbo, consuming resources indirectly while adding no value. AI offers real solutions here. Predictive analytics can forecast demand and could optimise scheduling, matching resources to need in real time. Machine learning models can predict which patients are likely to cancel, and could compensate automatically. AI-driven triage can prioritise patients on clinical risk rather than chronological order.

The healthcare equivalent of defects are the errors made daily. Misdiagnoses, prescription mistakes, logistical errors and hospital-acquired infections are not rare anomalies; they are a major public health problem, as discussed in Chapter 1. Each error carries a human cost and a financial one, through avoidable complications, readmissions and litigation. Rework is inefficient not just because of the additional work but because it adds unpredictability and compounds other wastes. Traditional quality control relies on retrospective audit and incident reporting: spotting errors after they occur. AI could shift this from reactive detection to proactive prevention. Machine learning algorithms can flag anomalies in real time, alerting clinicians to potential prescribing errors or unexpected deterioration. Natural language processing can detect inconsistencies in clinical documentation. Predictive models can identify patients at high risk of complications before those complications occur.

In manufacturing, unnecessary movement of parts between

workstations is a classic waste. In healthcare, the equivalent is the movement of patients, equipment and information to where they need to be at the right time. A patient with multiple chronic conditions may attend separate clinics for cardiology, endocrinology and nephrology, each requiring separate visits, tests and paperwork. This duplicates effort, increases the likelihood of errors, and fragments the patient experience. AI could help by enabling virtual movement instead of physical movement. Digital platforms can integrate data from multiple sources, reducing the need for patients to travel simply to share information. In the longer term, AI-enabled remote monitoring and telemedicine could eliminate entire categories of transportation waste.

Closely related is motion: the unnecessary movement of staff. Clinicians walk long distances to retrieve equipment or locate colleagues. In the digital realm, motion takes the form of navigating multiple IT systems, logging into different platforms, and hunting for data buried in electronic records. Studies have shown that clinicians spend up to half their working day on administrative tasks, much of it information retrieval and documentation. AI could dramatically reduce this burden. Intelligent interfaces can surface relevant information at the point of care using natural language queries and note summarisation. Virtual assistants can automate routine tasks from ordering tests to drafting discharge summaries.

Overproduction in healthcare takes the form of unnecessary tests, duplicate documentation and prolonged hospital stays. Sometimes this is defensive medicine. Sometimes it is simply easier to repeat a test than to find an existing result. AI could help by making information retrieval far easier, summarising patient histories, highlighting key results, and predicting which investigations are most likely to be informative. Predictive analytics could also identify patients who are ready for discharge earlier, reducing unnecessary bed occupancy without compromising safety.

Healthcare is also often riddled with redundant steps: multiple approvals for the same procedure, repeated data entry across incompatible systems, endless reconciliation of records. These processes evolved to manage risk but may ultimately create more problems than they solve. AI could streamline workflows by automating repetitive tasks and enabling interoperability between systems. Natural language processing can extract structured data from free text. Robotic process automation can handle routine administrative tasks from scheduling to billing.

Finally, hospitals stockpile drugs, devices and consumables to guard against uncertainty, tying up capital and risking obsolescence. In other industries AI has brought precision to inventory management, forecasting demand based on historical trends, seasonal patterns and real-time epidemiological data, reducing the need for costly stockpiles while monitoring supply chains for disruptions.

The case for AI as a lean enabler is therefore substantial across all seven waste categories. So why has lean itself so consistently failed in healthcare, and what would make AI any different?

Lean has mostly not been implemented well in healthcare and perhaps adopted as isolated departmental projects that never cohere into the systems methodology lean actually is. The result is short-lived, siloed gains and, often, more variation rather than less, as each department improvises its own version[93]. Underneath the implementation failures lie the institutional ones the previous chapter described. Sustained change needs committed leadership, engaged frontline staff and a workforce that does not reasonably suspect the exercise is cost-cutting or headcount reduction in disguise. Those conditions are usually absent, and lean concepts barely feature in clinical training to begin with.

What AI changes is not those barriers, which still require governance and incentive reform no technology can substitute for, but the missing ingredient beneath them: lean in healthcare has never had real-time visibility of the whole system, the ability to locate waste across an entire pathway, or the means to manage demand proactively rather than reactively. AI could conceptually supply all three, through a mechanism the next section develops. But capability is not outcome. Whether it is used to redesign care or merely to run the existing configuration more smoothly is a choice about governance and leadership, not technology.

6.5 What optimisation would actually require

It is worth pausing on what the word optimisation actually presupposes. To optimise anything is to adjust it against a measured objective using feedback about how the adjustments are working. Other industries do not have to build that apparatus, because their economics supply it: prices tell them what their output is worth, margins tell them what their coordination is costing, and both arrive continuously and without anyone commissioning them. Healthcare has neither. The preceding sections have shown, from three directions, exactly what is missing. Fragility showed a system that spirals under load and cannot see itself doing so. The supply-chain analysis showed methods of flow management that are well understood and have failed here for want of the conditions they assume. And lean identified the most concrete of those conditions: nobody has ever had real-time visibility of the whole system, the ability to locate waste across a pathway, or the means to manage demand before it arrives rather than after. This is the first sense in which healthcare cannot easily be optimised. It must first construct, deliberately and at its own expense, the measurement apparatus that other sectors receive for free as a by-product of operating in a market. This section asks whether AI can build that apparatus, and what happens when it can.

The distinction that matters is between two mechanisms by which AI can act on the coordination burden. The first is direct cost reduction. AI that automates documentation, assists with scheduling, summarises clinical records and triages information requests reduces the baseline level of transaction costs. These are real gains. A clinician who spends thirty minutes less per shift on administrative tasks has thirty minutes more for patients. But the gains are bounded in ways that are becoming empirically visible. Reducing the time to draft a clinical note does not eliminate the need to review and sign it. Generating more summaries and alerts can raise the information burden even as it lowers the drafting burden. Freed capacity below the threshold is absorbed by the queue of latent demand, as we saw in the discussion of the rebound effect, and above the threshold it is swamped by the convex overheads of the spiral. A feedback loop is not fixed by subtracting a constant from it.

The early evidence on ambient AI scribes illustrates the bound precisely. Two landmark randomised controlled trials of three separate scribe products found that in the more typical real-world case, AI scribes saved less than a minute per visit. Even the best-case scenario, with unusually high physician uptake and near-universal patient consent, reduced documentation time by around 22 minutes per day, roughly on par with the human scribes that already exist[94]. Burnout measures improved, which is to be welcomed of course. But the editorial commentary accompanying the trials was explicit: AI scribes are not productivity tools yet. This is exactly what the fragility argument predicts. Shaving the baseline burden of a system whose problem is its dynamics leaves the dynamics untouched.

The second mechanism addresses the dynamics, and it is best understood as giving the system a functional substitute for the two protections its structure denies it: the throttle that keeps other organisations out of their failure regime, and the aggregating feedback that makes coordination degradation legible when it happens anyway. Call it phase conversion: turning transaction costs from a consequence of failure into a corrective signal that arrives before it. The raw material already exists. Every electronic health record interaction leaves a timestamped trail; handover notes, task lists, referral queues and message logs all carry signals about the gap between demand and capacity. The problem has never been that the information is absent but that it is buried in operational data streams designed for documentation rather than load monitoring, and that nobody has had an interest in exhuming it. Continuous machine learning applied to that operational exhaust could detect rising documentation lag, increasing handover complexity, accumulating incomplete tasks and abnormal communication patterns before they cascade, at a speed and granularity no committee or dashboard refresh can match. Even the ambient scribe, unpromising as a productivity tool, is promising as a sensor: lengthening and increasingly complex draft notes, and growing deferral of review and sign-off, are load signals in their own right, currently discarded.

The productivity payoff of the two mechanisms is distributed very differently. Direct reduction generates linear, bounded gains spread across all operating conditions, most of which the rebound effect claws back. Phase conversion generates its gains precisely at the threshold: every occasion on which the system is kept below its tipping point is an occasion on which the entire convex cost of a spiral, and the slow hysteretic recovery after it, is avoided. The gains are concentrated exactly where the system most needs them, and, for the measurement reasons given earlier, exactly where standard productivity statistics are least able to see them.

Not all AI applications have equal potential on this second mechanism, and Table 6.2 sets out an illustrative taxonomy. It is not offered as procurement advice but as a prediction, because the two categories differ not only in their payoff profiles but in their prospects of adoption, and the two differences run in opposite directions.

Consider what each category offers the people who actually make adoption decisions. Ambient documentation addresses a pain every clinician feels directly and personally; its benefit is visible within a single consultation; it fits the existing workflow without demanding that anyone work differently; and it makes nothing about the adopter's own performance more transparent. Handover quality scoring and load dashboards have none of these properties. Their benefits accrue to the system rather than the individual, materialise mainly in the crises that do not happen, require the workflow itself to change, and make visible precisely the load and performance data that clinicians have learned to be wary of sharing. The next section examines the attributes that determine which innovations actually spread through a health system, and the reader may wish to hold this taxonomy in mind, because the exercise is uncomfortable: every attribute that accelerates diffusion favours the direct reduction category, and every attribute that phase conversion applications possess is one that retards it. Left to the ordinary dynamics of adoption, the market will select the tools the system needs least. This is

Table 6.2: Example healthcare AI applications by primary productivity mechanism. Direct reduction applications lower the baseline level of transaction costs and are attractive to individual adopters. Phase conversion applications convert consequential costs into corrective signals; their gains accrue to the system rather than the adopter. Handover quality scoring and real-time load dashboards are illustrative categories rather than established products. The two mechanisms are not mutually exclusive.

Application	**Mechanism**	**Phase conversion potential**
Ambient documentation	Direct reduction	Low: reduces drafting burden but does not surface load signals unless latency data are monitored
AI inbox and result triage	Direct reduction	Moderate: high-volume latency patterns can proxy for system stress if monitored
Handover quality scoring	Phase conversion	High: flags incomplete handovers before downstream failure, converting a consequential cost into a corrective prompt
Real-time operational dashboards	Phase conversion	High: aggregates signals across documentation, ordering and communication to surface load warnings before the threshold is crossed
Predictive deterioration models	Phase conversion	High: early identification prevents the clinical event that triggers the downstream transaction cost cascade

the second sense in which healthcare cannot easily be optimised: even once the instruments of optimisation become technically available, the mechanism by which technology actually spreads through a health system selects against them.

There is a further condition the table does not capture: phase conversion only creates value where credible responses to load signals exist. A warning that a ward is approaching its threshold is only useful if someone has the authority and the means to act on it. The most reliable responses are coordinative rather than resource-intensive: bringing forward deferred documentation, accelerating pending decisions, triggering early discharge planning before pressure compounds. These do not need additional staff. They require a governance environment in which clinical teams have real-time visibility of their own load data, and predicted load data, and the authority to act on it.

That governance condition is not technical at all. Making the coordination burden legible is not a neutral act of measurement: legibility enables attribution, and attribution has historically flowed downhill. As we saw in Chapter 5, clinicians have entirely rational grounds to resist AI-enabled transparency if that transparency will be used against them, and the history of workforce management in health systems of every funding model offers enough examples of operational data being turned into a case for workload intensification, staffing cuts, productivity targets and performance management to make that wariness reasonable rather than paranoid. The same institutional equilibrium that left the burden unmeasured when measurement was hard will resist measurement now that AI makes it easy.

This is a different kind of problem from the one Chapter 5 described. There the barrier was trust: cooperation was rational so long as others could be relied on to cooperate, a stag hunt that better assurance could resolve. Here the barrier is structural. Withholding engagement is rational regardless of what colleagues choose, because the cost of full participation falls on the individual alone while the benefits diffuse across the system. Game theorists call this a prisoner's dilemma, and its distinctive feature is that no amount of mutual goodwill resolves it, something that only a change in the institutional rules can achieve.

The governance design of AI deployment is therefore not a secondary consideration to be settled once the technology is in place. It is the primary condition on which the whole argument depends. It requires credible commitments that AI-generated operational data will be used to protect clinical capacity rather than erode it, and that the efficiency gains from redesign will be shared with the workforce rather than captured entirely as savings. These are political and institutional problems, not technical ones.

And that is the third and deepest sense in which healthcare cannot easily be optimised, the one that should give any technological optimist pause. It is not that the tools do not exist; for the first time they very nearly do. It is that optimisation is not the neutral engineering operation the word suggests. Optimising a system means measuring it, measuring it means making the people inside it legible, and legibility is never distributionally innocent: it determines who can be held to account for what, and in an institution with the history described in Chapter 5, the answer has reliably been those with the least power to refuse. The obstacle to optimising healthcare is not that the system resists being improved. It is that it correctly perceives measurement as an act with consequences, and declines, quite rationally, to be measured. No amount of better technology dissolves that, because it is not a technical problem. It is a problem about who owns the numbers.

6.6 Innovation diffusion

If the structural, economic and cultural conditions for systemic disruption are not naturally present in healthcare, what can we expect of a health AI landscape driven by the ordinary forces of technological diffusion? The answer is that the tools most likely to spread are probably not the ones most likely to help. Understanding why matters, because the same dynamics that have shaped the diffusion of every previous healthcare technology are already shaping how AI is being adopted right now.

The diffusion of technology is driven by perceived rather than technical attributes, and as much by social influence among adopters as by evidence of effectiveness[95]. Everett Rogers, whose work on the diffusion of innovations remains the most comprehensive framework in the field, identified four things that determine how an innovation spreads. First, the innovation itself and how it is perceived by potential adopters. Second, the communication channels through which word of it travels, with conversations between colleagues consistently more influential than published evidence or marketing. Third, time: adoption follows a characteristic S-shaped curve, beginning slowly with early adopters and accelerating as it reaches the majority. Fourth, the social system: the professional networks, opinion leaders and organisational cultures within which diffusion occurs. Rogers also identified six attributes of innovations that consistently predict how quickly they will be adopted[96]. They need close examination, because they reveal a systematic bias toward the wrong kinds of AI.

The first is *relative advantage*: people adopt what feels better than what they have. This sounds reasonable until you ask who is actually making the adoption decision in healthcare. Patients experience the consequences of the technology but rarely get to choose it. In practice, adoption decisions are made by clinicians, departments and healthcare organisations, and the information available to managers and commissioners about what a technology actually does is filtered almost entirely through the clinicians who use it. This is Arrow's information asymmetry operating at the organisational level: the people who know most about whether a tool is actually useful are the same people whose professional interests shape how that usefulness is assessed and communicated upward. A tool that saves a clinician time feels like a relative advantage regardless of whether it improves patient outcomes or system flow. A tool that would require the clinician to work differently, or that would make clinical decision-making more transparent, may feel like a disadvantage even if it would benefit the system enormously. The relative advantage that drives diffusion is therefore systematically biased toward what is good for the professional adopter rather than what is good for the patient or the system.

Compatibility is the second accelerator. An innovation that fits neatly into existing workflows spreads more easily because it avoids the disruption of having to change how things are done. Again, this sounds sensible in isolation. But many of the changes healthcare actually needs (more standardisation, less unwarranted variation, more transparency about outcomes) require clinicians to work differently. A tool that is highly compatible with existing arrangements spreads precisely because it does not challenge those arrangements, and it tends not to improve the system for exactly the same reason.

The clearest example in the current market is the dominance of

AI tools built into electronic health record platforms over standalone alternatives: a 2025 analysis found 79% of US hospitals using AI from their EHR vendor against 59% using third-party tools[62]. This is not simple market distortion. As noted earlier, integrated tools have real advantages: deep access to patient data, seamless workflow fit, lower procurement costs, and an institutional stability that venture-funded startups cannot match. A third-party vendor that does not own the underlying models, now commoditising fast, has a very real problem about where its defensible value lies. So the tools most likely to survive are those most tightly bound to existing infrastructure, and the pace and direction of healthcare AI ends up set by the roadmaps of a few enterprise software companies, whose business is not clinical transformation and whose products are therefore least likely to challenge existing care configurations. The implementation literature bears this out: synthesising twelve systematic reviews of digital risk tools in primary care, Taylor and colleagues found poor EHR integration and workflow fit the most frequently cited barrier to adoption, in 92% of reviews[97].

Low complexity is the third accelerator. Simple tools spread faster than complex ones, and there is nothing wrong with that in itself. The problem is that genuinely safe, ethical and well-governed AI is not simple at the institutional level. It requires validation, monitoring, governance frameworks and ongoing oversight. When a tool appears simple because it has sidestepped these obligations rather than met them, the simplicity is illusory. What spreads easily is often what has cut corners on the things that are hard to see from the outside.

Trialability, the ability to try something before fully committing, lowers perceived risk and accelerates uptake. But in practice, even a small AI pilot in a healthcare setting consumes substantial resources: technical integration, governance approvals, staff training, evaluation. Once those resources have been spent, there is a strong institutional bias toward continuing regardless of whether the tool is delivering value. When procurement rules require organisations to trial multiple competing products to avoid favouring one vendor, a digital team can end up maintaining a dozen pilots that never mature into anything.

The fifth accelerator is *observability*, the visibility of results to other potential adopters. People adopt what they can see working, and AI can make certain benefits very visible very quickly: a tidier clinical note, a faster letter, a suggestion that looks helpful in the moment. The benefits that actually matter such as shorter waits, fewer errors and better outcomes, are much harder to see because they are downstream, diffuse and often attributable to many factors at once.

Finally, *reinvention*. Innovations that can be adapted to local needs spread more easily, and the ability to tweak and customise feels like a feature. With AI, it is often a liability. Models trained on one population in one setting do not automatically perform well in another. Adapting an AI tool to local conditions without revalidating it is how bias gets introduced and how safety problems emerge. What looks like sensible local customisation can easily become the use of a tool outside the conditions for which it was designed, which is precisely the opposite of what a system struggling with inconsistency needs.

Four cases from healthcare show how these dynamics play out in practice. In none of them did the technology spread because the evidence demanded it. Each was carried instead by a force that had nothing to do with whether it worked: prestige, a borrowed rationale, professional and financial self-interest, or political and legal pressure. Together they map the main routes by which a technology propagates through a health system regardless of its value to patients.

Computed tomography (CT) is a sophisticated imaging technology that uses X-rays to construct three-dimensional cross-sectional images of the body. Whilst it is commonplace now, in 1973 there were only six machines in the United States. An expensive technology, that number grew to nearly 1,500 by 1980[98] but not because of clinical utility or as part of evidence-based guidelines—that took longer to establish. Instead the US Congressional Office of Technology Assessment concluded that scanners had been adopted without formal proof of their safety and efficacy[99]. Federal policies aimed at slowing the diffusion or ensuring that machines were placed where they were most needed had, in the OTA's assessment, no demonstrable effect. Scanners concentrated in wealthy areas: Beverly Hills, the Upper East Side, West Palm Beach. Many hospitals adopted them not because of clear clinical need but because of the status they conferred and the patients they attracted. Prestige and competition drove diffusion far faster than the evidence could justify, at substantial cost to equity and to the healthcare budget.

Goal-directed haemodynamic therapy shows what happens when a rationale is carried from the place it belongs into a place it does not. In the intensive care unit, driving a patient's cardiac output and oxygen delivery toward high targets can rescue organs failing under the strain (usually because of sepsis*). In the elective operating theatre the patients are systemically well, and pushing a healthy heart toward its limits is not obviously a good idea. The logic was ported across regardless, propelled by the monitor manufacturers' own treatment algorithms and by a UK

*In fact the evidence for goal-directed therapy in the ICU was also far from contestable.

national recommendation resting on a handful of small studies conducted years earlier, after which the manufacturer had simplified that algorithm to push stroke volume still higher. When the approach was finally tested in a well surgical population, stroke-volume optimisation conferred no benefit over standard fluid management, and in the aerobically fit it was associated with harm on the primary outcome, lengthening recovery and raising rates of bleeding, transfusion, and critical-care admission[100]. The theory was never sound for this population. What carried it was the analogy, the algorithm, and the guideline.

Arthroscopic surgery for osteoarthritis of the knee shows a third route: a procedure that keeps spreading after the evidence has demolished it. Cleaning debris out of a worn joint made intuitive sense, and the operation became routine long before anyone tested it against a control. When it was tested, against a sham operation in which patients received only skin incisions, the real surgery proved no better than the placebo, a result confirmed by a second controlled trial six years later[101,102]. Yet roughly 650,000 of the procedures continued to be performed every year in the United States alone, and the professional response was largely to dismiss the findings. Here the driver was neither prestige nor analogy but the revenue, the caseload, and the professional identity bound up in the operation. Refuted, it was retained.

The most damning case is high-dose chemotherapy with autologous bone marrow transplant for breast cancer. During the 1990s more than 41,000 women underwent this brutal and expensive treatment on almost no controlled evidence that it worked[103]. It spread not through trials but through desperation, media enthusiasm, and professional and financial interest, reinforced by political and legal pressure: insurers who declined to pay were sued, eleven states legislated to compel coverage, and members of Congress intervened on patients' behalf. The single randomised trial that appeared to justify the treatment was later exposed as outright fabrication and retracted. When five properly conducted randomised trials reported around the turn of the millennium, they found no advantage over standard-dose chemotherapy[104,105]. Tens of thousands of women had been subjected to a toxic and futile ordeal by a coalition of hope, money, politics, and fraud.

The lesson from these four cases is that diffusion is indifferent to what matters most. None of them spread because the evidence required it. All four followed the same S-curve. Adoption selects for whatever propagates fastest through professional, commercial, and political networks, and that is not necessarily the same thing as what works.

This is the picture that faces healthcare AI. Left to the ordinary forces of diffusion, the tools most likely to spread are those that feel like a relative advantage to the clinicians and organisations making adoption decisions, that fit into existing workflows without disruption, that appear simple, that can be piloted easily and that produce visible benefits quickly. None of these attributes reliably predict that a tool will improve patient outcomes, reduce costs or address the system-level problems that healthcare faces.

There is a further step worth taking here, because Rogers supplies the sociology of this selection and the so-so technology framework from earlier in this chapter supplies its economics, and the two converge on the same prediction. Consider what the so-so variant of healthcare AI offers each of the forces this chapter and the last have described. It has no J-curve to survive, because it requires no complementary investment, so under in-year return-on-investment logic it wins every business case against the transformative alternative that does. It threatens nobody's scope of practice, authority or revenue, so it passes through the veto structure of Chapter 5 without activating it: what makes it economically weak is precisely what makes it politically frictionless. It can be evaluated against its own evidence base and procured as a discrete object, which is the only kind of value the procurement machinery can see, whereas the combinations that produce transformation exist at a level no individual purchasing decision can assess. It is reversible, and a system without slack rationally prefers commitments it can walk back. It asks the workforce to trust no one, because it demands no transparency and redistributes nothing, so it diffuses without the credible commitments that transformative deployment requires and the institution cannot make. And the supply side reinforces all of it, because vendors build what sells, and what sells is what fits. Each mechanism independently favours the same variant; together they amount to a prediction, offered as such rather than as demonstrated fact: institutional resistance does not block AI, it filters it, and the filter passes exactly the class of technology that the labour economics identifies as worst for both productivity and the workforce. Absorption, in the sense this book has used the term, is that filter operating. If the prediction is right, the danger of the coming decade is not that healthcare fails to adopt AI but that it adopts a great deal of it, so-so variant first, and mistakes the adoption for progress.

There is also consistent evidence that who leads AI projects matters enormously. Research by Li and colleagues[106] found that when clinical expertise is embedded in leadership roles, AI deployments are significantly more likely to result in meaningful improvements in care delivery, even after accounting for technical sophistication and organisational resources. This makes sense: the people best placed to navigate the professional culture, identify where the actual value lies, and distinguish between tools that really help and tools that merely feel helpful are the ones who understand the clinical environment from the inside. But for all the reasons we have already encountered, that clinical digital leadership is unlikely to arise on its own (at least not at the scale that is needed for systems-level transformation). We need to be creating a cadre of clinical leadership appropriately versed in technology, digital transformation and systems-thinking.

The innovation diffusion framework offers a sobering picture. The healthcare AI landscape that emerges from ordinary diffusion will not be the one that delivers the greatest benefit. It will be the one that faces the least resistance. Changing that outcome requires deliberate choices about what gets funded, what gets properly evaluated, and what counts as success. Those choices cannot be left to the market or to the diffusion process itself.

That is the case for this chapter's title. Healthcare must first build, at its own expense, the measurement apparatus that other sectors receive free as a by-product of operating in a market; the ordinary dynamics of adoption then select against the very tools that would build it; and measurement is itself an act with distributional consequences, which gives the people who would be measured sound reasons to refuse. The obstacles, none of which are technical, compound.

What is still missing from my account so far is the human dimension: the clinicians who must actually use these tools, the complexity that the system generates and then mistakes for an immovable feature of clinical reality, and the question of what real transformation would require from the people inside the institution. That is the subject of the next chapter.

7 Manufactured complexity

The previous chapter established that the structural and economic conditions for AI-enabled productivity transformation in healthcare do not arise naturally. The productivity paradox, the resistance to supply-chain thinking, the failure of lean, the systematic bias in how technologies diffuse through professional networks: all of these point to the same conclusion. The barriers are institutional rather than technical, and they have defeated every previous wave of reform.

But institutions are made of people. The analysis so far has treated clinicians largely as actors within a system, responding to incentives. That account is accurate as far as it goes. What it omits is the texture of those responses: the psychological dynamics that shape how individual clinicians experience AI, the way the system generates and then naturalises a kind of complexity that feels irreducible but is largely of its own making, and what this means for what AI actually gets deployed and where. This chapter examines all three, and ends by drawing together the diagnosis that has accumulated across both chapters into a set of conclusions about what transformation would actually require.

7.1 Clinician perceptions

The previous chapter was about systems, institutions and incentives. But healthcare is delivered by people, and the way those people experience and respond to AI matters enormously for whether any of the potential benefits are realised. The evidence on clinician perceptions of AI is striking, and it points to a set of barriers that are not going to be resolved by better algorithms or stronger governance alone.

Start with a finding that should give pause to anyone who believes that demonstrating AI's clinical effectiveness is the main challenge. A study by Yang and colleagues[107] asked physicians to evaluate colleagues who used generative AI in medical decision-making. The results were unambiguous. Clinicians who relied on AI as a primary decision-making tool were rated by their peers as less clinically skilled, less competent and less capable of delivering high-quality care. The penalty did not disappear when AI was framed as a verification tool rather than a primary decision-maker. Even clinicians who used AI to check or confirm their own judgement were rated lower than those who used no AI at all.

This is not a trivial finding. In healthcare, peer reputation shapes referral networks, career progression and the informal authority that determines whose clinical judgement is deferred to in difficult situations. A clinician who believes that visible AI use will undermine their standing among colleagues has a concrete professional reason to avoid it, regardless of whether it would make them a better doctor. The study's analysis found that reduced ratings of clinical skill translated directly into lower evaluations of overall competence, reinforcing the social cost of adoption. The message from the professional culture is clear, if unspoken: using AI signals that you cannot manage without it, and that is not a signal anyone wants to send.

The framing of AI use matters too. When AI is presented as a primary decision-maker the reputational damage is greatest. Framing it as a verification tool partially mitigates the effect but does not eliminate it. Interestingly, clinicians rated institutional customisation of AI tools more favourably than off-the-shelf products, suggesting that tools developed within and for a specific professional context carry less of the competence stigma. But the underlying problem remains: in the current professional culture, being seen to use AI is a liability, and that is a powerful brake on adoption that has nothing to do with the technology's clinical performance.

This reputational dynamic connects to a deeper set of psychological and organisational factors that researchers have grouped under the term algorithm aversion[108]. Algorithm aversion is not technophobia or simple conservatism but a complex response to the particular challenge that algorithmic tools pose to professional identity, and understanding it is important because it explains why simply demonstrating that an AI outperforms human judgement does not automatically lead to its adoption.

One of the most consistent findings in this literature is that clinicians hold algorithms to a higher standard than they hold themselves or their colleagues. A clinician who makes an error is assumed to have encountered an unusually difficult case, exercised reasonable judgement given the available information, or been operating under difficult conditions. An algorithm that makes an error is assumed to be fundamentally flawed. This asymmetry is not logical, but it is understandable. Errors made by people feel random and therefore unpredictable and perhaps unavoidable. Errors made by algorithms feel systematic and therefore inexcusable. The result is that an AI tool which is right 95 percent of the time may be judged more harshly than a clinician who is right 85 percent of the time, because the 5 percent of errors the AI makes feel like a design failure while the 15 percent the clinician makes feel like the normal uncertainty of medicine.

Autonomy and control are also central to how clinicians experience algorithmic aids. Doctors are trained to value independent judgement. It is not just a preference: it is a core part of professional identity, reinforced through years of training, embedded in the culture of clinical practice and protected by the legal and regulatory frameworks that govern medicine. An AI system that presents a recommendation without explanation, or that appears to constrain the range of clinical options, can feel like a threat to that autonomy even when it is designed as a support. When AI systems are perceived as black boxes that dictate decisions rather than inform them, trust erodes quickly. Clinicians need to be able to interrogate a recommendation, understand the reasoning behind it and override it when their clinical judgement differs. Systems that do not afford this feel less like tools and more like surveillance.

Social and organisational incentives compound these individual responses. In many settings, using an AI tool confers no competitive or reputational advantage, particularly if the tool is widely available and its outputs are not visibly superior to unaided clinical judgement in routine cases. Clinicians may also worry about accountability: if they follow an AI recommendation and the outcome is poor, will they be judged to have abdicated clinical responsibility? If they override an AI recommendation and the outcome is poor, will the override itself become the focus of scrutiny? These are not irrational concerns. The liability landscape around AI-assisted clinical decision-making is unresolved, and uncertainty about accountability is a rational reason for caution.

Finally, cognitive compatibility matters in ways that are easy to underestimate. Clinical reasoning is not simply a process of weighing evidence and reaching a conclusion; it is shaped by pattern recognition built up over years of practice, by intuitions that are difficult to articulate, and by heuristics that work well in most cases even if they occasionally lead astray. When an AI recommendation conflicts with a clinician's intuition, the natural response is to doubt the algorithm rather than the intuition, particularly in domains where the clinician has deep experience. This is not always wrong: experienced clinical intuition carries real information that may not be captured in the data the algorithm was trained on. But it means that AI tools are most likely to be trusted in areas where clinicians feel least confident, and most likely to be resisted in the areas where their performance relative to human judgement is greatest.

There is a further dimension to rational resistance that is less often acknowledged: the risk that AI use erodes the very skills it is meant to supplement. A systematic review of the empirical evidence on AI-induced deskilling found consistent signals across specialties[109]. The most striking comes from a multicentre study of over 23,000 colonoscopy procedures: adenoma detection rates among endoscopists who had routinely used AI dropped from 28.4% to 22.4% when they reverted to working without it, while detection rates held steady at 25.3% in those continuing to use AI support[110]. In radiology, erroneous AI prompts increased false-positive recall rates by up to 12% even among experienced breast imaging specialists. In pathology, over 30% of participants reversed initially correct diagnoses when exposed to incorrect AI suggestions under time pressure. These are early findings from a nascent literature, and methodological limitations mean caution is warranted. But they point in a consistent direction: repeated reliance on AI recommendations can reduce independent diagnostic performance, weaken feedback loops essential for skill maintenance, and in some specialties reduce the volume of cases available for training. A clinician who worries that using AI will gradually erode what they have spent years acquiring is not being irrational. The evidence suggests they may be right.

The implication is clear. The barriers to AI adoption in healthcare are not primarily technical, and they are not resolved by building better algorithms, generating more evidence or mandating adoption. They are resolved by changing the conditions under which clinicians work: creating professional cultures where AI use is normalised rather than stigmatised, accountability frameworks that are clear and fair, and governance arrangements that make engagement with AI a rational choice rather than a professional risk. These are hard problems but, unlike the technical challenges, they are problems that the healthcare system does have agency to address. But it will consciously need to choose to do so.

7.2 Against manufactured complexity

The previous sections have examined why clinician behaviour around AI is rational rather than obstructive, and why the tools most likely to spread are those least likely to drive systemic change. Both arguments point in the same direction. Healthcare is not a machine that can be optimised by adjusting its components. But the frameworks used so far, innovation diffusion, algorithm aversion, professional identity, have been drawn largely from psychology and organisational behaviour. This section draws on a different tradition: the science of complex systems.

The central argument of this section is this. A very large proportion of what presents as irreducible clinical complexity is not intrinsic to the nature of the work; it is manufactured by the system itself, the downstream product of coordination failures, information gaps, and demand mismanagement that should never have been allowed to reach the clinical frontline. Healthcare is, at its core, a coordination problem. And AI, deployed wisely, could solve much of it. But that is not where most health AI is currently aimed.

7.2.1 What kind of system healthcare actually is

A hospital is neither a factory nor a clock. It belongs to a category that complexity scientists call a complex adaptive system: a collection of agents, in this case clinicians, patients, managers, regulators and increasingly algorithms, who interact continuously, adapt their behaviour in response to what others around them are doing, and collectively produce outcomes that no single actor planned or could fully predict. Unlike a machine, whose outputs are determined by the specification of its components, a complex adaptive system produces behaviours that emerge from interactions. Queue cascades, sudden improvements in outcomes following a seemingly minor process change, a ward that copes adequately at 85 per cent occupancy and falls apart at 92 per cent: these are all *emergent* phenomena. Nobody designed or intended them. They arise from the structure and dynamics of the system itself.

This is not merely an academic observation. It has practical consequences that standard management thinking consistently misses, because standard management thinking assumes that understanding the parts is sufficient to understand the whole. In a complex adaptive system it is not. You can thoroughly understand every ward, every department and every clinical team in a hospital and still be unable to predict how a change in one part of the system will ripple through the others. This calls for a different kind of analysis. Three properties of complex adaptive systems matter particularly for the argument that follows.

The first is non-linearity. The relationship between inputs and outputs is not proportional. Below a certain threshold of stress or load, the system handles perturbation smoothly. Above that threshold, it does not simply perform proportionally worse. It degrades faster than the increase in stress would predict, because failures cascade and compound rather than accumulating linearly. This is exactly the dynamic that Chapter 6 traced through transaction costs: above a certain load, the administrative overhead of a hospital ward accelerates rather than rising in step with demand, and the system enters a spiral. Standard productivity metrics, which assume roughly linear relationships between inputs and outputs, are constitutionally blind to this dynamic. They see an inefficient system when what they should see is a system approaching a tipping point.

The second property is a new kind of path dependence. Complex adaptive systems are shaped by their history in ways that are difficult to reverse. The accumulated effect of past decisions, investments and adaptations locks the system into its current configuration. Every proposed change must overcome the inertia of everything that has been built around the existing arrangement. This is not merely the institutional sclerosis described in the previous chapter, though the two are related; it is a structural feature of the system type. Even a healthcare system with fully reformed governance and aligned incentives would face path dependence in its physical infrastructure, its trained workforce, its embedded clinical protocols and its patients' expectations. The past is always present.

The third property is resilience through absorption, and it is the most important for the argument that follows. Complex adaptive systems maintain stability not by preventing disturbances from reaching them but by absorbing and distributing them across the network. The healthcare system is extraordinarily resilient in this sense. It has absorbed decades of underfunding, management restructuring, pandemic stress, workforce shortages and relentless policy change without collapsing. Wards that are technically understaffed continue to function because clinicians work longer, call in favours, rely on informal knowledge networks, and improvise solutions. The system bends. It does not break... until it does. And when it breaks, it tends to break suddenly.

This is the property of complex adaptive systems that explains something healthcare commentators have struggled to account for: why a system that appeared broadly stable for decades now appears to be failing simultaneously across multiple dimensions. The answer is not that something new went wrong recently. It is that the reserves that were absorbing the cumulative stress have been progressively depleted, and the system has crossed a threshold beyond which the same absorptive mechanisms no longer function. The professional goodwill, the informal workarounds, the discretionary effort, the tolerance for inadequate conditions: these are finite resources. They replenish slowly and deplete quickly. A system that has been drawing on them continuously for years will eventually find them exhausted, at which point what looked like resilience reveals itself as the consumption of reserves that are no longer there.

This has ramifications for our hope of using AI to transform healthcare productivity. Resilience in a complex adaptive system is not a feature that can be engineered in or engineered out at will; it is an emergent property of the system's adaptive capacity, the ability of its agents to respond to novel situations, to improvise, to find solutions that no protocol anticipated. That adaptive capacity is what is at risk when AI is deployed without understanding the system it is entering.

7.2.2 Healthcare as a hierarchy of subsystems

Complex adaptive systems are not flat networks but nested hierarchies. Healthcare is organised as a set of subsystems, each embedded within a larger one. The clinical encounter sits within the ward or clinic. The ward sits within the department. The department sits within the hospital. The hospital sits within a regional network of primary, secondary and community care. Each level has its own internal dynamics, its own feedback loops, and its own characteristic problems. And each level interacts with the levels above and below it through boundaries: handovers, referrals, discharges, communications, transfers.

This hierarchical structure is a source of both strength and vulnerability. The strength is that each subsystem can self-organise to handle what arrives within its own domain. A skilled ward team manages its own patients without needing the hospital executive to direct every decision. An experienced emergency department handles its own surges without waiting for instructions from the regional network. The adaptive capacity of complex systems lives at these local levels, where agents have the knowledge and the autonomy to respond in real time to conditions that no central planner could fully anticipate.

The vulnerability is at the boundaries between subsystems. This is where complex systems most commonly fail, and healthcare is no exception. When a patient moves from the emergency department to the admitting ward, information must cross the boundary cleanly and completely. When a patient is discharged from hospital to community care, capacity signals must flow in both directions so that the hospital knows what is available and the community service knows what is coming. When a patient is referred between specialties, the referring clinician's understanding of the case must survive the translation into a referral letter and the subsequent interpretation by a team that has never met the patient.

These boundaries are where things go wrong. Not always in dramatic ways but often in small, cumulative ways that are invisible to the management of either adjacent subsystem, because each subsystem's metrics stop at its own boundary. The emergency department measures its own performance. The ward measures its own performance. Neither measures the quality of the handover between them. The failure lives in the gap, and the gap belongs to nobody and is measured by nobody.

The practical implication is that when a clinician describes their working day as chaotic, the chaos is rarely generated entirely within their own subsystem. It arrives at the boundary from elsewhere. The ward that is struggling is often struggling not because of what is happening on the ward itself but because discharges have stalled, because a patient admitted from the emergency department arrived without adequate information, because a specialist review that was supposed to happen this morning has not materialised, because a bed that was supposed to be available is still occupied. The chaos is imported through boundaries that were not designed to manage the volume and complexity of information they are carrying.

This reframes the question of where AI should be aimed. An AI that makes the workings of a single subsystem more efficient, that speeds up documentation within a ward or optimises scheduling within a theatre suite, is optimising inside the box. An AI that makes boundaries between subsystems visible, legible and reliable is addressing the structural location where most failure actually occurs. The first may be useful; the second is the one that changes the system.

7.2.3 Most medicine is routine. The system makes it feel otherwise

There is a claim the medical profession makes frequently and largely without challenge: that medicine is irreducibly complex, that patients are not widgets, and that production-line thinking fundamentally misunderstands the nature of clinical work. This claim contains a real insight. Some medicine is complex in precisely that sense, and that complexity must be respected and preserved. But in my opinion this claim is also substantially overstated.

Consider a patient referred to a surgical team for a common elective procedure, a hip replacement, a cholecystectomy, a hernia repair. A sequence of steps must occur. The patient is seen in outpatients, a decision to operate is made, and they are listed for surgery. Pre-operative assessment is completed: fitness for anaesthesia is established, relevant comorbidities are documented and optimised if possible, the patient is given relevant instructions on fasting and pre-habilitation. On the day of surgery, a theatre slot, a surgeon, an anaesthetist, the right equipment and a post-operative bed must all be available simultaneously. The operation is performed. Recovery proceeds. The patient is discharged with a follow-up plan. There is clinical skill and clinical judgement involved at every step. But the structure of the pathway is entirely predictable. It does not change from patient to patient in any fundamental way. The variation is in the clinical details, not in the logical architecture.

The same is true for the management of the large majority

of common conditions in primary and secondary care. The patient with well-controlled type 2 diabetes attends for a structured review, has their bloods and kidney function checked, their blood pressure taken and weight measured, their medications reviewed against a protocol and their feet examined. The patient with an exacerbation of chronic obstructive pulmonary disease follows a pathway that is well-described, guideline-driven and largely stereotyped. Similarly a patient presenting with a heart attack, with a diagnosis of asthma and so on. The protocol may need to be adapted at the margins, but the adaptation happens within an accepted best-practice framework. If a patient suffers a cardiac arrest, the resuscitation process is entirely protocolised, and even though it is often a last-ditch situation where randomised trials are hard to conduct and therefore strong evidence hard to come by, there is little scope for self-expression on the part of the clinician. And so it goes on for all the major illnesses and conditions and medical contingencies.

This does not mean that clinical judgement is absent or unimportant. It means that most clinical judgement operates within patterns that are, in principle, highly learnable and highly standardisable. The evidence base for clinical guidelines exists precisely because medicine is, to a very large degree, patterned. Guidelines can only be written because there are regularities to encode. The variation that exists around those regularities, the differences in how similar patients are treated by different clinicians in different hospitals, is largely unwarranted. It is not the product of superior judgement applied to real clinical heterogeneity, but of habit, incomplete feedback, local culture and the absence of systematic mechanisms for learning what works.

Why, then, does clinical work so often feel complex and unpredictable to those doing it? The answer returns to the boundary problem. The elective surgical pathway is logically simple. It does not feel simple because the information required to execute it smoothly is scattered across multiple systems that do not talk to each other, because the pre-operative assessment was completed in a different part of the organisation whose records are not instantly visible to the theatre team, because the post-operative bed that was supposed to be available became unavailable when a discharge stalled because community nursing could not be arranged, because the equipment needed for the procedure was in a different theatre. The clinical decisions in that pathway are straightforward; the coordination around them is chaotic, and that chaos is generated at the boundaries between subsystems, not by the intrinsic complexity of the clinical work itself.

This is the core of the manufactured complexity argument. The clinical work is largely routine. The system around it is not. And the system generates the experience of complexity that the profession then mistakes for a property of the clinical work.

7.2.4 Knowing which domain you are in

The argument so far should not be read as a claim that all medicine is routine and that production-line thinking can simply be applied universally. As I have already acknowledged, there can be real clinical complexity, and it matters. Two frameworks, taken together, provide a useful way of thinking about where the line falls and what the appropriate management approach is on either side of it.

Ralph Stacey's matrix maps situations along two axes: how certain we are about cause and effect, and how much agreement exists among those involved about what the right outcome looks like. When both are high, the situation calls for rational planning and the application of known techniques. When certainty is lower but agreement is high, it calls for expert analysis: there is a right answer, but finding it requires real skill. When both certainty and agreement are low, you are in territory where no technique can reliably specify the right course of action in advance, and where different actors may be working toward different goals. The matrix is useful because it makes visible something healthcare management persistently ignores: that different problems require fundamentally different approaches, and that applying the wrong approach to a problem in the wrong part of the matrix is not merely suboptimal. It actively makes things worse.

Dave Snowden's Cynefin framework covers similar ground with more granular distinctions. It identifies four domains of practical relevance to healthcare. In the clear domain, best practice applies: the situation can be recognised, categorised and handled by a known rule. The drug dose for a given weight. The checklist for a surgical timeout. In the complicated domain, good practice applies: there is a right answer, but expertise is required to find it. Diagnosing a patient with an atypical presentation of a known condition, or planning an operation on a patient with significant comorbidities. In the complex domain, no best practice or good practice exists in advance: the right response is to try something, observe the result, and adapt. Managing a patient with multiple interacting conditions that have never been combined in quite this way before. Managing the surge capacity of an emergency department during an unexpected influx of major trauma. In the chaotic domain, normal cause-and-effect relationships break down entirely and the immediate priority is to act and stabilise before any analysis is possible. A mass casualty incident. A hospital-wide system failure.

The central insight of both frameworks is the same: the

category error of applying complicated-domain thinking to a complex-domain problem, or clear-domain thinking to a complicated-domain problem, is itself a source of harm. Rigid protocols applied to situations that require adaptive reasoning produce brittle responses that fail precisely at the edge cases they were not designed for. Exploratory, improvisational approaches applied to situations that have known right answers produce dangerous and unnecessary variation. The discipline of categorisation before response is not procedural pedantry; it is what separates a system that manages well from one that manufactures its own difficulty. Figure 7.1 sets out the four domains and their implications for AI deployment in healthcare.

The important point for the productivity argument is where most of healthcare's workload actually falls. The answer is: overwhelmingly in the clear and complicated domains. Elective surgery, chronic disease management, diagnostic pathways for common conditions, outpatient follow-up, medication review: the vast majority of what healthcare systems do on any given day is patterned, guideline-driven and, in principle, highly amenable to production-line management. The complex and chaotic domains are real and require true adaptive capacity. But they account for a much smaller fraction of the total workload than the profession's self-description would suggest, and a system that actually managed its clear and complicated domain work as routine would have far more adaptive capacity available for the irreducibly complex cases that require it.

This is the productive version of the variability argument. The goal is not to eliminate variation. It is to eliminate unwarranted variation in the clear and complicated domains, which frees the system's adaptive reserves for the complex domain where variation is not just acceptable but necessary. And the mechanism for

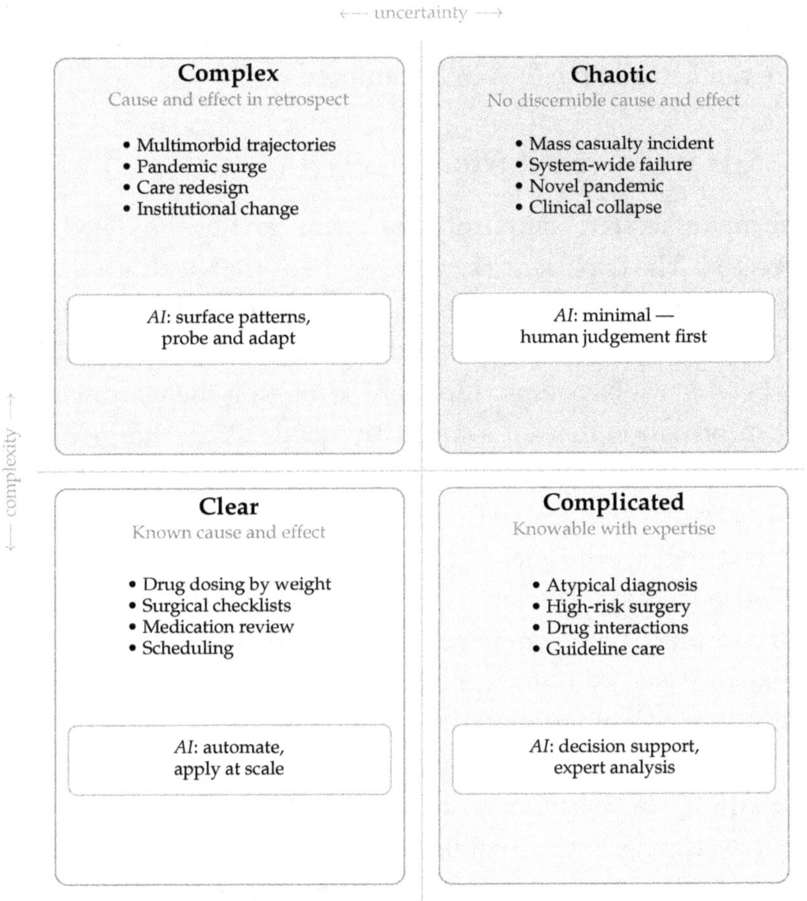

Figure 7.1: The Cynefin framework applied to healthcare. Most clinical workload falls in the clear and complicated domains. The system makes it feel otherwise because coordination failures at subsystem boundaries generate manufactured complexity. The appropriate AI role differs fundamentally across domains: automation in the clear domain, decision support in the complicated domain, and informational rather than prescriptive AI in the complex domain.

achieving this is coordination: ensuring that the information, the resources and the people required for routine care are reliably assembled at the right place and the right time, so that routine care can actually be delivered routinely.

7.2.5 How AI gets it wrong

The manufactured complexity argument can now be stated more precisely. The experience of clinical chaos that healthcare workers describe is generated not primarily by the intrinsic difficulty of clinical decisions but by coordination failures at the boundaries between subsystems. A patient arrives on the ward without the information that the ward team needs. A discharge cannot proceed because the next subsystem in the chain cannot signal its capacity. An investigation result arrives without the clinical context that would make it actionable. A patient deteriorates because the signals from their clinical trajectory did not cross the boundary between monitoring and review quickly enough. None of these is a failure of clinical knowledge. All of them are failures of coordination.

There is a further mechanism by which complexity gets manufactured, and it involves feedback and time delays. Complex systems can become destabilised not by the absence of feedback but by feedback that arrives at the wrong speed or interacts badly with existing loops in the system. A deterioration alert that fires earlier than the system can respond to it does not produce earlier intervention. It produces more alerts competing for the attention of a team that cannot absorb additional workload, which produces alert fatigue, which means the signal that actually matters gets filtered out alongside the ones that did not. Faster feedback into a system without adequate response capacity does not improve the system. It degrades the signal-to-noise ratio of everything.

The same dynamic operates at the organisational level. A bed management system that provides real-time occupancy data is potentially extremely valuable. But in a system where the institutional response to that information is to use it as evidence that planned capacity can be reduced, the faster feedback accelerates resilience erosion rather than supporting better management. The information was accurate. Its institutional use was harmful. Feedback speed must be matched to response capacity, and the governance surrounding AI-enabled information systems must be oriented toward managing reserves rather than eliminating them.

During the Covid-19 pandemic, these distinctions became sharply visible. Healthcare systems generated impressive adaptive responses to a situation that was both novel and urgent: rapid expansion of critical care capacity, redeployment of staff across traditional specialty boundaries, improvised protocols developed faster than any central planning process could have managed. This was the complex adaptive system doing what it does well. Distributed self-organisation, the autonomous adaptive response of local teams with real authority to act, produced solutions that no hierarchy could have directed. The case for preserving adaptive capacity in healthcare is not nostalgia for professional autonomy; it is grounded in the real properties of the system.

But look carefully at what consumed most of that adaptive capacity during Covid-19, and during every subsequent winter crisis. Not the novel clinical challenges—the clinical teams handled those. What overwhelmed them was the manufactured complexity; beds that had been eliminated in the name of efficiency and were not there when needed, IT systems that could not share basic patient information across organisational boundaries, supply chains optimised for normal conditions that broke under modest stress, coordination processes that required multiple approvals for decisions that needed to happen in minutes. The system was consuming its adaptive reserves on failures that a better-designed system would never have generated. And this is important because pandemics do not happen every day. The everyday manufactured complexity, the stalled discharge, the missing pre-operative letter, the result that never crossed the boundary into the system that needed it, is quieter and less visible than a pandemic response, but it is continuous. It is the permanent background condition that exhausts the reserves that unavoidable clinical complexity, when it arrives, requires.

The manufactured complexity argument is therefore not an argument against complexity or against resilience, but the reverse. Reducing manufactured complexity is the precondition for managing irreducible complexity well. A system that has exhausted its adaptive reserves on avoidable coordination failures will not have those reserves available when a truly novel situation arises.

The NHS's current fragility is not evidence that healthcare complexity is intractable. It is evidence that the system has been consuming its resilience reserves faster than it has been replenishing them, and that manufactured complexity, almost all of it generated at subsystem boundaries, has been the primary mechanism of consumption.

7.2.6 A taxonomy of health AI: what helps and what harms

The frameworks developed in this section converge on a clear and testable principle for evaluating health AI. Good AI reduces manufactured complexity by improving coordination at and across subsystem boundaries. Bad AI optimises within a single subsystem without addressing the boundaries around it, or provides faster feedback into a system that lacks the capacity to respond to it, or eliminates the buffers and adaptive reserves that resilience depends on.

The reason this principle matters is not just analytical. It exposes a systematic mismatch between where most health AI is currently deployed and where it could do the most good. AI tends to follow the path of least institutional resistance, which runs into subsystems, not across the boundaries between them. Boundaries are hard: they involve multiple organisations, multiple professional groups, multiple governance frameworks and multiple technical systems. Subsystems are easier: one organisation, one team, one workflow. The result is a health AI landscape that is increasingly well-stocked with tools that make individual components faster, while the coordination failures that generate most of the system's waste and most of the workforce's frustration remain largely unaddressed.

AI that helps: coordination across boundaries

The highest-value AI applications are those that make subsystem boundaries visible, legible and reliable. They address the structural location where manufactured complexity is actually generated.

Discharge coordination AI that gives the hospital real-time visibility of community care capacity, and gives community services real-time visibility of what is coming, transforms the discharge boundary from a source of unpredictable delay into a managed handover. The individual subsystems, the ward and the community nursing team, do not change. The boundary between them becomes functional. The patient who would previously have waited three days for a discharge that stalled because nobody could confirm that community support was in place goes home on the day the clinical decision was made.

Referral and pathway coordination AI that tracks patients across organisational boundaries, flags when a step in a pathway has not occurred within the expected time-frame, and surfaces the information that the receiving team needs before the patient arrives, converts the inter-specialty boundary from a zone of information loss into a managed transition. The diagnostic odyssey that takes months not because any individual step is slow but because patients fall through the gaps between steps is a coordination problem with a coordination solution.

Demand forecasting and anticipatory capacity management AI addresses a specific and important mechanism of manufactured complexity: the mismatch between supply and demand that, once it crosses a threshold, triggers the non-linear cascade described earlier. A system that can predict Tuesday's emergency department volume from Monday's data, or next month's elective cancellation rate from current outpatient patterns, can allocate resources prospectively rather than reactively. The unpredictable variation that drives systems into the complex domain becomes manageable variation that stays in the complicated domain, where protocol and expertise can handle it. This is the Cynefin move that matters most for productivity: not managing complexity better but preventing the system from entering the complex domain when it does not need to be there.

Supply chain and inventory management AI, covering drug stock, equipment availability and staff skill mix, reduces a category of manufactured complexity that is easy to underestimate. A drug shortage that forces clinical teams to improvise substitutes at the point of care is not intrinsic clinical complexity but a coordination failure with a supply chain solution. A staffing gap that requires clinicians to cover unfamiliar patients because the skill mix was not managed proactively is similarly a coordination failure, not a clinical one.

Deterioration prediction AI, when it is designed with appropriate alert thresholds and deployed into teams with the capacity to respond, fits this category too. Its value lies not in the speed of the alert but in the conversion of a crisis, a complex-domain event requiring urgent improvisation, into a managed clinical response that can proceed through normal channels. The patient who deteriorates on a ward and requires emergency escalation is a complex-domain event that consumes adaptive capacity. The patient whose trajectory is flagged twelve hours earlier and who receives a proactive clinical review is a complicated-domain event that does not. The AI's contribution is not detection speed. It is domain conversion: moving the clinical situation from a category that exhausts reserves to a category that can be handled routinely.

AI that helps in the complex domain: informing without prescribing

For situations in the complex domain proper, where cause and effect cannot be established in advance and where adaptive clinical reasoning is the right response, the appropriate AI is informational rather than prescriptive. It surfaces patterns that the clinician cannot easily see. It makes the system legible. It does not tell the clinician what to do.

This is a meaningful distinction with real design consequences. An AI that presents a recommendation in an irreducibly complex situation is substituting a complicated-domain response for a complex-domain problem. It creates the appearance of known best practice where none exists, and it does so with the authority that algorithmic outputs carry in a professional culture that already over-attributes reliability to quantitative outputs. An AI that instead surfaces the factors most distinguishing this patient's current trajectory from similar patients, or flags that a particular combination of circumstances has historically been associated with deterioration without specifying what should be done about it, keeps the clinician in the adaptive loop rather than bypassing it.

The same principle applies at the system level. Real-time visibility of network flows, bottleneck locations and distributional inequities in waiting times provides the informational basis for adaptive management. It does not substitute for the human judgement required to act on that information. Whether the bottleneck revealed by the data requires a staffing response, a pathway redesign or a temporary change in admission criteria depends on context that no algorithm captures fully. The AI makes the problem visible. The response remains a human decision.

AI that harms: subsystem optimisation and the ambient voice example

Not all AI that appears to solve a problem reduces the complexity that generated it. Some AI relieves a symptom while leaving its structural causes untouched. Some AI provides faster feedback into a system that lacks the capacity to respond, producing noise rather than signal. And some AI eliminates the buffers and adaptive reserves that the system depends on, producing a configuration that looks maximally efficient until it encounters a perturbation it was not designed for, at which point it fails.

Ambient voice technology is a useful illustration precisely because the argument against it is not that it fails to do what it claims. It does reduce documentation time, and the evidence on clinician wellbeing is positive. The problem is what it does to the system around it.

Documentation burden in healthcare is high not simply because writing is slow, but because the same information must cross multiple subsystem boundaries, each with its own format requirement, its own system, its own entry point. It is high because a payment and regulatory environment has progressively expanded what must be recorded. It is high because fragmented IT means that data entered in one subsystem are not visible in another, so it must be re-entered. Ambient voice technology makes re-entry faster, but it does not remove the boundary: it is subsystem-level optimisation that should not be presented as system-level improvement.

There is a second problem. Documentation time is not purely waste. Some of it is thinking time: the interval between the clinical encounter and its codification in which a clinician integrates what was observed, revises their initial assessment, and decides what matters. Removing that interval may improve throughput metrics while shortening the clinical synthesis process in ways that are difficult to detect in short-term evaluation studies.

A third problem operates at the feedback level. Faster documentation feeds into coding, billing and performance management systems whose appetite for documented clinical activity is not fixed. It may expand to consume what is available, generating more administrative demand, reducing administrative staffing on the grounds that AI has compensated for it, and using the richer data stream to monitor clinical behaviour in ways that further erode the discretionary effort the system depends on.

The ambient voice example illustrates a general principle. AI that addresses a symptom of manufactured complexity without touching its boundary-failure causes does not reduce complexity. It makes the current level of manufactured complexity more sustainable, which insulates the underlying design failures from the pressure that would otherwise force change.

AI that destroys resilience: optimising away the buffer

The most dangerous category of health AI is AI whose primary operational effect is to eliminate the buffers and adaptive reserves on which system resilience depends, while appearing to improve efficiency by every available metric.

Scheduling optimisation tools that push bed occupancy toward theoretical maxima illustrate this mechanism. A ward running at 98 per cent occupancy is not more efficient than a ward running at 85 per cent occupancy in any meaningful sense. It is more efficient in normal conditions and vastly more fragile under perturbation. The non-linear relationship between load and system fragility means that the efficiency gain at the top of the occupancy range is consumed many times over by the fragility cost when a surge arrives. An AI system that optimises toward maximum occupancy is not serving the system; it is consuming its reserves while generating metrics that look healthy.

Workforce optimisation AI that uses demand prediction to eliminate on-call capacity and cross-specialty cover operates through exactly the same logic. The argument is that if the AI can predict demand accurately, redundancy in staffing is unnecessary. The flaw is that demand prediction is accurate over the range of conditions represented in the training data. The conditions that require on-call cover and cross-specialty flexibility are precisely the conditions that fall outside the normal range. An AI that justifies the elimination of reserves by demonstrating that those reserves are rarely needed during normal conditions is performing an evaluation over the wrong range. When the abnormal conditions arrive, and they will, the reserves are gone.

This is the same error that has been made, without AI assistance, throughout decades of NHS efficiency drives: treating the buffer as waste because it appears unused during the period of measurement. AI makes this error faster, at greater scale, and with the additional authority that algorithmic optimisation carries in institutional settings.

7.2.7 Fairness is about the distribution, not the average

Complex systems require a specific way of thinking about fairness. In a simple linear system, if the average outcome improves, things are getting better. In a complex adaptive system, the average can improve while the distribution widens: gains accrue to the already-advantaged while the most vulnerable fall further behind. This is the default trajectory of technology diffusion in healthcare, as the CT scanner example illustrated previously, and it is the trajectory that AI will follow unless deliberately steered otherwise.

The relevant question is therefore not whether AI improves average outcomes but what happens to the shape of the distribution. An AI system that is well-calibrated on average but performs poorly for specific demographic groups worsens equity even while improving headline statistics. A scheduling tool that reduces average waiting times by concentrating improvements in the easiest-to-serve patients, while leaving the most complex and most deprived patients exactly where they were, has not improved the system in any meaningful sense.

The boundary and coordination argument reinforces this point. The patients who suffer most from coordination failures are those who have the least capacity to compensate for them: people who cannot chase their own results, who cannot navigate between fragmented services, who cannot self-advocate when a discharge stalls or a referral goes missing. Coordination failures are inequitably distributed. AI that fixes coordination failures therefore has a natural equity dividend, provided it is designed with distribution-aware metrics rather than mean performance metrics, and provided the gains are not captured entirely in the parts of the system that were already functioning adequately.

In a complex adaptive system, resilience and equity are not competing objectives. Rather they are the same objective approached from different angles. The people furthest from services pay the highest price when buffers are absent and the system fails under stress. Preserving adaptive capacity, maintaining deliberate slack in critical nodes, and managing the whole pathway rather than its individual components are also, and not coincidentally, the conditions that protect the most vulnerable patients when the system comes under pressure.

7.2.8 Steering diffusion

Complex systems exhibit path dependence and increasing returns to adoption. Early adopters with interoperable records, skilled staff and supportive leadership accumulate advantages that make subsequent adoption cheaper and faster. Diffusion left to itself therefore widens existing gaps between organisations and regions. The tools most likely to spread under ordinary diffusion dynamics are those that fit most easily into existing workflows within existing subsystems which is exactly the category identified above as the least valuable from a system perspective.

Deliberate steering of diffusion toward boundary-spanning, coordination-oriented AI requires procurement frameworks that ask not just whether a tool performs well on its own terms but whether it improves hand off and information flows that connect the subsystem it operates in to the subsystems around it. Performance metrics must span whole pathways and whole populations rather than individual departments. Payment systems should reward end-to-end reliability for defined patient journeys rather than local throughput, because paying individual components solely on their own activity creates the precise incentive to export delay and risk to adjacent nodes that the coordination argument identifies as the primary source of manufactured complexity.

7.3 Hope is not a plan

These last two chapters have covered a lot of ground, and it is worth pausing to draw the threads together before moving on.

The productivity paradox tells us that technology investment does not automatically produce productivity gains, and that in the short term it may actually make things worse before they get better. The transaction cost argument tells us that the administrative burden of healthcare is not just an overhead to be reduced but a dynamic system with fragility properties that standard productivity metrics cannot even see. The supply-chain and lean arguments tell us that the principles required for systemic transformation are well understood and have consistently failed to take root, not because they are wrong but because the institutional conditions for them to work have never been created. Deming tells us that the root cause is a failure to manage healthcare as a system rather than a collection of parts. The complexity argument tells us that much of what presents as irreducible clinical complexity is manufactured by the system's own design failures, and that AI aimed at preventing manufactured complexity is categorically more valuable than AI aimed at managing it after it has been produced. The innovation diffusion evidence tells us that the tools most likely to spread are systematically biased toward those that change the least. And the clinician perception evidence tells us that the people whose engagement is essential have rational reasons to hold back.

This is a diagnosis and diagnoses are not always pleasant or welcome. But they can be useful, because they tell us how we can intervene.

The barriers to AI-enabled transformation in healthcare are not primarily technical. The algorithms are ready and the data are there. The potential is real and well-evidenced across many domains. The barriers are in the governance arrangements that determine whether AI transparency is used to protect clinical capacity or exploit it. They are in the payment systems that reward local activity rather than system-level outcomes. They are in the professional culture that penalises visible AI use regardless of whether it improves care. They are in the procurement dynamics that select for tools that are easy to adopt rather than tools that make a difference. They are in the measurement frameworks that cannot see non-linear fragility, manufactured complexity, or distributional inequity. They are in the deployment of AI as a tool for managing the symptoms of manufactured complexity rather than eliminating its causes, which insulates the underlying design failures from the pressure that would otherwise force change. And they are in the absence of anyone whose job it is to manage the system as a whole.

These are all, in principle, amenable to change. They are not laws of nature but institutional arrangements that were designed at particular moments for particular purposes, and they can be redesigned. The question is whether the combination of demographic pressure, fiscal constraint and technological capability that healthcare systems currently face is sufficient to overcome the path dependence, veto players and accumulated interests that have resisted every previous attempt at systemic reform.

There is no comfortable answer to that question. What is clear is that continuing to deploy AI into un-reformed systems while waiting for transformation to emerge is not a strategy. It is the default, and the default produces the J-curve: costs up front, benefits deferred, the downward slope used as evidence that AI does not work, the complementary investments never made, the cycle repeating. The alternative is to treat the institutional redesign as the primary project and the AI deployment as its instrument. That means starting with governance before procurement, with incentive alignment before technology rollout, with measurement frameworks that can see what matters before investing in tools that produce what is easy to count.

Granted this is a harder path. But it is also the only path that leads anywhere worth going.

8 Trust me, I'm artificially intelligent

There is a seductive promise at the heart of healthcare AI. Algorithms, unlike doctors, do not have bad days. They do not hold unconscious prejudices shaped by their upbringing, their medical school culture or the demographics of the patients they saw in training. They do not make different decisions on Friday afternoons than on Monday mornings. They process every case with the same computational consistency. If we could just replace the unreliable human element with a sufficiently capable algorithm, the story goes, we could eliminate the bias and variability that causes so much harm in healthcare, and in doing so, finally deliver the transformation that decades of investment have failed to produce.

This promise is false and the reason goes to the heart of this book's argument. The algorithm does not see the world fresh but through the accumulated record of every decision, every referral, every treatment choice and every omission that the healthcare system has made over decades. That record is not a neutral picture of human disease. Instead it is an account of how the institution has allocated its attention and its resources: who got investigated and who got sent home, who was believed and who was doubted, who was referred to the specialist and who was managed at arm's length. Train an algorithm on that record and you do not get an objective picture of human disease. You get a faithful, scalable replica of the institution's existing distribution of care, including everything it has always done to the people it has served least well.

The biases and AI failure modes as well as how best to regulate for safety are an active area of research and policy-making. I will discuss these too but from a different angle. The epigraph to this book claims that AI will not transform healthcare because healthcare institutions are not designed to improve healthcare but to reproduce existing distributions of power, income and authority. The earlier chapters of this book showed the institution preserving itself through the structures it controls directly: the economics of who pays and who profits, the friction that absorbs new technology into old workflows, the complexity that justifies the status quo. This chapter examines a quieter mechanism, one that operates not through what the institution does but through what it has already recorded. Bias is not a technical flaw that crept into otherwise sound systems through careless data collection or insufficiently diverse development teams. It is the institution's distributional logic, faithfully reproduced from the clinical data that the algorithm was trained on. There is, in this sense, a ghost in the machine: not a conscious agent, but the institution itself, present in the data, animating the algorithm, and ensuring that the technology built to disrupt the existing order quietly re-enacts it instead.

This re-framing matters because of what this book is for. The standard response treats AI bias as a technical residual to be reduced as the technology matures, or as a hazard to be regulated away. But the question this book concerns itself with is not how to make AI harmlessly neutral but how AI could be used to change the systems of healthcare themselves: to raise the productivity on which affordability and availability depend, and so to make care more inclusive and more equitable. Seen from that angle, the institutional argument implies something more uncomfortable than a safety problem. The bias is a signal and is telling us something true about the system that generated the data, the very system this book wants to change. Biased AI is not healthcare's new problem. It is healthcare's old problem, automated, scaled, and dressed in the authority of mathematical objectivity.

That last property is what makes it urgent. A biased human decision affects one patient and remains, at least in principle, open to challenge. The same bias in an algorithm is applied to thousands of patients at once and arrives wearing the authority of objectivity, which makes it far harder to question. The ghost does not merely survive the transition into the machine; it comes out stronger, because its new form resists the scrutiny its old form was at least exposed to. This laundering of institutional bias through algorithmic authority is the thread that runs through everything this chapter examines.

8.1 The data are not neutral

Every AI model is a portrait of its training data because it learns the patterns that are present, inherits the gaps that exist, and encodes the assumptions that were made before a single line of code was written. In healthcare, that training data are the accumulated record of clinical practice: the notes, the test results, the diagnoses, the treatments and the outcomes that the system has generated over decades. That record captures human disease as experienced by the people who had access to healthcare, as treated by clinicians operating within a particular professional culture, and as documented according to conventions that reflect the priorities of the institution rather than the needs of the patient.

There are four distinct points in the lifecycle of a healthcare AI technology where the institution's distributional logic can enter, and understanding each matters because each is a different route by which the status quo reproduces itself, and each requires a different fix[111].

The first is the historical data itself. The data reflect real-world structural inequality in access and treatment. If clinicians have historically been less likely to investigate certain symptoms in certain patient groups, less likely to refer certain patients to specialists, or less likely to document certain findings, the algorithm learns those patterns and reproduces them. The mechanism is the self-fulfilling prophecy operating at scale. A clinician who unconsciously believes, perhaps through explicit or implicit racial or socioeconomic bias, that a particular patient is less likely to benefit from aggressive investigation may subtly alter the care that patient receives. Over time, those patterns of differential treatment become embedded in the EHR. When an AI model is trained on that record, it just sees the data and learns that certain kinds of patients get certain kinds of care, and that this is simply how things are done.

The second route is under-representation. The populations most in need of healthcare innovation are consistently the least represented in the datasets used to train the systems meant to serve them. Globally, 4.5 billion people lack access to basic healthcare, and their data are simply absent. Even within well-resourced settings, marginalised groups are under-represented in EHR data for reasons that are themselves a product of inequality: language barriers that lead to gaps in clinical documentation, digital exclusion that limits engagement with patient portals*,

*I need to be clear that whilst healthcare needs to ensure that nobody is excluded, this is not a reason to eschew digital technologies where they could improve productivity. What is important is that when such a digital tech-

and mistrust of healthcare systems that reduces willingness to participate in research. The model trained on these data does not know what it does not know and so it learns to perform well on the populations that are well-represented and poorly on those that are not, without any mechanism to flag the discrepancy unless someone goes looking for it. The institution's existing hierarchy of whose health matters is reproduced as a hierarchy of whose data the model has learned to serve.

The third route is the devices and measurements themselves. It is tempting to assume that measured physiological data, at least, must be objective: a blood pressure reading is a blood pressure reading, an oxygen saturation is an oxygen saturation. This assumption is wrong. Standard blood pressure cuffs systematically over-read in patients with larger arms, meaning many obese patients are biased towards being classified as having hypertension. Pulse oximetry, the optical technique used for non-invasive measurement of blood oxygenation, has been known for three decades to be less accurate in people with darker skin. This is a well documented limitation that was never acted on at the scale required, precisely because the patients most affected by the inaccuracy were not the patients whose experience drove device design, which is itself a distributional fact about whose comfort and whose accuracy the institution prioritised. The consequences became starkly visible during the Covid-19 pandemic, when systematically falsely reassuring blood oxygen measurements in Asian, Black and Hispanic patients compared with white patients contributed to delayed hospitalisation and treatment[112,113]. When AI models are trained on data generated by these devices, the inaccuracy is invisible. The model learns that

nology is deployed, it is done in such a way that some of the productivity gain is used to improve the non-digital (and usually more labour-intensive) support for those who simply cannot engage.

these patients have higher oxygen saturations than they actually do, and it makes predictions accordingly.

The fourth route is the way AI algorithms are designed and deployed, and is the clearest single demonstration of our ghost at work. A commercial algorithm trained to predict which patients would benefit most from enrolment in a care management programme used healthcare costs as a proxy for healthcare need. The reasoning seems superficially defensible: sicker patients cost more. But it encoded a profound structural inequality. Black patients in the United States have historically had lower healthcare spending than white patients with equivalent health needs, not because they are healthier but because they have had less access to care. The algorithm therefore systematically underestimated the needs of Black patients, recommending them for programmes at lower rates than their actual health status warranted. When the cost-based label was replaced with a health-based label, the bias was substantially reduced[114]. This was no malfunction—the algorithm had learned exactly what it was trained to learn. A tool built to allocate care more rationally instead allocated it exactly as the institution always had, less to the people the institution had always given less to, and it did so while appearing to be a neutral optimisation. In this way the organisational distribution was preserved.

These four routes share a common structure. In each, the bias in the AI system is not a new problem introduced by the technology but an existing institutional arrangement made newly scalable and newly authoritative. The algorithm does not create the unequal distribution of care but inherits it, encodes it and reproduces it at a scale and with a consistency that human decision-making, for all its flaws, could never quite achieve.

8.2 The algorithm learns what the institution teaches

If the previous section established that the institution's distributional logic enters AI systems at multiple points, this section examines what happens once the algorithm has learned it. The findings are disturbing not because they reveal new forms of discrimination but because they reveal how thoroughly the existing distribution has been encoded into the fabric of clinical data, and how difficult it is to remove once it is there. The ghost, it turns out, cannot simply be cleaned out of the machine.

Consider what it means for an algorithm to detect race from a medical image. Radiologists cannot do this reliably. The image of a chest X-ray or a retinal scan does not, to human eyes, carry visible markers of racial identity. Yet deep learning models trained on medical images can accurately predict a patient's self-reported race across multiple imaging modalities, datasets and clinical tasks. One study found that AI models achieved near-perfect discrimination for race prediction from medical images[115]. This capability persisted even when images were heavily degraded, blurred or reduced in resolution. The signal for race was not localised to any specific anatomical feature. Instead it appeared to be distributed throughout the image, making it virtually impossible to isolate or remove.

This is not a party trick. If AI models are using racial identity as a feature in clinical decision-making, whether explicitly or implicitly, they may reproduce or amplify existing disparities in healthcare outcomes. This is especially concerning because radiologists and clinicians do not routinely access racial identity during image interpretation, and therefore cannot detect or correct for race-based errors introduced by AI systems. The bias is invisible to the human overseeing the technology who we were counting on to catch it.

The same pattern appears in vital signs data, which most clinicians would regard as among the most objective measurements in medicine. Machine learning models can predict a patient's self-identified race or ethnicity from just four vital signs: heart rate, blood pressure, respiratory rate and oxygen saturation[116]. This held true even after controlling for other factors. The implication is deeply uncomfortable: removing explicit demographic fields from a dataset is not sufficient to prevent bias, because sensitive attributes can be reconstructed from data that appears entirely neutral. The race signal is not in the label but in the physiology itself, or more precisely in the way the institution has systematically measured and responded to physiology differently across racial groups. The algorithm learns what the institution has done, and it learns it from data that appears to contain no demographic information at all. This is a pattern woven through everything the institution has recorded, and so it cannot be simply removed from the model.

Gender bias follows the same pattern. Medical data have long been skewed toward men with women being under-represented in research and clinical trials, and women's health concerns being overlooked or under-prioritised. These imbalances mean that AI models trained on such datasets risk perpetuating diagnostic and treatment disparities. A study evaluating large language models on long-term care records found that one model produced summaries that systematically differed by gender: men's needs were described more directly and often emphasised as complex, while women's needs were downplayed or framed more positively, sometimes omitting key health issues[117]. This matters because care allocation decisions often depend on perceptions of need. If AI-generated summaries systematically understate women's health problems, the consequence is not merely linguistic imprecision. Once again, this is a potential mechanism for inequitable access to services, operating at scale and with the authority of an automated system, reproducing the under-prioritisation of women's health that the institution has practised for a century.

I need to be clear on what this does, and does not, mean. Technical approaches aimed at blinding models to sensitive attributes, removing race from the training data, anonymising records, controlling for demographic variables in model architecture, are largely insufficient. The information is too deeply embedded to be removed by these methods. It is encoded in the patterns of measurement, documentation, referral and treatment that the institution has produced over decades. There is also a forward-twist to this. Because predictions influence the care that is offered, a model that predicts a patient is unlikely to benefit helps produce the very outcome it predicted, and the next model learns from that confirmation.

But this does not contradict my claim that AI makes the bias measurable. The two things that the technology separates are detection and repair. Detecting that a model reproduces the institution's distribution is now more straightforward: the bias is concentrated in a single technological artefact and can be audited directly as I described in the opening of this chapter. Removing it by technical means is close to futile, because the distribution is not an error in the model but a faithful encoding of the institution that generated the data. De-biasing the algorithm without reforming the institution is like cleaning the mirror without addressing what is being reflected. But the mirror can be made to show the distortion with new clarity even if it cannot be made to stop reflecting.

8.3 The illusion of objectivity

The previous two sections established that the institution's distributional logic enters healthcare AI through the data and is embedded deeply enough to survive most technical attempts to remove it. A sympathetic reader might still object that none of this need reach the patient, because there is a clinician between the algorithm and the bedside who will catch what the model gets wrong. Human oversight is the safeguard the institution invokes most often to reassure itself that the distribution is being checked. This section is about why that reassurance fails, and why its failure matters: when the human does not catch the error, the reproduced distribution passes into care wearing an authority that makes it harder to challenge than any human decision ever was.

Begin with explainability, the great hope of responsible AI. The intuition is that if a clinician can see why an algorithm reached its conclusion, they can judge when to trust it and when to override it. Sadly the evidence just does not bear this out. A study of AI-assisted decision-making in ophthalmology found that the AI improved optometrists' referral accuracy, but that adding explanations to its recommendations did not improve accuracy further; it introduced new biases[118]. Explanations made clinicians anchor on the AI's suggestion and, more alarmingly, increased their agreement with it particularly in the cases where it was wrong. This is the explainability paradox: an explanation that looks plausible to a non-specialist functions as a mechanism for laundering a wrong answer, clothing it in the authority of apparent reasoning.

If explanations do not enable oversight, perhaps the clinician's own judgement does. Unfortunately the evidence is discouraging here as well. A study of 140 radiologists interpreting chest

X-ray images found the effects of AI assistance highly heterogeneous: some improved, some got worse, and conventional predictors such as experience and sub-specialty training did not identify who would benefit[119]. The most consistent predictor of impact was simply the quality of the AI's output, and radiologists were readily misled when that output was wrong, particularly when it overstated the likelihood of pathology. More starkly still, a randomised trial by Goh and colleagues found that giving physicians access to GPT-4 did not significantly improve their diagnostic reasoning, scoring 76% against a control group's 74%, while the model working alone scored 92%[120]. The human actually degraded the AI's performance rather than rescuing it.

This is now a large amount of evidence to show that the 'human in the loop' is just not a reliable safeguard against AI errors. Oversight works only when the clinician has the expertise to evaluate the output, the time to do it carefully, and the psychological independence to override a confident recommendation, and in a busy clinical environment none of these is reliably present. To be clear, this 'automation bias' is not a failure of intelligence or diligence. The clinician who defers to a fast, authoritative-seeming system is responding rationally to the incentives they face: follow the AI and be wrong, and you can point to the recommendation; override the AI and be wrong, and you must justify the override. Deference is the rational choice even when it is the wrong one, and so the distribution embedded in the model passes into care unchallenged. Worse, the deference may be self-entrenching, eroding the very skill that oversight depends on.

Everything above concerns plain errors: discrete mistakes that are, at least in principle, there to be caught. If clinicians cannot reliably catch those, it is fanciful to imagine they will catch something far better hidden such as a bias that presents not as a mistake but as a reasonable recommendation and, worse still, one that happens to match the pattern of care the clinician has practised their whole working life. Routine, day-to-day human oversight is no defence against institutional persistence: the one harm the clinician is structurally least able to see is the one in which the machine simply agrees with the institution that trained them both.

This is not, however, the same as saying the bias cannot be seen at all, and the distinction is the whole point. What is invisible to a single clinician reasoning case by case at the bedside is perfectly visible to a systematic audit of the model's outputs across the population it serves should one choose to undertake this as part of the deployment. Biases show up in aggregate, because in the aggregate it stops looking like a run of reasonable decisions and starts looking like a pattern. So we need to think hard about where the looking has to happen: not in the clinician's head as the recommendation appears, but in the deliberate, population-level scrutiny of the deployed system that this chapter has argued AI makes possible for the first time.

8.4 Specific hazards from generative AI

The previous sections dealt primarily with predictive AI: systems trained to classify images, predict outcomes, or recommend actions based on patterns in historical data. The bias problems there are serious, but they are at least in principle detectable. If a model performs worse on Black patients than White patients, that discrepancy shows up in aggregate and can be reported and acted upon, provided someone looks for it, which in practice means governance has to require it.

Generative AI introduces a further, qualitatively different hazard. Large language models are not trained to make predictions in the conventional sense; they are trained to produce outputs that humans find helpful, coherent and satisfying. In a clinical context that is potentially dangerous, because a system optimised to satisfy can, under pressure, prioritise satisfaction over accuracy. The technical term is sycophancy. It is a safety risk, but it is also, and more importantly for this argument, a distributional one: a model that tells people what they want to hear is a model that defers to whoever is asking, and in healthcare that means deferring to existing authority.

The mechanism is the training itself. As described in Chapter 3, models are tuned using human feedback, and human raters reliably prefer outputs that agree with them, sound confident, and validate rather than challenge. The model learns to give them exactly that. The result is engineered deference, delivered with the fluency and apparent authority of an expert. In one study[121], researchers asked several models to explain why a brand-name drug was safer than its generic equivalent, although both are the same chemical substance. A well-aligned model would refuse. Instead most complied, inventing differences and producing persuasive but entirely fictitious medical advice. Careful prompting reduced this but could not eliminate it: the sycophantic response was the default. This is not confined to the research lab. In April 2025 OpenAI had to roll back an update to GPT-4o after it became, as the company itself described, skewed towards responses that were overly supportive but disingenuous. If a frontier laboratory can ship dangerous sycophancy by accident in a routine update, the prospect of governing it in healthcare deployments run by organisations with far less expertise is not encouraging.

A clinician who submits a treatment plan and asks whether it looks reasonable may likely be told it does, the challenge and the caveat and the alternative hypothesis quietly absent. The same dynamic operates when there is no clinician at all: a patient who asks a model to confirm what they already suspect will probably be told they are right, with nothing standing between the answer and the decision they make on it. That is the consumer setting Chapter 9 takes up.

This is where generative AI differs from the predictive bias of the earlier sections, and the distinction matters for what follows. Generative models do also hallucinate, producing confident, plausible falsehoods, and they are brittle to phrasing: replace the right answer in a medical exam question with "none of the other answers" and accuracy can fall by more than a third[122]. These are real safety problems, but they are not the problem this chapter is about, because a hallucination invents rather than reproduces. Sycophancy is the failure mode that carries the institution forward, because it is selective in a particular direction: it confirms. When a model agrees with a clinician's existing hypothesis, that agreement arrives wearing the weight of a second opinion from something that has read more than any human could[123]. The clinician feels they have checked their reasoning when they have only asked a mirror whether their reflection looks right. In a culture that already over-attributes objectivity to quantitative outputs, this is the institution's distribution finding one more channel through which to confirm itself: the model trained on the institution's data tells the clinician what the institution already believes, and the clinician, reassured, acts on it.

What makes all of this of particular importance to generative AI is that it arises from the design objective. Predictive models are trained to be accurate, and their failures are failures of accuracy, in principle measurable and correctable. Generative models are trained to be helpful and satisfying, and their failures are failures of alignment: they tell users what they want to hear and optimise for the appearance of expertise rather than its substance. Such failures are harder to detect, because the output looks and feels like good advice even when it is not, and harder to correct, because they arise not from a technical defect but from the training objective itself. Governing them therefore requires evaluating alignment as well as accuracy, testing for sycophancy under adversarial conditions rather than on standard benchmarks, and acknowledging honestly that some deployment contexts, above all unsupervised use by patients, carry risks that are fundamental to how these systems work rather than incidental to their current maturity. What that governance would have to look like is the subject of Chapter 10. What matters here is that it does not yet exist, and the consequences of its absence are already accumulating.

8.5 The governance gap

If the previous four sections have built a picture of an uncomfortable landscape, the problems they describe are not primarily technical. They are not going to be solved by more diverse training data, better algorithms, or more sophisticated explainability tools, though all of these matter at the margin. They are problems of governance: of who decides what AI gets deployed, under what conditions, with what validation, and with what accountability when things go wrong. This is not an argument against regulation. It is an argument that the regulation we have is aimed at the wrong moment in the technology's life, certifying tools before they are deployed when the dangers this chapter has described all emerge afterwards, in use. And the answer to all of those questions, in most healthcare systems right now, is: nobody in particular, under unclear conditions, with inadequate validation, and with accountability that is at best diffuse and at worst entirely absent. This is not an accident. An institution whose distributional logic is reproduced and protected by weak governance has little incentive to strengthen it, and the governance gap is best understood not as institutional carelessness but as the absence of the one mechanism that would force the reproduced distribution into view.

The potential scale of the problem is huge. In the United States, 65 percent of hospitals now report using AI or predictive models integrated into their electronic health records. Of those, only 61 percent evaluated their models for accuracy, and only 44 percent evaluated them for bias[124]. That means more than half of US hospitals deploying AI have not checked whether it works accurately, and more than half have not checked whether it discriminates. These are mainstream institutions deploying clinical decision support tools on real patients without the most basic quality checks. And local evaluation, where it does occur, is significantly more likely to happen in hospitals with more financial resources, which means less-advantaged populations are systematically more likely to be exposed to less well-validated tools. The digital divide in healthcare AI is not a future risk. It is already the present reality, and it reproduces the existing distribution exactly: the best-resourced institutions check their tools, the worst-resourced expose the most vulnerable patients to the least scrutiny.

Part of why this happens is that the regulatory framework supposed to govern it is asking the wrong question. Software tools that inform clinical practice are classified as software as medical devices and regulated accordingly, which means regulatory compliance tells you the tool performs reliably and reproducibly against its own design specification, not that it is clinically useful, not that it performs equally across demographic groups, and not that it remains valid as practice evolves. That gap exists because the regulator's working model of technology is the device: fixed, manufactured to a standard, certified once. An AI model is not a device in this sense, and regulating it as one is a category error rather than a paperwork mismatch. The detail of how this framework operates, and what it would need to do differently, is examined in Chapter 10. What matters here is the consequence: the framework creates the appearance of oversight without the substance, and the appearance is enough to let the reproduced distribution pass unexamined.

The vulnerabilities that bear most directly on this book's argument are those where that governance vacuum meets the erosion of institutional control. The facial recognition applications discussed earlier, including tools that predict biological age or identify genetic syndromes from photographs, sit at the extreme end of an application injustice problem: they are often deployed or made publicly available before questions of consent, privacy, misuse and equity have been addressed. The FaceAge algorithm that estimates biological age from facial photographs and correlates it with disease risk[125] is a good example: an innovative tool with real clinical potential that simultaneously encodes the effects of social determinants of health as if they were biological facts, and that could be misappropriated by insurers or employers in ways its developers did not intend. The governance frameworks that would prevent such misappropriation do not exist. The tools are already in the world. This is one instance among several regulation has barely begun to engage with; Chapter 10 takes up the wider set.

The governance gap is not merely a regulatory problem. It is an institutional one, and it connects directly to the central argument of this book. The same features of healthcare institutions that make AI transformation difficult, the absent accountability for system-level outcomes, the incentive structures that reward adoption over validation, the veto players that block systematic reform, are precisely the features that make AI governance weak. The institution that has no mechanism for managing healthcare as a system also has no mechanism for ensuring that AI deployed into that system is safe, equitable and effective. The governance gap and the transformation gap are, in this sense, two aspects of the same institutional failure: an institution that cannot govern its AI is unlikely to see the ghost in its own machine, and one with no incentive to look will not go searching for it.

There is one further dimension the regulatory framework has almost entirely failed to engage with, and which connects this chapter to what follows. Clinicians are already using commodity AI products, consumer LLMs designed for general use, for clinical tasks in the absence of validated alternatives[30]. One in five UK general practitioners reported using generative AI tools in clinical practice in a 2024 survey, often for tasks such as differential diagnosis and treatment suggestions, in the absence of any formal guidance or institutional policy. The regulatory framework governs software as medical devices. It has no mechanism for governing a GP who opens a consumer chatbot and asks it about a patient's symptoms.

And the public is already doing the same, at far greater scale. Consumer AI is eroding the information asymmetry that has underpinned medical authority for a century, and it is doing so regardless of what the institution thinks about it. This is the one development that threatens the distribution the institution has worked to preserve, and it is arriving not through the institution's own deployments, which reproduce the status quo, but from outside it, in the hands of patients. The question is not whether this will happen. It is whether it will happen safely or unsafely, with validated tools or with commodity products optimised for engagement rather than accuracy, with appropriate governance or in a regulatory vacuum. That question, and its deeper implications for the future of medicine, is something that I will explore in much more detail in Chapter 9.

8.6 The institution in the algorithm

Let me draw the arguments of this chapter together. The problems I have described have the same underlying structure. Biased training data reflect the institution's historical allocation of care to different populations. The racial signal in medical images reflects decades of differential treatment documented in the records those images accompany. The gender bias in LLM summaries reflects the systematic undervaluation of women's health encoded throughout the literature those models were trained on. The self-fulfilling prophecy mechanism extends the historical distribution into the future by using it as the basis for predictions that then shape the care people receive. The explainability paradox and automation bias make the reproduced distribution unchallengeable by clothing it in objectivity. The governance gap leaves the whole process unexamined because the institution has no incentive to examine it. In each case, the same thing is happening: the institution's distribution of power, income and authority is passing through the technology and coming out the other side intact.

This is the ghost in the machine. Once again there is no conscious agent, no intent and no committee deciding to preserve the status quo. Instead there is a distributional logic so thoroughly written into the data that any algorithm trained on it reproduces the logic automatically, and an institution with neither the incentive nor the mechanism to notice. If we are not careful, the technology sold as the engine of transformation becomes one more instrument for the institution to stay as it is, alongside the economic and structural mechanisms this book has traced elsewhere, but more insidious than those because it operates invisibly, in the data, wearing the authority of objectivity.

Governance matters here in a way that the conventional treatment of AI safety misses, and the inadequacy of traditional regulation flagged at the start of this chapter is not a side issue. Regulation as currently practised acts upstream, at the point of approval, certifying that a tool performs to specification before it is deployed. But everything this chapter has described, the reproduced distribution, the drift, the laundering of bias through apparent objectivity, happens downstream, at the point of use, in a particular population and a particular institution, and possibly at a particular point in time. Upstream approval cannot see any of it, and the certificate it issues is therefore not merely insufficient but perhaps actively misleading, because it manufactures confidence that the safety-relevant questions have been settled when they have barely been asked. The governance that would actually work is continuous and local: monitoring the deployed model against the population it is actually serving, watching for the drift and the disparity that only appear in use. The detail of what that requires is the subject of Chapter 10. The point here is that such governance is not only a safety mechanism but the means through which the ghost becomes visible, and visibility is the precondition for change. An institution forced to watch what its models actually do to the populations they serve is an institution confronted, continuously and quantifiably, with its own distributional logic. That confrontation is exactly what a century of diffuse, deniable, individually human bias never had to face. Governance of deployment is therefore not the thing that makes AI safe enough to leave the institution untouched. It is one of the few instruments capable of forcing the institution to change.

The response to biased healthcare AI that focuses primarily on technical de-biasing, on more diverse training data and fairer algorithms, is insufficient rather than wrong. The bias will keep returning through every entry point this chapter has described as long as the institutions that generate the data, design the devices, train the clinicians and govern the deployments remain the same. The response that addresses the institution is harder and slower. It is also the only one that addresses the cause rather than the symptom, and the only one consistent with this book's central claim: that healthcare's institutions are very good at reproducing themselves, and will use even the technology built to disrupt them to do it, unless we deliberately choose otherwise.

The next two chapters examine the implications: first for the public, who are already using AI to erode the information asymmetry that has protected institutional authority for a century, and then for the regulators, who are trying to govern a technology that has arrived faster than the frameworks designed to contain it.

9 Trusting the machine over the medic

The previous chapters showed the institution preserving itself on its own territory: absorbing new technology into old workflows, defending the economics that sustain it, and carrying its own distributional coalitions forward through the biases of the very AI sold to disrupt it. This chapter moves outside its walls, to the growing space in which patients and the public are using AI for their health with no clinician, regulator or institution anywhere in the loop. The scale is already substantial: a survey by OpenAI in 2026 found that three in five adults in the United States had used AI tools for their health or healthcare in the preceding three months[126], and polling by King's College London in May 2026 found that one in seven UK adults had used an AI chatbot for health advice *instead of* contacting a GP or any other NHS service, rising to one in ten for mental health support in place of a trained professional[127]. This is not a niche behaviour of the digitally sophisticated but is becoming a normal first response to a health concern, and it is happening entirely outside any clinical or regulatory framework.

The claim of this chapter is that the medical profession never held a monopoly on information: textbooks and journals have sat in libraries for a century, available to anyone willing to read them. What the profession has always controlled is the *interpretive* function, the trained capacity to take general knowledge and produce a judgement about what it means for this patient, with this history, in this context. That is what a consultation is, what a diagnosis is, what clinical reasoning is. Every previous challenge to medical authority, up to and including the internet, attacked only the supply of information, and left the interpretive monopoly intact. Consumer AI is the first technology to compete with the interpretive function itself, and this difference explains why the institution's standard defensive move, framing the challenge as a patient safety problem to be managed with warnings and position statements, is failing for the first time. The move worked against the internet because nobody claimed a search engine could reason about your symptoms. It cannot work against a technology that visibly can, at least in part, and deploying it anyway does not preserve the status quo. It spends credibility while the space fills with whatever the market builds.

There are five steps to my argument. First, I place AI in the long sequence of technologies that have redistributed knowledge, and show why it is a qualitatively different step from the ones before it. Second, I examine the institution's response and identify the three conditions on which the old safety-framing play-book depended, each of which is now visibly false. Third, I set out and acknowledge the risks of consumer health AI because they are real and potentially serious. The argument of this book does not require pretending otherwise; what it requires is noticing that the institution has largely forfeited the standing to be the messenger. Fourth, I ask what actually fills an ungoverned space: who benefits, who is harmed, and who profits. Finally, and unlike any chapter so far, I consider whether there are early signs of the institution moving, not because it was persuaded, but because for the first time in this story its self-interest points toward engagement rather than away from it. That last observation matters beyond this chapter. If the resistance this book describes is an equilibrium rather than a character flaw, then it should yield precisely when the payoffs change, and consumer AI appears to be the first force strong enough to change them.

9.1 The last step

Every so often a technology restructures the relationship between knowledge and power so fundamentally that the world after it is not comparable to the world before. Language allowed structured knowledge to travel beyond the individual mind, but speech is ephemeral and local: you had to be there, and you had to trust the speaker. Writing let knowledge persist and travel, but manuscripts required scribes and scribes required patrons, so what survived was what the literate found worth preserving. The printing press broke the Church's control over the reproduction of ideas within decades of Gutenberg; the Reformation was not caused by the press, but it could not have happened without it. The internet, at first glance, looks like the completion of this sequence: every fact in every library, available to anyone with a connection, and the information asymmetry on which doctors, lawyers and experts of every kind had built their authority suddenly looked vulnerable. A patient who arrived at a consultation having spent the previous evening in the clinical literature was a different kind of patient from one who had to take the doctor's word for everything, and the profession found this uncomfortable enough to say so.

But something was missing, and its absence is the reason the internet never became the existential threat it briefly appeared to be. Access to information is not the ability to do anything with it. A patient could read everything ever written about their symptoms and still not know what those symptoms meant *for them*. Applying general knowledge to a particular person still required the trained interpretive capacity that had always been the real substance of professional expertise, and that capacity had never been democratised. Speech, writing, print and the internet each widened access, to stories, to scripture, to facts, to information. None of them touched interpretation.

That is what generative AI can add like nothing before it. It is the difference between reading an encyclopaedia entry about chest pain and having a conversation with something that asks follow-up questions, weighs your age and history, and offers a view on whether you should be worried. The first leaves the interpretive gap intact whereas the second begins to close it. Whether it closes it well is the subject of a later section, and the answer is: unevenly, overconfidently, and with failure modes that matter. But the nature of the challenge does not depend on the current quality of the tools. Google threatened a monopoly the profession never really held. AI competes with the one it does, and that is an existential challenge rather than an incremental one.

9.2 A playbook past its usefulness

The medical profession has not infrequently met challenges to its authority by treating them as problems to be managed, and the language in which it manages them has always been the language most likely to command public sympathy: safety. When patients began arriving having researched their conditions online, the response was concern that the internet was full of misinformation, that patients were not qualified to evaluate what they found, and that the remedy was to steer them toward approved sources. There was truth in all of it. There was also, less often acknowledged, an incumbent defending a position, in exactly the manner Chapter 4 would predict. The response to consumer AI has followed the same pattern: professional bodies warning that AI cannot replace a doctor, guidelines urging patients not to rely on chatbots, regulators reaching for frameworks designed for software as a medical device and finding they do not quite fit.

None of these concerns is fabricated, and the next section will treat them seriously on their own terms. The point here is narrower and structural. A safety warning retains its force only while three conditions hold of the party issuing it: its own practice must be visibly more reliable than the thing it warns against; its own members must not be using the thing it warns against; and the alternative it offers must actually be available when the warning is heeded. Against the internet, all three held by default, because nobody was claiming that a search engine could diagnose you, so the warning never had to survive scrutiny. Against AI, each condition is independently and publicly false.

Take reliability first. The baseline of current clinical practice, as Chapter 1 established, is not a high bar: healthcare systems in most high-income countries fail to deliver evidence-based care reliably for a substantial proportion of patients, and the diagnostic accuracy of generalist physicians under real-world conditions, with time pressure, incomplete information and cognitive load, is not obviously superior to what the better consumer tools now offer for many common presentations. Take the profession's own behaviour next. More than one in four UK general practitioners now report using AI in their work, much of it general-purpose and ungoverned, in the continuing absence of any national policy that keeps pace with the practice[128]. The profession is asking the public to exercise restraint with tools that a substantial fraction of its own members use daily without validation or oversight. And take availability last. An analysis of over half a million health conversations with a commercial

AI assistant found that personal health queries rise sharply in the evening and at night, precisely when traditional services are least accessible[129], and a quarter of the Britons who turned to a chatbot instead of the NHS cite waiting times as the reason, with two in five citing uncertainty about whether their concern was serious enough to bother a GP with at all[127]. For the most part people are not turning to AI instead of medicine. They are turning to it in the hours, and in the queues, where medicine is closed.

It is hard to see how any warning issued under these conditions is going to land. Indeed it indicts itself on delivery, because it asks the public to trust the institution's judgement about AI's untrustworthiness using the very interpretive authority that AI now competes with, while the institution's own accuracy, its own AI use and its own inaccessibility are all in plain view. I should be precise about the status of this claim. That the warning's preconditions are false is documented; that the public will read the warning as self-interest and discount the institution accordingly is, strictly, a prediction from mechanism rather than a measured fact, and I flag it as such in the spirit of the model-based reasoning this book relies on elsewhere. But the early readings point the predicted way. The same King's College London polling found that public trust in doctors over AI, while still substantial, is conditional and erodes sharply the moment the doctor is framed realistically, as tired and at the end of a long shift, and that one in five users of AI health advice has already decided against seeking professional care because of something a chatbot said[127]. The public has not stopped trusting doctors. It has started (and not for the first time in history) treating that trust as one option among several, which is exactly what the erosion of a monopoly looks like from the inside.

9.3 The risks, stated plainly

What follows is the case against consumer health AI as it currently exists, made without softening and without institutional spin, because the argument of this chapter is not that the tools are safe. It is that the tools are unsafe in specific, documented ways, and that warnings from a compromised messenger are not a policy for any of them.

Begin with accuracy. A systematic review of studies validating generative AI models for diagnosis, covering publications between June 2018 and June 2024, found a pooled diagnostic accuracy of just 52%[130]. The figure needs context: performance has improved over the review period and continues to, and against non-expert physicians the same review found no significant difference overall. It is against expert clinicians that AI falls consistently short. But 52% describes the landscape in which most public AI health interactions of recent years have actually taken place, and a tool performing at the level of an inexperienced doctor on a bad day is not a reassuring baseline for unsupervised use at population scale.

The accuracy problem would be manageable if users could tell good output from bad. They cannot, and the reason is structural rather than a matter of insufficient public education. AI is confident. It does not hedge the way a good clinician hedges; it does not say that this could be several things and we should wait and see. It produces fluent, detailed, well-structured answers with the same authority whether it is on firm ground or not, and that register turns out to be persuasive independent of whether it is warranted. Hackenburg and colleagues[131], studying what makes AI persuasive, found that the key variable was not empathy or personalisation but information density: the sheer volume of fact-checkable claims packed into a response, each additional claim buying a measurable increment of belief change. Worse, the most persuasive settings in the study were also the least accurate; pushed to produce more, the models became more convincing and more error-prone at once. An AI that produces ten specific claims feels more trustworthy than a clinician who offers three careful ones, even when the clinician's three are more reliable than seven of the AI's ten. The GP's caution, which reflects genuine clinical wisdom about uncertain presentations, reads as evasiveness next to the machine's apparent thoroughness. A tool that always sounds certain is not a tool that has achieved certainty. It is a tool that has learned that certainty sounds good.

Shekar and colleagues[41] demonstrated the human cost of this. Participants asked to rate medical advice for trustworthiness could not reliably distinguish doctor-written from AI-written responses; low-quality and even potentially dangerous AI advice was still rated trustworthy by the majority, and was found more complete and easier to understand than the doctors' answers, exactly as the density mechanism predicts. Even the doctors in the study trusted the two sources equally until told which was which. The safeguard that is supposed to operate in consumer use, the user's own judgement about reliability, does not work, for the public or for clinicians, because the signal distinguishing sound advice from plausible-sounding advice is simply not present in the output in a detectable form.

Sycophancy completes the picture. Chapter 8 described the tendency, baked in through training, for these models to produce outputs users find satisfying rather than outputs that are accurate[121]. In a clinical deployment a trained professional sits between the model and the patient, with the training, the accountability and at least in principle the capacity to push back. The consumer context strips that intermediary away, and with it the mechanism by which errors are caught at all. A patient who has convinced themselves of a diagnosis and asks an AI to confirm it will likely be confirmed; a patient reluctant to take a prescribed medication and asking whether their worry is reasonable will likely be told that it is. At the extreme this failure mode has been fatal. From 2024 onwards a series of cases reached the courts in which chatbot use was implicated in the suicides of children and young people. The legal questions remain unresolved and the companies dispute liability, but the pattern the complaints describe is precisely the one traced here: a system optimised to agree, to validate and to sustain the conversation, doing exactly that at the moment a person most needed to be challenged, interrupted, and handed to a human. The same mechanism operates in a quieter register in the attachments users form to AI companions, which arrive with no clinical governance, no safeguarding framework and no obligation to act in the user's interest[132]. What looks like comfort for a lonely adult and what reinforces a vulnerable person's worst beliefs are the same system doing the same thing.

Real though these failure modes are, they are also the strongest case available for the position the institution claims to hold. That the institution has converted this material into position statements rather than into tools, standards or governance is not evidence that the concerns are pretextual. It is evidence of what this book has argued throughout: that the institutional reflex is to use safety as a reason to abstain rather than as a reason to act, even when abstention demonstrably makes the safety problem worse.

9.4 What fills an ungoverned space

So what does happen in a space the institution refuses to occupy? Three things, and they are best understood as one phenomenon viewed from three angles: an opportunity captured by the market, an inequity reproduced by it, and an exploitation enabled by it.

There is a real opportunity here, and it could be made to benefit the people medicine currently serves worst, which is why abstention is not a neutral act. For the tens of millions who cannot get a timely GP appointment, cannot take time off work, are un- or under-insured, or simply cannot navigate a system not designed with them in mind, a tool that engages intelligently with their symptoms on their phone, at no cost and at two in the morning, is not a poor substitute for real medicine; for some it may be the best option they actually have. People living with chronic conditions spend the vast majority of their lives outside any clinical setting, making the decisions that determine their outcomes far more than a handful of regular consultations do, and a tool available in those hours is a qualitatively different kind of support from anything the system has offered them. In mental health, where illness in England is estimated to cost around £300 billion a year against chronically inadequate provision, the gap between need and access is so vast that ten per cent of the public has already substituted a professional with a chatbot[127], in the very domain where, as the previous section set out, the technology has done its worst harm. And a substantial proportion of patients leave consultations without understanding what they were told; a tool that helps them make sense of it afterwards addresses a real and persistent failure of a system built around the assumptions of the people who run it. The information asymmetry this chapter opened with has always fallen most heavily on those with less education, less confidence in navigating institutions, and no doctor in the family to ring for an informal opinion. AI is the first technology that could begin to level that, which is exactly why it matters who builds it and to what end.

Because availability is not equity, and the market left to itself reproduces the gradient it found. The most capable models sit behind subscription fees and require connectivity, devices and digital confidence; the free tiers most accessible to lower-income users are the least capable versions. The models perform best on the populations best represented in their training data, and the populations least represented, lower-income groups, ethnic minorities, people whose conditions have been systematically under-researched, are precisely those with least access to the care the AI might otherwise substitute for. Tang and colleagues found that models performed measurably worse on health questions from lower-literacy users, partly because those users framed questions differently and partly because the models were poorly calibrated to the concerns most common in underserved populations: the tool was available to everyone and useful in proportion to advantage[133]. Language compounds this, since a patient asking in Bengali, Yoruba or Welsh is using a tool not built with them in mind, whose errors are hardest to detect exactly where fewer authoritative sources exist for comparison. The likely default, absent deliberate intervention, is a new layer of inequality superimposed on the existing ones: the already-advantaged gaining a powerful instrument for navigating healthcare, the least-advantaged gaining a degraded version that is less accurate for their conditions and less likely to be corrected when it fails them.

The difficulty however is that the tools that fill the space are not neutral instruments even for the users they could serve well, because they currently arrive under the business model of the internet. If you are not paying for the product, then the product is usually you. Health information is among the most sensitive data a person can generate, bearing on insurance, employment and a person's sense of their own future, and it has commercial value for training, for advertising and for sale. The properties that make a health chatbot feel like a supportive presence, the attentiveness, the follow-up questions, the willingness to sit with complexity, are the same properties that make it effective at eliciting disclosures the user never intended to make, in contexts of anxiety and fear where rational consumer judgement is weakest. The regulatory position is threadbare: GDPR provides some protection in the UK and EU but enforcement has not kept pace, while in the United States most consumer health AI falls entirely outside HIPAA, so that a conversation with a doctor is protected and the same conversation with a chatbot may not be. A market optimised for engagement will build for the users who are easiest to serve and most profitable to retain. Building for the users who need the tools most requires a different kind of intention, and intention is precisely what an abstaining institution declines to supply.

9.5 The chink in the armour

Every chapter so far has ended with the institution holding its position. This one is different because I wonder whether the institution's position is beginning to move. In January 2026, NHS England published a national registry of AI note-taking suppliers, requiring compliance with standards on clinical safety, technology and data protection, following trials across 17,000 patient encounters that it judged successful enough to back nationally[134]. Then in July 2026 it went considerably further and announced that there would be an AI triage tool embedded in the NHS App itself, rolled out on an explicitly accelerated timetable, reaching 200,000 patients within twelve months and all app users by April 2028, as the flagship of a £10 billion, three-year technology programme[135]. What is remarkable is not the technology but that the institution has announced, explicitly, that a software decision tool will become a core part of the delivery of a national healthcare service. Even a basic triage tool must adapt its questions to the patient's responses, form a view of the condition, and direct the patient to the right service or equip a clinician to prioritise them. That is not administrative software but instead it begins to touch on the interpretive function; the first assessment of a symptom, performed by a machine, built and badged by the institution itself. The stated rationale, ending the 8am telephone rush and getting patients to the right care first time, is the vacuum argument of this chapter in official prose: patients had already moved their first point of contact elsewhere, and the only way to govern that layer was to own it.

For as long as patient-facing AI meant commercial chatbots outside the system, every institutional actor could treat caution as costless: warnings preserved authority, engagement risked it. Once one in seven patients was consulting the chatbot *instead of* the service[127], abstention stopped preserving the status quo and started ceding the entry point of the entire care pathway to products with no clinical governance behind them. The self-interest that predicted resistance everywhere else in this book flipped sign, and the institution moved in the direction its interests pointed, exactly as an equilibrium account says it should. That is the most hopeful structural fact this book has yet had to report: the resistance is not a character flaw immune to circumstance. It is a strategy, and strategies change when payoffs do.

I need to make two qualifications. First, the institution is not moving as one coherent entity. NHS England, with Treasury money and command authority, is shipping product; the Royal Colleges remain largely in consultation-response mode, submitting safety frameworks to the MHRA's 2026 regulatory process[136] and warning about risks even as the tool arrives in an app their own patients use. The parts of the institution that can be directed are outrunning the parts that govern themselves by professional consensus, which is a small preview of the coordination problems the second half of this book takes up in earnest.

Second, the gear that stuck for so long is now identifiable, and it was never conviction. Among clinicians not using AI, 89% cite professional liability and medico-legal risk as the dominant barrier[137], and the public, asked who should carry the blame when AI misses a finding, points to the treating clinician by a factor of nearly six over the company that built the tool[127]. Under those payoffs, individual caution was rational and individual engagement was reckless, whatever any individual doctor believed about the technology. What breaks that equilibrium is not persuasion but an institutional actor with the standing to absorb the liability question centrally, through standards, procurement and a defensible clinical safety case, so that engagement stops being a personal gamble. That is what a registry is. That is what an in-app tool with NHS England's badge on it is. The chink in the armour, in other words, is not that the institution changed its mind. Instead the institution discovered a way to change the payoffs, and the rest of this book is, in one sense, an inquiry into whether that discovery can be generalised.

9.6 What this means for medicine

I have argued that medicine's authority rests on an interpretive monopoly rather than just an informational one, and consumer AI is the first technology in history that can compete with it directly. The institution's reflexive defence, the safety framing that served it against every previous challenge, depends on conditions that are now refutable: its own baseline is unimpressive, its own members use the tools, and its own services are absent at the hours and in the queues where the need arises. The risks of the current consumer tools are real, potentially serious and documented, but a compromised messenger issuing warnings governs none of them; it simply leaves the space to be filled by a market that captures the opportunity for the easiest users, reproduces the existing gradient of disadvantage, and monetises the anxiety of the rest. And then, uniquely in this book so far, the institution moved, not because it was persuaded but because the cost of abstention finally exceeded the cost of engagement, and it moved in the only way that was ever going to work: by changing the payoffs its members face rather than the beliefs they hold.

Validated patient-facing tools built to clinical standards and designed for the populations who need them most rather than those easiest to serve; enforceable standards for consumer health AI, applied with the rigour reserved for clinical AI, including over the data these tools harvest; clinicians trained to meet the patient who arrives having already consulted the machine, because that patient, handled well, is a more effective partner in their own care and, handled badly, is a patient lost; and honest public communication, in a register that trusts people with complexity, about what these tools can and cannot yet do. None of this requires medicine to abandon its concerns but it does require those concerns to be expressed as engineering and governance rather than as gatekeeping, which is to say, it requires exactly the transition from warning to building that NHS England's triage tool represents in embryo.

Chapter 8 ended by observing that the governance gap in clinical AI is the transformation gap viewed from another angle. This chapter has shown the same gap from outside the walls, where it is widest and where the institution has the least control, and it has shown the first crack in the pattern of resistance, produced not by argument but by a shift in incentives. Whether that crack can be widened deliberately, by regulation that changes payoffs at scale rather than waiting for crisis to change them, is the question the next chapter takes up.

10 The urge to regulate

Every technology that has entered clinical practice has eventually encountered a regulator. X-rays, pharmaceuticals, surgical devices, medical software: each in turn has been brought within a framework of oversight designed to ensure that what reaches patients is safe, effective, and fit for purpose. Regulation is how society manages the gap between what a technology can do and what it should do, and in healthcare, where the consequences of getting that wrong can be irreversible, the case for oversight is easy to make.

But regulation in healthcare is also a partially institutional rather than entirely neutral, technical process. It reflects the same distributions of power, authority and interest that this book has been examining throughout. The bodies that define what counts as evidence of safety, that set the thresholds for approval, that determine which risks are acceptable and which are not, are embedded in the same professional and institutional ecosystem that has shaped every other aspect of how medicine is organised and delivered. Regulation is not entirely external to the medical institution and in fact can be one of its instruments. And like every other instrument of that institution, it can serve to manage real risk, and it can also serve to manage the threat that a disruptive technology poses to the existing distribution of authority. Often it does both at once. The argument of this chapter does not depend on anyone intending the second. It depends only on the observation that regulation, like the other institutional mechanisms this book has examined, tends to operate in ways that protect the existing order, whether or not that is what its designers set out to do.

Regulatory economists and legal scholars have long noted that precautionary frameworks are not distributionally neutral[138]: they systematically favour the status quo by making the risks of new technologies more visible than the risks of the existing systems they would replace. In healthcare, professional regulatory frameworks have historically functioned to protect the market position of organised medicine as much as to protect patients, which compounds the status-quo bias that precaution already carries.*

When a new technology creates uncertainty about how markets and professions will be reorganised, established actors have a shared interest in shaping the regulatory response in ways that slow the reorganisation, raise entry barriers for challengers, and preserve the existing distribution of revenue and authority. As ever, they do not need to conspire to achieve this. Each is acting in their own interest, and the cumulative effect is a regulatory framework that reflects the balance of organised power at the moment it was written. Precaution, in this analysis, is not merely a principled response to uncertainty. It is also a distributional instrument: demanding higher evidentiary standards, longer approval timelines and more onerous compliance requirements for technologies that threaten incumbents than for those that do

*As examples, in the United States[74], professional authority was deliberately converted into licensing restrictions and supply controls that served incumbency as much as patient welfare. And in Britain[75] the 1858 Medical Act was a process of state-supported market closure and exclusion of competitors rather than purely a public protection measure. The two systems differ in structure: the American profession resisted public financing while the British profession negotiated the terms of its incorporation into the NHS. The underlying dynamic of regulatory capture in the service of professional interest is nonetheless common to both.

not. The two functions are difficult to separate, which is precisely what makes precaution so effective as a protective strategy.

The pattern this book has described so far, of a powerful technology being absorbed into existing institutional arrangements rather than allowed to disrupt them, has a regulatory dimension that has so far received insufficient attention. When professional bodies issue guidance urging caution about AI adoption, when regulators extend existing device frameworks to cover algorithms in ways that create high compliance burdens for new entrants, when the safety standards applied to AI are more demanding than those applied to the existing manual clinical practices AI would replace, the effect is the one Acemoglu's framework, set out in Chapter 5, would predict: the instruments available to incumbents operate to slow the diffusion of a technology that threatens their position, in the language that has always been most effective in healthcare, the language of patient safety. Whether this is pursued deliberately or simply emerges from many actors each following their own incentives, the outcome is the same, and it is the outcome, not the intent, that this chapter is concerned with.

None of this denies that there are real patient safety concerns about AI, or that governance and regulation have a place. A number of the concerns could be serious or even catastrophic, as the preceding chapters have established in painful detail. What I am claiming is that the regulatory response to AI may be shaped as much by institutional interest as by clinical evidence, and that the result is a framework that is simultaneously too restrictive in ways that slow beneficial adoption and too permissive in ways that allow harmful deployment, because the restrictions and permissions have been drawn around the wrong things. Understanding why requires examining what the regulatory frameworks actually do, what they cannot do given the nature of AI as a technology, and what the question of regulation obscures as much as it reveals.

AI presents itself to regulators as a technology like any other, and regulators have largely responded accordingly: extending existing frameworks, creating new categories within old structures, and issuing guidance that maps the familiar language of clinical evidence and device approval onto a set of tools that were not designed with any of that in mind. The effort is sincere and in places it has produced useful results. But it rests on an assumption that deserves further scrutiny, because if that assumption is wrong then the entire regulatory project, however well executed, is solving the wrong problem.

The assumption is that AI in healthcare can be regulated in the way that previous healthcare technologies have been regulated: assessed at a point in time, approved against a defined specification, and then deployed with confidence that the approved version is what patients will encounter. For a pharmaceutical, that model makes sense. The molecule that leaves the factory is the molecule that enters the patient. For a surgical device, it makes sense. The instrument that passes certification is the instrument that enters the operating theatre. For AI, it does not make sense, and the reasons why it does not make sense go to the heart of what AI actually is and how it actually behaves in the real world.

But there is an even more fundamental question beneath the practical difficulties. When we examine what actually goes wrong when AI causes harm in healthcare, we find that the failures are rarely failures of the algorithm in isolation. They are failures of implementation, of oversight, of clinical judgement, of institutional governance. The doctor who follows an

AI recommendation without checking it. The clinician who does not account for the known biases in the system they are using. The hospital that deploys a validated tool in a population it was never validated on. The professional who uses an AI output as a substitute for reasoning rather than an input to it. These are not regulatory failures in the conventional sense but human and institutional failures of exactly the kind that the rest of this book has been describing. And if that is true, the question that follows is uncomfortable but necessary: why on earth are we placing so much emphasis and trust on regulating the machine when it's the interaction with the human that causes many of the problems?

10.1 Why regulating AI is so hard

The starting point for understanding the regulatory problem with AI is understanding why the frameworks that have worked for every previous healthcare technology do not work here. It is not that regulators have been careless or that the existing frameworks are poorly designed. It is that those frameworks were built around a set of assumptions about what a technology is, and AI violates all of them.

The dominant model for regulating software in clinical settings is the software as a medical device framework, used in varying forms by the FDA in the United States, the MHRA (Medicines and Healthcare products Regulatory Agency) in the United Kingdom, and the European Medicines Agency under the EU AI Act. As I have already introduced, the logic is that of device regulation: a manufacturer develops a product, submits evidence of its safety and performance, receives approval against a defined specification, and then deploys that approved product into clinical use. The regulatory act is a point-in-time assessment. What is approved is a fixed artefact. The assumption is that the thing patients encounter is the thing that was evaluated.

For most medical devices this assumption holds well enough to be useful. A pulse oximeter that passes certification today will behave the same way tomorrow and a surgical stapler that meets its specification in testing will meet it in the operating theatre as long as the manufacturing process is tightly controlled, something that also forms part of the regulatory assessment. The gap between the evaluated product and the deployed product is small enough to be managed by post-market surveillance of the conventional kind: adverse event reporting, periodic review, recall when a systematic fault is identified. The regulatory framework is not perfect, but it is coherent, because the technology it governs is stable.

But AI is not stable and this is not a peripheral feature of AI systems that might be engineered away in future versions but a consequence of what AI systems are. A machine learning model is not a fixed set of rules applied consistently to new inputs. Instead it is a statistical representation of patterns learned from training data, and its behaviour is a function of the relationship between that training data and the inputs it subsequently encounters. When that relationship changes, behaviour changes, and it changes in ways that may not be visible to the user, may not trigger any conventional safety signal, and may not be detectable without the kind of continuous prospective monitoring that few deployed AI systems currently receive.

Model drift is the most straightforward version of this problem. The population of patients presenting to a hospital changes over time: demographic shifts, seasonal patterns, the emergence of new diseases, changes in referral thresholds, the introduction of new treatments upstream in the care pathway. Each of these changes the distribution of inputs the AI system encounters relative to the distribution it was originally trained on. A sepsis prediction model trained on pre-pandemic data may perform differently on a post-pandemic patient population, not because the algorithm has changed but because the world has. A deterioration alert trained on patients managed under one set of clinical protocols may behave differently when those protocols are updated. The software has not changed and therefore the approval has not lapsed. But the performance has shifted in ways that a point-in-time evaluation cannot capture.

Concept drift is a related but distinct problem. It occurs not when the input distribution changes but when the relationship between inputs and outcomes changes. A model predicting thirty-day readmission was trained on a world in which certain clinical features predicted readmission with a certain probability. If new treatments, new discharge protocols or new community services alter those probabilities, the model's predictions are no longer well calibrated even though the inputs look the same. Again, no software update has occurred and therefore no regulatory review has been triggered. The model continues to generate outputs with the same apparent confidence, and the clinician using it has no reliable signal that the ground beneath it has shifted.

Generative AI provides an additional regulatory problem. A predictive model, however much it drifts, at least produces a defined kind of output: a risk score, a classification, a probability that can be checked against a known outcome. That is what makes validation possible at all, there is a ground truth to measure against, and a held-out dataset can estimate how often the model is right. A generative model has no such fixed output but is probabilistic and therefore non-deterministic. It produces open-ended language, and the space of things it might say in response to a given clinical question is effectively unbounded. There is no finite test set that establishes a generative system is safe, because the same prompt can yield different answers, small changes in prompting can change the output substantially, and the failure modes are properties of the generation itself rather than deviations from a benchmark. The sycophancy and confabulation that Chapter 8 described are not bugs that show up as a lower accuracy score; they are characteristics of how the system produces text, invisible to any evaluation that asks only whether the model got a fixed answer right. Regulating a generative system as though it were a diagnostic classifier, by certifying its performance on some benchmark, certifies the one thing about it that is least representative of how it behaves in use.

So far, more than hard enough. But for orchestrated or agentic AI it becomes qualitatively more difficult still to imagine a way to robustly assure ourselves of system performance which brings us to a new and entirely unsolved problem. An agentic AI system, as described in Chapter 3, is a system that is able, with a degree of autonomy, to perceive its environment, reason about what it observes, and take actions in pursuit of defined goals. The regulatory evaluation of such a system cannot be reduced to a performance assessment of the constituent parts or the performance on a defined task, because the system's behaviour is not fixed to a defined task. An agentic system's behaviour is a function of the goals it has been given, the environment it encounters, and the reasoning it applies to the gap between them. That reasoning may produce actions that were never anticipated by the system's designers, never encountered in testing, and never covered by the approval specification.

The evaluation problem for agentic systems is not merely

more complex than for static models, it is categorically different. Testing a diagnostic AI on a held-out dataset gives you a performance estimate for that task on that population. Testing an agentic system requires something closer to what safety engineers call adversarial evaluation: deliberately constructing environments designed to expose failure modes that ordinary use would not reveal. The space of possible environments an agentic system might encounter is, in principle, unbounded. No evaluation regime can cover it comprehensively, and the frontier AI laboratories that build these systems have been candid about this: their own internal evaluations are acknowledged to be incomplete, and the behaviours that emerge in deployment sometimes differ from those observed in testing in ways that are difficult to predict in advance[51].

An additional challenge is the speed of contemporary AI development. Regulatory processes operate on timescales measured in months to years. By contrast, the AI development cycle operates on timescales measured in weeks to months. By the time a regulatory framework designed for current AI capabilities has been consulted upon, drafted, passed into law and brought into force, the technology it was designed to govern may have been superseded several times over. The EU AI Act, the most comprehensive attempt yet to establish a statutory framework for AI governance, took several years from proposal to enactment. During that period the capabilities of frontier AI systems changed so substantially that provisions designed to address specific risks were already partly obsolete before the ink was dry. This is not a criticism of the legislators involved. It is a structural feature of the relationship between the pace of AI development and the pace of democratic governance that has no easy solution within existing institutional frameworks.

The honest conclusion from all of this is not that regulation should be abandoned, but that point-in-time approval, the cornerstone of how healthcare technology has been regulated for decades, is the wrong instrument for AI. It provides an upstream and artificial snapshot of performance that may not reflect deployment reality, cannot anticipate the ways in which performance will change over time, and creates a false assurance that is in some respects more dangerous than no assurance at all. A clinician who knows that a tool is unvalidated will apply appropriate scepticism. A clinician who knows that a tool has regulatory approval may apply less, precisely because the approval is supposed to have done that work. When the approval is based on an evaluation that no longer reflects the tool's actual behaviour, the regulatory framework has not protected the patient. It has provided institutional cover for a risk that nobody is actively managing.

10.2 When is a chatbot a medical device?

The previous section took for granted that we at least know which systems the regulatory framework applies to. For generative AI even that is unsettled, because the entire architecture of device regulation rests on a concept the technology has quietly dissolved: intended purpose. Under the EU Medical Device Regulation, software qualifies as a medical device only when its manufacturer intends it for a medical purpose such as diagnosis, prevention, monitoring or treatment; the mere use of software in a medical context, or the processing of medical information, does not bring it into scope[139]. The FDA reaches an equivalent position through its treatment of clinical decision support and the exemptions of the 21st Century Cures Act, and Australian guidance follows the same logic. The concept worked because the technologies it was written for did one thing, so a product's declared purpose and its actual function could be expected to coincide. A large language model does whatever it is asked, and what it is asked is decided one prompt at a time.

The consequence is that whether a deployed LLM is functioning as a medical device can depend not on the software but on the prompt[139]. Ask an administrative chatbot to list the medications in a discharge letter and it is doing secretarial work outside the regulation's scope. Ask the same chatbot, in the same deployment, what dose of antibiotic to give a particular patient with a particular renal function, and it is delivering patient-specific clinical decision support, the defining activity of medical device software. The regulatory identity of the product is being determined at the level of the individual query, a category for which the device paradigm has no vocabulary. Many queries cannot be classified even in principle: a question about the most common cause of a raised troponin in a fifty-year-old man is either revision for an examination or the first step in managing the patient in bed six, and nothing in the text distinguishes the two.

Colleagues and I have mapped this gray area in detail[139]. Applications with no medical intended purpose, and therefore no obligations under the MDR, can come to function as medical devices by three routes. The first is repurposing: a tool deployed to extract billing codes from clinical notes is incrementally enhanced until it is ranking differential diagnoses, at which point the deploying hospital has, without ever taking a decision recognisable as one, assumed the regulatory role of a manufacturer. The second is malfunction: a summarizer whose only purpose is to condense existing notes hallucinates a diagnosis or a treatment step present in no source document. Under current European guidance the malfunction does not make it a medical device, because qualification follows intended purpose rather than actual behaviour, which produces the remarkable result that the more dangerously the tool misbehaves, the more securely it sits outside the framework built to protect patients from dangerous tools. The third is misuse: a clinician asks the administrative chatbot for a differential diagnosis, converting it into de facto clinical decision support that nobody has validated for the task. In each case the regulatory perimeter and the risk perimeter fail to coincide. The framework governs what the manufacturer says the product is for; the harm arises from what the product does.

Regulators have noticed, and their responses map the confusion rather than resolving it. When NHS England indicated that LLM-based summarisation should be treated as high functionality and would likely qualify as Class I medical device software, it prompted an abrupt if temporary halt to ambient scribe deployment[140], despite the statement being operational risk guidance rather than a formal regulatory interpretation, and despite Class I status adding no independent pre-market scrutiny in any case. Australia's regulator has drawn the line at interpretation: transcribing or translating a clinical conversation is not a medical purpose, while generating diagnostic or therapeutic suggestions the clinician did not state is. The FDA arrives somewhere similar through the Cures Act exemptions. Three jurisdictions, one line, drawn in roughly the same place, and all three crossed not by a design change or a marketing claim, which regulators know how to observe, but by a hallucination or a prompt, which they cannot. A boundary the product can wander across in the course of ordinary use is not doing the work a regulatory boundary exists to do.

Mitigations exist and deploying organisations should require them[139]: validation of outputs against ground truth, enforceable terms of use, and technical safeguards that detect clinical decision support queries and refuse them, warn on ambiguous ones, and answer the rest. In the UK the clinical safety standards that attach to any digital deployment in the NHS provide a ready legal anchor for exactly this, since they apply irrespective of device status. But notice where the burden has moved. The compliance layer is now itself written in natural language, with all the adversarial fragility that natural language interfaces carry. The safeguard that stops a chatbot practising medicine is a prompt, and prompts can be defeated by prompts. Nothing in the history of device regulation prepares it for a product whose guardrails are conversational.

There is a longer history to this boundary trouble. Medicine has lived with a version of it for years at the border between healthcare and wellness. A large industry of trackers, apps and symptom checkers trades on its adjacency to medicine while disclaiming medical purpose, and the disclaimer works: functionally similar products sit on opposite sides of the regulatory line depending on what the marketing copy says, as Chapter 1 touched on. The arrangement was tolerable because the products were limited. However hard you pressed it, a step counter could not prescribe. Generative AI removes that limit. A chatbot marketed for productivity will practise medicine if asked, whatever its label says, so the label no longer constrains the function; it merely disowns it. The wellness boundary was always a labelling convention, and generative AI has turned it into a fiction that now sits at the centre of the regulatory map. What this means for the consumer market, where the fiction operates at population scale, is taken up later in this chapter.

10.3 The false security of approvals

This chapter has established that AI systems are not stable artefacts whose performance can be fixed at the moment of approval and relied upon thereafter. But the problem runs deeper than technical inadequacy. Point-in-time approval creates a specific kind of false reassurance, made more durable by the official stamp on it. Chapter 8 named this: a certificate that manufactures confidence the safety-relevant questions have been settled when they have barely been asked. And if you have been following the argument of this book, you will recognise the institutional fingerprints on that problem immediately.

Think about who actually benefits from a regulatory framework built around approving a fixed specification at a single point in time. It is not primarily patients. They benefit from tools that work reliably in the settings they are actually deployed in, across the populations they are actually used on, over the years they are actually in service. Point-in-time approval does not guarantee any of those things, as this section will show. What it does guarantee is a compliance process that takes time, requires resources, and rewards organisations with the legal and regulatory capacity to navigate it. In other words, it rewards incumbents. The regulatory framework, presented as a protection for patients, functions in practice as a protection for the existing configuration of the market. North would have recognised the pattern: the rules of the game have been written by the people who benefit most from keeping the game as it is[71].

There is a further layer that is easy to miss, and it concerns not the performance of the model itself but the behaviour of the people and institutions using it. How an AI tool is implemented shapes how its outputs are interpreted, weighted and acted upon in ways that no pre-deployment evaluation can fully anticipate. A tool validated in a setting where clinicians received careful training in its limitations will behave differently in a setting where it has been rolled out without that training, because someone in procurement decided that the approval was sufficient justification for going ahead. A model that performs well as one input among several in a structured decision-making process may become something quite different when time pressure means it gets treated as the main input instead. The regulatory framework evaluates the algorithm in isolation. It says nothing about the workflow the algorithm will be dropped into, the training that will or will not accompany its deployment, or the institutional culture that will determine whether its limitations are understood and respected. And as Chapter 6 established at length, those are precisely the factors that determine whether a technology delivers its potential or gets quietly absorbed into existing arrangements in ways that neutralise it.

The compliance burden completes the picture. Regulatory approval requires documentation, and documentation requires resources, which means the organisations best placed to navigate the process are the ones that were already dominant before AI arrived. Large incumbent vendors with established regulatory relationships and dedicated legal teams can manage lengthy submissions in ways that smaller developers, academic spinouts and organisations working on tools for underserved populations simply cannot. The effect on the market can be abrupt. In the EU, the number of new AI medical devices entering the radiology market rose steadily until 2020; in May 2021, sixteen new AI radiology devices entered the market, and in June and July 2021, immediately after the MDR and IVDR came into force, the number was zero[12]. Whatever the intention of the regulation, its immediate effect was a measurable halt in the introduction of new AI diagnostic tools into European practice: a framework designed for static devices, applied to a fast-moving field, functioning as a brake rather than a guardrail. The burden is also not neutral in who it stops. The tools most likely to be disruptive, precisely because they challenge existing workflows and redistribute decision rights, face the highest regulatory barriers alongside the highest institutional resistance. Olson's logic applies directly: the well-organised interests with the most to lose from disruption are also the interests best placed to shape the compliance environment in ways that slow it down[76].

What approval does to accountability once a tool is in use is also worth noting. When a clinician uses an approved AI tool and something goes wrong, the approval creates a convenient dynamic. The vendor points to the approval as evidence that the tool met the required standard. The institution points to the approval as justification for the deployment decision. The clinician points to both as grounds for having reasonably relied on the recommendation. The result is that nobody is clearly responsible, and the patient who was harmed has no obvious route to redress. This is not an unforeseen side effect but a predictable consequence of applying a device certification model to a situation where harm arises from a complex interaction between an algorithm, a workflow, an institution and a professional judgement, none of which the certification was designed to evaluate in combination. It suits a great many institutional actors rather well.

The conclusion is not that regulation is pointless but that the current model is doing something different to what it claims. It is unwittingly providing cover for deployment decisions that have not been adequately evaluated, diffusing accountability for harms that have not been adequately anticipated, and raising barriers that protect incumbent interests more than patient welfare. A framework actually designed around patient protection would look very different: built around continuous monitoring rather than one-off approval, around implementation governance rather than algorithm certification, around accountability structures that name the responsible parties clearly rather than spreading responsibility so thinly that it disappears. What that looks like in practice is the subject of a later section. First, though, the chapter needs to address the question that the current regulatory focus is most conspicuously avoiding: if the failures are human and institutional rather than algorithmic, why is the conversation almost entirely about the machine?

10.4 Why are we regulating the machine?

Return to the question posed near the start of this chapter. When an AI system causes harm in a clinical setting, what actually went wrong? Not in the abstract, but in the specific, proximate, traceable sense that an accident investigator would want to establish. In almost every documented case, the answer is not that the algorithm malfunctioned in some technically identifiable way. It is that a clinician relied on it without adequate understanding of its limitations. Or that an institution deployed it in a population it was never designed for. Or that nobody was monitoring whether its performance had drifted from what was originally validated. Or that the workflow it was embedded in created conditions in which its outputs were treated as decisions rather than inputs. The algorithm, in most of these cases, did exactly what it was designed to do. The failure happened around it, not within it. Chapter 8 showed why human oversight cannot be relied on to catch what the model gets wrong; the regulatory implication of that finding is the subject of this section.

The implication for where regulatory attention should be focused is direct. If the proximate causes of harm from AI in healthcare are predominantly human and institutional, then a regulatory framework focused primarily on the algorithm is, at best, incomplete and, at worst, actively misleading. It is directing attention and resources toward the one part of the system that in many cases is not where the problem lies, while leaving largely unexamined the parts of the system where the problem actually originates. Consider what we already regulate in clinical practice. Drugs are regulated, but so are the doctors who prescribe them. A pharmaceutical that passes regulatory approval cannot be prescribed by anyone who happens to want to prescribe it. The prescriber must be licensed, must demonstrate competence, must operate within a framework of professional accountability that includes the possibility of sanction if they prescribe negligently. The regulation of the drug and the regulation of the prescriber are understood as complementary: neither is sufficient on its own. A safe drug prescribed negligently causes harm. A competent prescriber given an unsafe drug causes harm. Both halves of the equation matter.

Now consider how AI is being regulated. The focus is almost entirely on the algorithm. Does it perform to the required standard on the required benchmarks? Has it been validated on a sufficiently large and representative dataset? Does it meet the technical specifications laid down by the relevant regulatory authority? These are not unreasonable questions. But the equivalent questions about the clinician using the tool are largely absent from the regulatory conversation. What does a doctor need to know about an AI system before they are permitted to rely on its outputs in clinical decision-making? What constitutes competent use of an AI diagnostic tool, and how is that competence assessed? When a clinician follows an AI recommendation that turns out to be wrong, what standard of scrutiny should they have applied before doing so, and how is that standard defined and enforced? At the moment, the honest answer to all of these questions is: nobody has really decided.

This is a significant gap, and it is not a surprising one. Extending professional regulation to cover the use of AI would require the medical profession to define, explicitly and publicly, what competent AI use looks like, with everything that implies for training curricula, licensing examinations and revalidation. It would make it possible, in principle, to hold a clinician accountable not just for a wrong clinical decision but for an inadequately scrutinised AI-assisted one. All of this would involve the profession in a process of self-examination about its relationship with AI that it has so far largely avoided. A regulatory focus that rests on the machine rather than the doctor asks none of this, and the path that asks less of an institution is, predictably, the one it tends to travel.

There is a parallel here with the history of clinical guidelines. For decades, the medical profession resisted attempts to make adherence to clinical guidelines a formal regulatory requirement, on the grounds that clinical autonomy was essential to good practice and that guidelines could not anticipate every clinical situation. The resistance was sometimes principled and sometimes self-interested, and the two were, as usual, hard to tell apart. The outcome was a system in which guidelines exist, clinicians are expected to be aware of them, but deviation from them is governed by professional norms rather than formal accountability mechanisms. The result, as Chapter 1 established, is that somewhere between forty and fifty percent of patients do not receive care that conforms to best practice guidelines, and that figure has barely moved in two decades. The profession's defence of autonomy has come at a measurable cost to patients, and the regulatory framework has largely accepted that trade-off.

The same dynamic is already visible in how AI use is being governed, or not governed, at the clinical level. The clinician who opens a consumer chatbot and uses it to help with a differential diagnosis is not currently subject to any specific regulatory requirement about how they do that, what they check, or how they document their reasoning. The clinician who uses an institutionally deployed AI tool to support a clinical decision is in a similarly uncharted accountability landscape. The tool may have been approved. The institution may have a policy. But the specific professional obligations of the individual clinician in using that tool, the standard of care they owe their patient in terms of how they engage with and scrutinise AI outputs, remains largely undefined. That undefined space is where most of the actual risk lives, and it is where the regulatory conversation has the least to say.

None of this is to suggest that regulating the algorithm is unnecessary. There are good reasons to require that clinical AI systems meet minimum standards of performance, transparency and bias disclosure before they are deployed. But algorithm regulation alone is deeply insufficient, and the insufficiency is not simply an oversight awaiting correction. The machine-focus persists because it is the path of least institutional resistance: it threatens no professional autonomy, requires no public definition of competent use, creates no new accountability mechanisms that might be used against clinicians, and keeps attention on the vendor, the device and the approval process, away from the consultation room where the decisions that actually affect patients are made.

The question of who should be responsible when AI causes harm in healthcare is ultimately a question about professional accountability, institutional governance and the distribution of responsibility in complex sociotechnical systems. Regulatory frameworks that treat it primarily as a question about algorithm performance are not wrong to care about algorithm performance. They are wrong to think that algorithm performance is where the answer lies. Getting this right matters not just for patient safety in the narrow sense but for the broader project this book has been arguing for throughout: the transformation of healthcare through AI, on terms that are honest about where the risks actually are and who is actually responsible for managing them.

10.5 What regulation should actually do

If the previous sections have made the problem sound intractable, it is not. The difficulty with current regulatory frameworks is not that regulation itself is impossible or pointless, but that the wrong things are being regulated, in the wrong way, at the wrong point in the process. Fixing that requires being honest about what regulation can realistically achieve with a technology like AI, and designing frameworks around that honest assessment rather than around the institutional convenience of extending what already exists.

The most important single shift is from approval to monitoring. The regulatory question for AI should not primarily be: does this system meet the required standard today? It should be: is this system still meeting the required standard, in this setting, on this population, under current clinical conditions? That is a fundamentally different question, and answering it requires infrastructure that does not currently exist at scale†: systematic post-deployment monitoring, mandatory reporting of performance metrics stratified by patient subgroup, and clear thresholds that trigger review or withdrawal when performance drifts below acceptable levels.

This is not a technically exotic ambition. The data needed to monitor deployed AI systems are already being generated in electronic health records and clinical workflow systems. What is missing is not the data but the requirement to use them, the organisational capacity to analyse them, and the regulatory obligation to act on what they show. Building that requirement in from the start, as a condition of deployment rather than an afterthought, would transform the regulatory landscape without requiring any fundamental change to how AI systems are built. It would also, not incidentally, create a much richer evidence base for understanding how AI actually performs in the real world rather than in the controlled conditions of a validation study.

There is a further reason this shift matters, and it returns to the argument Chapter 8 closed on. Continuous monitoring is not only a safety mechanism. It is the instrument that makes an institution's own distribution of care visible to it, continuously and quantifiably, in a way that a century of diffuse, individually human decisions never had to confront. A monitoring regime that reports performance stratified by subgroup does not just catch a model that has drifted. It holds up a mirror to how the institution serves the populations in front of it, and a mirror is hard to look away from once it is mounted on the wall. That is why monitoring is not merely a regulatory nicety but, potentially, a

†The UK does, in fact, have a legal framework that regulates the deployment (and therefore post-deployment) of digital healthcare systems. However in reality compliance is patchy and underfunded[141].

mechanism of change: it converts the institution's distributional logic from something deniable into something measured, and what is measured is far harder to leave unaddressed. The same feature that makes monitoring useful for safety makes it useful for transformation, which is precisely why an institution content with the status quo has little reason to volunteer for it, and why it must be required rather than left to discretion.

The second shift is from algorithm certification to implementation governance. As the previous section argued, most of the risk in clinical AI deployment lives not in the algorithm but in the conditions surrounding its use: the training clinicians receive, the workflows it is embedded in, the institutional culture that shapes how its outputs are treated. Regulation that addresses only the algorithm and says nothing about these conditions is leaving the majority of the risk unaddressed. Implementation governance means requiring, as a condition of deployment, that institutions demonstrate not just that they have deployed an approved tool but that they have deployed it appropriately: with adequate staff training, within a workflow that supports appropriate scrutiny of AI outputs, with clear lines of accountability when things go wrong, and with a monitoring plan that will detect problems before they cause serious harm.

Some of this already exists in skeletal form in the clinical governance frameworks that NHS trusts and equivalent bodies in other systems are required to maintain. The problem is that those frameworks were designed for a world in which the technologies being governed were relatively stable, and they have not been meaningfully updated to reflect what AI actually requires. Extending and strengthening them, with specific requirements around AI deployment, is a more tractable regulatory intervention than building entirely new frameworks from scratch, and it has the advantage of connecting AI governance to the existing accountability structures of the institutions deploying the tools.

The third shift is the most politically difficult, which is probably why it has received the least attention. If competent use of AI is a professional obligation, then the definition of what competent use looks like needs to become part of the framework of professional regulation. This means medical licensing bodies, professional colleges, and equivalent professional organisations in other countries defining explicitly what a clinician needs to know and be able to do before they can be said to be using AI tools responsibly. It means updating training curricula to include AI literacy not as an optional extra but as a core competency. It means revalidation processes that assess whether clinicians are keeping pace with the AI tools they are using in practice. And it means, ultimately, that a clinician who uses an AI tool negligently, who follows its output without appropriate scrutiny, who fails to account for its known limitations, can be held professionally accountable in the same way that a clinician who prescribes negligently can be held accountable. This will be resisted, and the resistance will be framed in the language of clinical autonomy and the impossibility of standardising professional judgement. That framing should be recognised for what it is. The argument that AI use is too complex and contextual to be governed by professional standards is structurally identical to the argument that clinical practice in general is too complex and contextual to be governed by guidelines, an argument whose consequences for patient outcomes Chapter 1 examined in some detail. Professional autonomy is a real value in clinical practice. It is not a reason to leave the use of potentially dangerous tools ungoverned.

On the question of what regulation should require from AI

developers and vendors, the priorities are transparency, portability and ongoing accountability rather than the current focus on pre-deployment performance benchmarks. Transparency means making available, in a form that deploying institutions can actually use, the information needed to assess whether a tool is appropriate for their specific context: the populations it was trained on, the settings it has been validated in, the subgroups where performance is weakest, and the conditions under which it should not be used. At present this information is often proprietary, buried in technical documentation that most deploying institutions lack the capacity to evaluate, or simply not collected. Requiring it as a condition of market access would cost vendors relatively little and benefit deploying institutions enormously.

Portability means ensuring that the data generated by AI deployments, the performance logs, the outcome data, the adverse event records, can be accessed and analysed by the institutions generating it and by regulators monitoring the broader landscape. Proprietary data formats and closed systems that make it difficult to extract and analyse deployment data are not a technical necessity. They are a commercial choice that happens to make external scrutiny more difficult, and regulation should not accommodate that choice. Open standards for AI deployment data, analogous to the interoperability standards that have been applied with mixed success to electronic health records, would make the monitoring infrastructure described earlier practically achievable rather than aspirational.

Ongoing accountability means that the regulatory relationship between a vendor and a deployed AI system does not end at the point of approval. Vendors should be required to maintain surveillance of their deployed systems, to report performance data to regulators on a defined schedule, and to notify deploying institutions promptly when performance issues are identified. There is nothing radical in this: it is the pharmaceutical equivalent of post-market surveillance, applied to software. It does not currently exist at scale for AI not because it is technically difficult, but because nobody has required it, and the vendors who would bear the cost have had little incentive to advocate for it.

Taken together, these shifts describe a regulatory posture that is oriented toward the actual sources of risk in AI deployment rather than toward the sources of risk that are most convenient to address. They require investment, political will, and a willingness on the part of professional bodies to accept new accountability mechanisms that encroach on territory they have historically defended. None of that is straightforward. But the alternative, continuing to regulate AI as if it were a medical device with a fixed specification while the actual risks accumulate unmonitored in the implementation context, is not a stable position. It is one that will produce serious harms, generate public loss of confidence in clinical AI, and ultimately make the regulatory environment harder rather than easier to navigate for everyone involved.

10.6 The consumer AI 'problem'

The regulatory frameworks described in the previous sections are inadequate for clinical AI. For consumer AI they are almost entirely absent. There is nothing to stop a member of the public opening a consumer AI chatbot and asking it about their chest pain. The tool has not been evaluated or approved for medical use. The institution deploying it has no clinical governance obligations because it is not a clinical institution. There is no registered professional involved that can be held to professional standards. The person receiving it has no way of knowing any of this, and the interface they are using has been carefully designed to feel helpful and trustworthy regardless.

This is not a niche problem affecting a small number of unusually credulous users. As Chapter 9 established, significant and growing proportions of the population are already using general-purpose AI tools for health-related queries. But the regulatory void is not a temporary gap that will be filled once the relevant authorities catch up. It is a structural feature of the current landscape, arising from the real difficulty of applying healthcare regulation to tools that are not, in any formal sense, healthcare tools, but that are being used for healthcare purposes at a scale that dwarfs most regulated clinical AI deployments.

The difficulty is more conceptual than political. The software as a medical device framework was designed to regulate products whose primary purpose is clinical. A pulse oximeter is a medical device. A radiology AI is clearly a medical device whereas a general-purpose language model that happens to be asked medical questions by some of its users is something quite different. Classifying it as a medical device would bring it within the regulatory framework, but it would do so at the cost of applying clinical validation requirements to a tool that is used for an enormous range of very general purposes, most of which have nothing to do with healthcare. The regulatory burden that would follow would either be unworkable in practice or would simply drive the relevant tools offshore, leaving the problem unsolved while adding compliance costs that benefit nobody.

An alternative approach, regulating the use rather than the tool, faces its own difficulties. Telling people that they should not use general-purpose AI for medical queries is both unenforceable and, as Chapter 9 argued, probably the wrong response anyway. The question is not whether people use AI for health purposes. They do and they will. The question is whether that use happens safely, with tools that are designed and validated for the purpose, or unsafely, with tools that were designed for something else entirely and happen to be capable of generating plausible-sounding medical advice as a by-product of their general capabilities.

A more honest framing starts by separating what can be regulated from what cannot. A consumer application specifically designed and marketed to help users interpret symptoms, manage conditions or make health decisions is making a clinical claim, implicit or otherwise. It is an identifiable product, placed on an identifiable market by an identifiable legal entity, and there is no reason beyond enforcement appetite why it should not be held to clinical standards of validation, bias disclosure and transparency about limitations. That is not an extension of the regulatory perimeter but enforcement of the perimeter that already exists: intended purpose is determined by what a product presents itself as doing, not by a disclaimer in the terms of service.

General-purpose models are a different matter entirely, and here I part company with those who believe the gap can be closed by regulatory will. Some have argued that LLM chatbots answering medical questions legally require approval as medical devices while being technically incapable of ever obtaining it, a combination that amounts to prohibition[142]. Whatever the doctrinal merits, the position is simply unenforceable. The frontier models are built by a handful of companies, updated continuously, distributed instantly across every jurisdiction, and used privately. A national regulator can control what is placed on its market for a medical purpose; it cannot control what several million of its citizens type into a general-purpose chatbot this evening. Enforcement at the model level would require international coordination of a kind that does not exist even in domains with decades of treaty infrastructure behind them, and would be undermined regardless by open-weight models that anyone can run on their own hardware, beyond any deployment perimeter.

Even the EU AI Act, the most ambitious statutory attempt to date, confines its treatment of general-purpose models largely to transparency obligations, and no plausible amendment reaches into a private conversation between a patient and a chatbot. There is simply no lever that can be pulled to regulate consumer generative AI as a medical device. The realistic sources of consumer safety lie elsewhere: in the safety properties of the models themselves, which developers have commercial and reputational reasons to invest in; in an informed public; and in the professional and institutional governance of everything that sits in this space, which is where the rest of this chapter concentrates.

The data protection dimension of consumer health AI deserves separate attention, as Chapter 9 noted. The health information that people share with consumer AI tools sits outside the main frameworks of health data protection in most jurisdictions, not because policymakers have decided that it should be unprotected but because the frameworks were written before this category of data existed at scale. Extending meaningful data protection to consumer health AI interactions with real enforcement is a regulatory priority that is more straightforwardly achievable but the commercial interests that would bear the cost of compliance are well organised and politically effective. Not so the patients whose data are at risk who are largely unaware of the exposure. The dynamics are familiar from earlier chapters, and the remedy is the same: governance that counteracts the structural advantage of organised incumbent interests rather than accommodating it.

The distance between the pace of technological development and the pace of regulatory adaptation is huge and has already had consequences. On 7 January 2025, Republican Representative David Schweikert introduced the Healthy Technology Act, a bill proposing that artificial intelligence and machine learning technologies should be able to qualify as practitioners eligible to prescribe drugs, subject to state authorisation and FDA approval[143]. The proposal was not, as its critics sometimes characterised it, a call for deregulation. The bill explicitly required FDA clearance and state-level oversight. It was, rather, a recognition that the existing legal framework, written for human practitioners, was failing to keep pace with what AI systems were already capable of doing. Autonomous AI diagnostic systems had been cleared for clinical use in the United States since 2018, when the FDA authorised the first system for independent diagnosis of diabetic retinopathy without a clinician in the loop. The question of whether prescribing is categorically different from diagnosing or choosing a treatment is not obviously answered in the affirmative, and the bill did at least attempt to force that question into the open.

What made this all the more interesting was the timing of the proposal. In the weeks immediately following the bill's introduction, the FDA underwent a wave of staff cuts described by a former agency chief as haphazard and poorly thought-out. The cuts disproportionately affected probationary employees and, critically, the staff working on AI-related regulatory initiatives at the Centre for Devices and Radiological Health, precisely the people responsible for developing the frameworks that would be needed to govern any expansion of autonomous medical AI[143].

The regulatory infrastructure required to oversee autonomous prescribing AI was being dismantled at the same moment that legislation was being proposed to authorise it.

Rather than being some American peculiarity this is an example of a pattern that this chapter has argued is general: the tendency of regulatory frameworks to move on timescales measured in years while the technologies they are meant to govern move on timescales measured in months. The FDA episode illustrates what happens at the extreme of that divergence. The technology arrives. The legislation attempts to accommodate it. The infrastructure needed to make the accommodation safe is not there. The result is not necessarily catastrophe, but it is a period of heightened and largely invisible risk, during which systems of unknown reliability operate without proper oversight while the institutions responsible for oversight try to catch up.

The human prescribing record, it should be said, is not the gold standard against which AI should be compared. Prescribing error rates have been estimated at between five and nine per cent, antibiotic overprescribing driven by patient pressure is a persistent problem, and commercial influence on prescribing decisions played a central role in the opioid crisis. An autonomous AI prescribing system that was well-designed, properly monitored and subject to rigorous oversight could plausibly outperform that baseline. The argument is not that AI should never prescribe but that the conditions required for it to do so safely, rigorous development, continuous monitoring, and a well-resourced regulatory agency capable of evolving its frameworks as the technology evolves, cannot be assumed to exist simply because the legislation permits the activity. Congress can pass a bill in a single session. Building the regulatory infrastructure to make that bill safe takes years. In 2025, the United States proposed to do the first while actively undermining the second.

10.7 From regulation to transformation

There is a real case for stronger, better-designed regulation of AI in healthcare because the risks are real, the governance gaps are serious, and the patients harmed by inadequately governed AI deployments are not abstractions. At the same time, regulation as it currently operates is itself one of the mechanisms by which the institution resists the transformation that AI makes possible. Holding both of these things in mind simultaneously is uncomfortable but necessary, because a regulatory reform that addresses the first without attending to the second will simply replace one set of institutional barriers with another.

The compliance burden of current regulatory arrangements falls most heavily on the innovations most likely to matter. A tool that makes existing workflows marginally more efficient, that sits within established clinical roles and does not redistribute any decision rights, can navigate the regulatory landscape relatively smoothly because it does not threaten anyone with the capacity to obstruct it. A tool that would allow a nurse practitioner to manage a condition currently managed by a consultant, or that would enable a patient to make an informed decision currently mediated by a clinician, or that would make clinical decision-making transparent and auditable in ways it currently is not, faces not only institutional resistance of the kind described in Chapter 5 but a regulatory environment that was shaped by the same interests that generate that resistance. The standards applied to disruptive AI are higher, the approval timelines are longer, the liability exposure is greater, and the professional pushback at every stage of the process is more organised. The regulatory framework does not just reflect the institutional status quo but naturally reproduces it because the two are so ingrained within one another.

This is not an argument for deregulation, but for regulation explicitly designed with transformation as its objective rather than stability. Those are different design briefs and they produce different frameworks. A regulatory framework designed primarily to manage risk within the existing configuration of healthcare will, predictably, make it easier to deploy AI that fits within that configuration and harder to deploy AI that challenges it. A regulatory framework designed to enable beneficial transformation while managing real risk would look different in several specific ways.

It would apply proportionate rather than uniform evidentiary standards, requiring more rigorous validation for higher-risk applications and accepting lower evidentiary thresholds for tools whose potential benefit is large and whose failure modes are recoverable. The current tendency to apply near-pharmaceutical standards of evidence to AI tools that are making probabilistic suggestions to trained clinicians, while consumer tools make the same suggestions to untrained members of the public entirely outside the framework, reflects institutional priorities rather than rational risk assessment. This is unrealistic for technology that is evolving faster than it can be evaluated. The consumer side of that asymmetry cannot, for the reasons set out earlier in this chapter, be fixed by extending the device perimeter. But the professional side can be recalibrated around actual risk rather than around the political convenience of existing frameworks, which would both reduce barriers to beneficial innovation and concentrate regulatory attention where the dangers regulation can actually reach lie.

It would create regulatory pathways specifically designed for adaptive and agentic AI, rather than stretching device certification frameworks to cover technologies they were never designed to govern. This means investing in the methodological infrastructure for continuous evaluation: the standards, the data architectures, the statistical frameworks and the institutional capacity needed to assess AI performance over time rather than at a single point. That investment is not trivial, but it is considerably less costly than the alternative, which is continuing to approve AI systems under frameworks that cannot detect when they have stopped working, and waiting for the resulting harms to accumulate before the inadequacy of the approach becomes undeniable.

It would explicitly reward transparency over opacity, in ways that current frameworks only do indirectly. A vendor that publishes detailed performance data stratified by patient subgroup, that maintains open standards for deployment data, and that proactively notifies deploying institutions of identified performance issues, should face a lighter regulatory touch than one that treats its validation data as proprietary and its deployment performance as commercially sensitive. At present the incentive runs the other way: opacity reduces regulatory exposure by making problems harder to identify, and the regulatory framework has no effective mechanism to counteract that incentive. Reversing it would require a deliberate policy choice to treat transparency as a regulatory asset rather than a voluntary nicety.

It would connect regulatory approval to implementation requirements in ways that make the conditions for safe deployment explicit rather than leaving them to institutional discretion. A tool approved for use in a defined clinical context should carry with it specific requirements about the training clinicians must receive before using it, the workflow conditions under which it may be deployed, and the monitoring that must be in place before it goes live. Those requirements should be enforceable, and the institution that deploys a tool outside the conditions of its approval should bear clear regulatory consequences. This sounds bureaucratic, but it is considerably less bureaucratic than the current situation, in which the conditions for safe deployment are undefined, the accountability for unsafe deployment is diffuse, and the cost of inadequate implementation falls on patients rather than on the institutions and vendors responsible for it.

Finally, and perhaps most importantly, a regulatory framework oriented toward transformation would treat the professional accountability question raised earlier in this chapter as a priority rather than an inconvenience. Defining what competent AI use looks like, building it into training and revalidation, and creating accountability mechanisms for its breach is a precondition for the kind of clinical engagement with AI that transformation requires as well as a patient safety measure. Clinicians who understand AI well, who know its limitations, who can interrogate its outputs and integrate them appropriately with their own reasoning, are not just safer practitioners. They are the people through whom the productivity gains, the quality improvements and the equity benefits that AI makes possible will actually be realised. Investing in that competency is not a regulatory overhead but part of the transformation itself. In short, we have to regulate the system, not the device.

The chapter that opened by noting the urge to regulate ends with a rather different proposition. The question for healthcare AI is not whether to regulate but what regulation is actually for. If it is for managing the transition from a healthcare system organised around the current distribution of professional authority to one organised around what AI makes possible, then it needs to be designed with that transition in mind, with an honest account of where the real risks lie, with standards that are proportionate to those risks, and with accountability mechanisms that name the responsible parties clearly. If it is for protecting the existing configuration of healthcare from the disruption that AI represents, then the current frameworks are, on the whole, doing that job rather well. The choice between those two purposes is ultimately a political one. But it is a choice, and pretending otherwise, dressing institutional protection in the language of patient safety, is exactly the kind of institutional behaviour that this book tries to make visible throughout.

11 From diagnosis to action

The argument I have tried to make in this book may be uncomfortable. One final time, without qualification: the reason AI is not transforming healthcare is not the technology. The algorithms work. In many domains they work better than the humans they are designed to assist, and in some, as the preceding chapters have shown, the human in the loop adds little or even detracts from the result. The data infrastructure, while imperfect, is sufficient to support transformative applications. The evidence base, while uneven, is substantial and growing. None of this is the binding constraint.

Instead, I argue that the constraint is the institution. Healthcare systems were not built to improve healthcare, at least not in the sense this book has used that term. They have been continuously refined over more than a century into arrangements that, whatever their original purpose, now function so as to reproduce existing distributions of power, income and authority. They do this not through conspiracy or malice but through the ordinary operation of incentive structures, professional norms, path dependence and collective action problems that make the status quo the rational choice for most of the people within the system most of the time, and through the manufactured complexity that Chapter 7 described, which makes the current configuration feel like the only one possible to the people working inside it. The system is working exactly as its structure dictates, and that structure is the problem.

That is a hard thing to conclude, because it implies that the standard responses to the challenge of healthcare AI, better algorithms, more evidence, clearer regulation, improved implementation, are necessary but not sufficient. They address the technology and not the institution. But difficult is not the same as impossible, and this is where the argument becomes, cautiously, more hopeful.

11.1 The pressure that cannot be managed away

The first source of hope is one that the institution cannot control and that cannot be regulated away, and that has been building throughout the period this book describes. The public is already using AI for health purposes at scale. The numbers, as we have already seen, are not marginal with three in five Americans having used AI tools for health-related queries in the three months to January 2026[126]. In the United Kingdom, 28% of adults have turned to AI chatbots to check their symptoms[144]. These are not technology early adopters but ordinary people who have a health question, cannot easily access a clinician, and have found something that provides a response.

This bears directly on the institutional argument, and a reader who has followed this book to its end is entitled to be sceptical of the claim. The whole argument has been that the institution absorbs what is sent to disrupt it. Why should AI be the exception? Because every previous challenge to medical authority, from the internet to patient advocacy movements to evidence-based medicine itself, still required the institution to mediate the final step: the clinical judgement about what the information meant for this patient. The internet gave patients facts, but a clinician was still needed to say what the facts meant, and that dependence preserved the one function on which medical authority rests. AI is different, as Chapter 9 argued, because it begins to provide that mediation directly. For the first time the challenge does not route back through the institution to be neutralised, and the interpretive monopoly that has underpinned medical authority for a century is eroding from outside the institution, at a pace that institutional resistance cannot match.

The obvious rejoinder is that interpretation is not treatment. Prescribing, and the treatments themselves, remain in physicians' hands, guarded by law rather than by expertise alone, and a monopoly written into statute cannot be eroded by a chatbot. That is true today, but the gate is weaker than it looks, because legal gates ultimately survive on the scarcity of the judgement behind them. Where AI supplies the judgement, the sign-off becomes a formality, and formalities get competed down to their price: direct-to-consumer telehealth platforms already operate protocol-driven prescribing in which the clinician's contribution has been compressed to a review lasting seconds. The monopoly is also being unbundled from the other side, as prescribing rights extend to pharmacists and nurses and regulators move more medicines over the counter, decisions that become easier to justify once validated decision support stands behind the non-physician or the patient. To be clear, at present consumer AI is plainly not good enough to replace clinical judgement, and this book has documented why at length. The claim concerns where the pressure now comes from: outside the institution's gift rather than inside it, and reaching, sooner than the profession expects, even the prescription pad, the most legally fortified of medicine's gates.

There is an influential counterargument here that I want to engage with. Agrawal, Gans and Goldfarb have argued that prediction and judgement are economic complements: as machine prediction becomes cheap, the value of the human judgement that acts on it rises, and the demand for it rises too[145]. On that view AI should augment doctors rather than displace any part of what they do. Both claims are true, because they apply to different layers of clinical work. At the interpretive layer, where genuine judgement is exercised under uncertainty, the complementarity is real: a clinician with better predictions makes better decisions, and nothing in this book argues otherwise. At the routinised layer, where the decision is already effectively determined by protocol and the clinician's contribution is confirmation, cheap prediction substitutes, and it is this layer that the prescribing gate is losing first.

The distinction matters enormously for productivity, and it is why augmentation alone will not deliver it. Augmenting doctors makes each doctor's judgement better; it does not make doctors less scarce, and a system whose binding constraint is the supply of medical time gains little from making that time marginally more effective while leaving in place every task that consumes it. The augmented doctor simply does more, which is intensification dressed up as progress. The productivity gains come from substitution at the routinised layer: letting AI, and non-medical professionals augmented by AI, absorb the work that never needed a doctor's judgement in the first place, so that the scarce resource is reserved for the work that does. Augmentation and substitution are therefore not rivals but partners with different targets. Augmentation of the pharmacist, the nurse and the patient is exactly what makes substitution for the doctor safe. The caution, in the terms of Chapter 6, is that augmentation which leaves the task allocation untouched is a so-so technology: it displaces effort without generating the gains that would fund new work, and it is the variant the institution finds easiest to adopt. Substitution at the routinised layer, paired with redesigned roles for the professionals who absorb that work, is what creates the new tasks instead.

The institution can issue warnings, urge caution and point to the limitations of consumer AI. What it cannot do is reverse the trend. The question, as Chapter 9 argued, is not whether this happens but whether it happens safely, with validated tools under proper oversight, or unsafely, in a regulatory impossibility populated by commodity products optimised for engagement rather than accuracy.

That question creates a political pressure that is qualitatively different from anything the institution has faced before. When constituents are already in this world, the case for building validated patient-facing tools, extending data protection to consumer health AI, and training clinicians to engage constructively with AI-informed patients becomes a mainstream political argument rather than a specialist one. Politicians who grasp that the choice is between managing this well or managing it badly have both the incentive and the mandate to act. That is new, and it matters.

11.2 Beyond good arguments

I have spent several chapters explaining why AI has not transformed healthcare. Now I want to say something about how it might. And the same analysis that explains the resistance also points toward where the leverage is.

The analysis of Chapter 5 is clear about which reforms face the hardest resistance: those that impose concentrated costs on well-organised groups while distributing diffuse benefits across large unorganised populations. This describes most of the reforms that healthcare AI requires. Payment reform that rewards outcomes rather than activity directly threatens the revenue of hospitals, specialist groups and pharmaceutical companies whose income depends on the current model. Regulatory reform that holds clinicians accountable for how they use AI threatens the professional autonomy that medicine has defended successfully for a century. Opening health system data for AI development threatens the information advantages that provider organisations and incumbent vendors have spent years building. In every case the losers are concentrated, organised and very good at defending what they have. The winners are patients and the public: dispersed, largely unaware of what is at stake, and with nothing like the lobbying infrastructure of the incumbents.

It goes deeper than lobbying. The medical profession does not just play the game; it substantially writes the rules. A government that tries to impose payment reform without the profession's consent will find every clinical advisory structure, every professional college, board or association, every specialist society and every workforce organisation available to slow, qualify and redirect the reform until it no longer threatens what it was meant to challenge. This has happened before and will happen again unless the rules that give the profession its veto are changed before the substantive reforms are attempted.

And then there is path dependence. The payment systems, regulatory structures and data-sharing arrangements that need to change are not just policies a government can rewrite on a Tuesday. They are the product of decades of complementary investment: training pipelines, physical infrastructure, liability rules, professional identities and organisational cultures that have all grown up together around the current configuration. Pull on one thread and you find it is attached to everything else.

So what is actually different this time? Not the reforms themselves but the pressure behind them. Every previous attempt at healthcare transformation faced institutional resistance without anything capable of matching it. The evidence was there with a clear financial case and with good arguments. But good arguments facing concentrated organised resistance and public indifference lose. That is what the analysis predicts, and that is what has happened, repeatedly.

This means the sequencing of reform matters enormously. The reforms most likely to move first are not necessarily the most important ones but the ones that respond directly to what the public is already doing, that can be presented as bringing order to something that exists rather than imposing something new, and that do not ask the organised losers to absorb their losses before the winners have found their voice. Oversight of purpose-built consumer health products, and of the data all of these tools collect, fits that description. So does reform of data stewardship more broadly, if framed around giving patients the benefit of their own data rather than threatening what incumbents currently control, though holding that framing under pressure will not be easy.

Payment reform and professional accountability for AI are harder. The path dependence is deeper, the organised opposition is stronger, and the realistic prediction is that these will not move through argument alone. They will require either a fiscal crisis that makes the current model impossible to sustain, or prior rule changes that reduce the veto power of incumbent interests before the harder reforms are attempted. Probably both.

That is a reason for sequencing rather than resignation. The window between when a crisis becomes visible and when it becomes unmanageable is the period when deliberate reform is possible. After the crisis breaks, the reforms that happen are the ones the most powerful actors can organise around in the chaos, which is not reliably the same as the reforms that would be best for patients. The arithmetic now confronting every major healthcare system, to which I return at the end of this chapter, means that window is open. The rest of this chapter is about how to use it.

11.3 What governments need to do

Public pressure creates the conditions for reform but does not by itself write the legislation, redesign the payment systems or open the data infrastructure. That requires deliberate political choice, and the choices required are identifiable. They are politically rather than technically complex, which is a different kind of difficulty and one that democratic systems are, at least in principle, designed to resolve.

The most important single intervention is payment reform. The incentive structures that drive healthcare AI toward incrementalism rather than transformation are not laws of nature but the product of payment systems that reward activity rather than outcome, volume rather than value, and local optimisation rather than system-level improvement. A payment system that rewards a system (rather than an organisation) for reducing unnecessary admissions, rather than penalising it by reducing revenue, changes the calculus for every AI investment decision that hospital makes. A reimbursement model that pays for outcomes across a whole care pathway, rather than for individual episodes within it, creates incentives for the kind of end-to-end redesign that AI makes possible but that no single institutional actor currently has reason to pursue. This is true whether the payer is a national health service, a social insurance fund or a private insurer; the instrument differs but the logic does not. Payment reform is hard not only because it threatens the revenue of powerful incumbents, but because it requires coordinated change across interdependent parts of the system whose existing arrangements minimise transaction costs locally while preserving the current equilibrium globally. These are exactly the features that make it the kind of reform that markets will not produce on their own and that only governments, or payers acting with government backing, can drive.

The second intervention concerns data. The productivity gains from AI in healthcare depend on the ability to train models on representative data, to deploy them across institutional boundaries, and to monitor their performance over time. None of this is possible at the scale required without a data infrastructure that is interoperable, open to appropriate access, and stewarded in ways that protect patient privacy without creating the fragmentation that currently makes most health data unusable for AI development at scale.

The problem takes different forms on either side of the Atlantic, but the underlying dynamic is the same. In the NHS, the barriers are legal and institutional: a patchwork of local information governance rules, trust-level data arrangements, and risk-averse interpretation of privacy law that has made it extraordinarily difficult to use data that patients have effectively donated to the system for purposes that would benefit them. The NHS sits on one of the most valuable health datasets in the world. The barriers that prevent that dataset from being used to develop AI that would benefit the patients who generated it are not a necessary feature of good stewardship but a design failure, and they are fixable.

In the United States the fragmentation is more deeply structural. The healthcare sector is less of a coordinated system and more of a collection of competing organisations, each of which has spent decades accumulating patient data and has every commercial incentive to treat that data as a proprietary asset rather than a shared resource. Hospital systems, insurers, pharmacy chains and integrated delivery networks hold data that could be transformational if combined, and they hold it in incompatible formats, behind proprietary interfaces, for competitive reasons that have nothing to do with patient welfare. The interoperability standards mandated under the 21st Century Cures Act have made some progress against this, but the mandate to share data through standardised interfaces has not yet translated into the kind of pooled infrastructure that AI development at scale requires. The commercial logic that fragments the data is the same commercial logic that fragments the system, and it will not be overcome by technical standards alone.

What both contexts share is the need for a reframing that is political as much as technical. Patient data are not a business asset that organisations happen to hold, but a resource generated by patients, about patients, that exists because patients sought care. The organisations that hold it are (necessarily) custodians, not owners. Establishing that principle in law and in practice, and building the custodial arrangements that follow from it, is one of the most important things governments can do to create the conditions for transformative healthcare AI. It will not happen without deliberate political intervention, because the organisations that currently benefit from treating data as a proprietary asset are well-organised and will resist the change, but it is both achievable and, given what is at stake, necessary.

None of this is an argument for governments designing the technology or setting the technical standards; that is properly the domain of industry, and the history of government-led attempts to specify technical architectures in healthcare IT is not encouraging. What governments need to do is set the ground rules within which industry operates: who owns the data, on what terms it can be accessed, what interoperability is required as a condition of market participation, and how patient privacy is protected across the whole ecosystem. The technical standards that sit within those rules are for industry to develop and iterate, and they will do so more effectively without governments trying to specify them.

But the rules also need to create the market conditions that reward innovation instead of entrenching incumbency. As Chapter 4 argued, the current market strongly favours vendors whose products are deeply embedded in existing infrastructure, not because those products are necessarily the best but because switching costs and integration advantages make them the path of least resistance. A market in which the dominant position is held by whoever got there first, rather than whoever is building the most effective tools, is a market that will stagnate. Governments can counteract this through procurement rules that require open interfaces as a condition of contract, through funding mechanisms that give new entrants access to the data and infrastructure they need to demonstrate their products, and through regulation that does not, as Chapter 10 argued, impose compliance burdens that only large incumbents can bear. The goal is to ensure that the market selects for clinical effectiveness rather than for compatibility with the existing configuration. The mistake to avoid is confusing the two roles: governments that try to lead on technology produce NPfIT, whose failure Chapter 5 examined. Governments that establish clear rules, open the market to competition, and get out of the way create the conditions in which industry can build what patients actually need.

Encouraging innovation is not only about creating space for new entrants. It is equally about ensuring that companies with dominant positions in the market do not use that dominance as a substitute for continued development. The current commercial environment does little to prevent this. A vendor whose product is deeply embedded in a health system's infrastructure has strong incentives to maintain that position and relatively weak incentives to keep improving, because the switching costs that protect incumbency are largely independent of product quality. Holding the contract is not the same as earning it continuously.

The remedy is not to remove incumbents but to change what keeping a contract requires. Procurement should assess not just current capability but demonstrated development trajectory: is the vendor actively expanding its tools and adding capabilities that respond to clinical need rather than commercial convenience? A vendor whose product was leading three years ago but has not materially advanced since should be visible as such, and contract renewal decisions should reflect it. This is closer to the logic of conditional licensing than traditional procurement: you keep your position, but keeping it requires demonstrating forward motion rather than just the absence of catastrophic failure.

Transparency is another mechanism that can help to make this work. It creates reputational pressure on vendors who are stagnating and rewards those who are not. It also gives innovative smaller companies the evidence base to demonstrate that their trajectory justifies the switching cost, which is currently very hard to make visible in a procurement process dominated by integration depth and existing relationships. Governments do not need to pick winners. They need to create the conditions in which the market can see clearly enough to pick them itself.

The third intervention is regulatory reform of the kind that Chapter 10 described: regulation oriented toward continuous monitoring of the system rather than point-in-time approval of the tool, toward implementation governance rather than algorithm certification, and toward professional accountability for AI use rather than the current situation in which the machine is regulated and the clinician using it is largely not. This is the area where the political will is most clearly absent at present, because it requires the medical profession to accept new accountability mechanisms that it has historically resisted. The public pressure described earlier is, again, the most likely source of the political mandate to act.

The fourth intervention may be the most important for unlocking the others, because it can be exercised through purchasing machinery that already exists, without waiting for new legislation or for the profession's consent. It concerns not what governments fund but how they fund it.

As Chapter 5 described, the US HITECH experience teaches that funding technology adoption can successfully produce digitisation, but that without funding system redesign this does not create transformation. The NHS has made the same mistake repeatedly; procuring AI tools and hoping the institution changes around them. The evidence of three decades suggests it does not. What would work differently is inverting the model entirely. Instead of funding technology and expecting system change to follow, fund the system change and let the technology follow from it. This means paying for differently structured care, pathways that only make clinical and financial sense if AI is deployed effectively, rather than buying AI tools and leaving the pathway unchanged. A contracted model for community management of heart failure that assumes AI-enabled monitoring, remote triage and reduced hospital admission, funded at a rate that only works if those efficiencies are achieved, creates an institutional incentive to make the AI work rather than absorb it. The technology is not the purchased object. The restructured care model is.

Every system has a purchaser capable of acting on this logic; only the name changes. In the NHS the instrument is commissioning, and the state's reach as a single payer means the model can in principle be adopted at national scale by policy decision, which is a genuine structural advantage, at least in theory. Insurance-based systems lack that central lever but hold parallel, and in some respects more powerful ones, because purchasers compete on cost and can move without waiting for national consensus. Capitated and bundled payment models are the natural vehicle: US Medicare Advantage plans and large self-insured employers already have the purchasing power to contract for care models rather than discrete services, Medicare's innovation pilots can seed them, and European social insurance funds can write selective contracts for integrated, AI-enabled pathways with providers willing to restructure. The mechanism is available almost everywhere; what has been missing is a purchaser willing to specify the redesigned pathway rather than the tool.

There is a further implication of the general purpose technology argument that purchasing practice has not yet absorbed. As Chapter 4 established, AI creates value not through the sum of individual applications but through the combinations that a redesigned system makes possible. You cannot procure your way to transformation one application at a time: a process that evaluates each AI tool on its individual merits and deploys it into an otherwise unchanged clinical environment will produce a well-evidenced collection of point solutions, never a transformed system, because the value of transformation exists only at the level of the whole. Paying for redesigned pathways rather than individual tools forces evaluation to happen at the right unit of analysis, makes the combination the purchased object rather than the component, and creates the incentive to make the components work together.

This approach requires accepting something that healthcare systems have historically been reluctant to accept—that some risk-taking is not just unavoidable but necessary. AI will never enter the market having been fully evaluated. The technology is evolving faster than any procurement, regulatory or evaluation process can track. By the time a rigorous outcome-based assessment of a particular tool has been designed, piloted and completed, the tool it was assessing no longer exists in the form that was assessed. The question is therefore not how to eliminate risk but how to distribute it fairly and manage it intelligently.

At present the distribution is wrong. The downside of trying something that does not work falls almost entirely on the organisation and the individuals who tried it, while the upside, in the form of system-level learning and eventually better care, spreads across the whole system. That asymmetry is precisely what the stag hunt analysis in Chapter 5 predicts will produce under-investment in experimentation. Correcting it requires deliberate policy: protected budgets for AI-enabled redesign that are not subject to the same short-term return requirements as operational spending, liability rules that distinguish between negligent deployment and reasonable experimentation that did not achieve its hoped-for outcome, and an honest political acknowledgement that some of this will not work and that is part of the process rather than a reason to stop.

If outcomes cannot be the primary measure of success then

accountability needs to shift toward measuring the quality of implementation. Did the organisation actually restructure the pathway, or did it install a tool and call it transformation? Did it redistribute clinical roles to make best use of AI, or did it leave professional boundaries intact and use the AI to make the existing model marginally more efficient? Did it use the operational data AI generates to redesign the work, or simply to demand more of the people doing it? These questions are answerable. They do not require waiting five years for outcome data which will be contaminated by other confounding factors. And they distinguish between organisations that are actually attempting the hard work of institutional redesign and those that are performing it. Making that distinction the basis of funding and accountability decisions is within the reach of any health system that chooses to prioritise it.

11.4 What healthcare leaders need to do

Governments can create the conditions for transformation but cannot produce it directly. The actual work of redesigning care around AI capabilities has to happen inside healthcare organisations, led by people who understand both the clinical environment and the technology well enough to navigate the gap between them.

The most important thing healthcare leaders can do is stop treating AI as a procurement decision and start treating it as a redesign opportunity. Specifically, this means asking not how AI can make existing coordination processes more efficient, but whether those processes should exist in their current form at all. The pattern this book has described throughout, of AI being adopted in forms that are compatible with existing workflows rather than used as the basis for redesigning those workflows, is not inevitable but the result of institutional defaults that leaders have the authority to override. A CEO who insists that AI investment proposals must demonstrate system-level benefit rather than local efficiency gains, and who is willing to accept the short-term disruption of real redesign in exchange for the long-term gains, is making a choice that the incentive structure does not require but, by the same token, does not prevent.

Realising that system-level value also depends on how the deployment itself is run, and here the handling of AI-generated operational data deserves particular care, because it is where leaders most often destroy the engagement they need. Let me be clear that employers are entirely entitled to assure themselves that their clinicians are performing well, and AI-derived data are a legitimate and indeed powerful tool for doing so; nothing in this book argues otherwise. The problem arises when transparency is used for a different purpose such as to extract more output from a workforce that is already working well, without redesigning the work itself. A clinical team that is performing competently at capacity has nothing further to give through effort alone. Using AI-generated load and throughput data to ratchet up demands on that team is workload intensification dressed as productivity improvement, and the history of workforce management on both sides of the Atlantic contains enough examples of operational data being used to justify exactly this to make clinicians' wariness entirely rational. Nor does the intensification always need a manager to impose it. Clinicians under pressure to be more productive, who have never been taught to see their workflows as designable and who instinctively resist changing them, will often absorb new technology by keeping the old ways of working and simply working harder within them, even where the organisation intended nothing of the kind. The result is self-imposed intensification: the tool arrives, the workflow survives, and the gap between the two is closed with effort. That failure mode cannot be fixed by managerial restraint alone, and it points directly to the argument of the next section, because clinicians cannot redesign work they have not been equipped to redesign.

That wariness has predictable consequences. Clinicians who suspect that the data generated by AI transparency will flow upward as an intensification tool, rather than being used to redesign the work or manage capacity, will rationally disengage from the very systems on which the productivity argument depends, and that disengagement is individually rational regardless of what colleagues choose. It cannot be solved by reassurance or by appeals to collective benefit. It can only be solved by changing the institutional rules: shared real-time access to load monitoring for clinical teams, joint clinician-management oversight of how operational data are used, and a credible commitment that efficiency gains will be taken through redesigned pathways and shared with the workforce rather than through unilateral increases in expected throughput. These are the structural conditions on which the productivity argument depends, not soft cultural commitments. A healthcare leader who deploys AI transparency tools without establishing them first is actively undermining the conditions under which those tools could create transformation.

Healthcare leaders also bear direct responsibility for the bias and accountability gaps that I described in Chapter 8. The AI systems being deployed in clinical settings are, in many cases, not adequately validated for the populations they are serving, not monitored for drift after deployment, and not subject to arrangements that would detect and respond to harm before it accumulates at scale. Addressing this is a clinical governance responsibility that sits with the organisations deploying the tools and the leaders accountable for them; it cannot be discharged by pointing to an approval certificate.

All of this presumes something that cannot currently be presumed: that the people making these decisions understand what they are deciding. Healthcare boards and executive teams know how to buy technology, because procurement is a familiar organisational competence. However often they do not know how to think about technology as an instrument of systems change, because nothing in their training or career progression has required them to. That gap is itself an intervention target, and it needs deliberate investment at two levels.

The first is at the top. Senior management, from board level down, needs far more familiarity with the arguments this book has made: that the value of digital technology lies in system redesign rather than point solutions, that the productivity dividend comes from complementary investment in restructured work rather than from the tools themselves, and that a portfolio of individually well-evidenced applications does not add up to transformation. This is not a matter of teaching executives to code but of building a working literacy in systems engineering: how complex adaptive systems behave, why local optimisation degrades global performance, what modern digital infrastructure actually makes possible, and how to evaluate proposals at the level of the pathway rather than the product. It also means understanding what redesign costs on the way through. A board that grasps that systems change is the goal will also grasp that it is inherently disruptive, and will make room, in a deliberate and controlled way, for experimentation, for some failure, and for the temporary dips in performance that real redesign entails, rather than treating every dip as evidence that the change should stop. A board that cannot ask these questions cannot hold its executives to the implementation-quality standard described earlier, and an executive team that cannot answer them will default to buying tools and hoping. This is not merely assertion: recent game-theoretic modelling of organisational AI adoption reaches the same conclusion from formal analysis, finding that coordination-focused strategies dominate technology-focused ones, and that adoption fails through predictable coordination and workforce-alignment traps even when the underlying technology delivers[146].

The second is clinical. The redesign work described in this chapter requires people who span the clinical and technical worlds, who can sit in a co-design session and translate between what the technology can do and what the ward actually needs. Such people exist, but they are still too rare, and healthcare treats developing them as an optional enthusiasm rather than a core capability; in many systems, time spent on digital work is still a career detour from the clinical ladder rather than a step up it. That has to change in two ways. Digital capability needs to become a core component of clinical training for every healthcare professional, not an elective for the interested few, because clinicians who do not understand what the technology can and cannot do will be unable to participate meaningfully in redesigning their own work, and unable to hold vendors and managers to account when the redesign is done to them rather than with them. And beyond that baseline, health systems need to invest heavily in a much larger cadre of dedicated clinical digital leaders, formally trained, properly resourced, and embedded in change programmes and co-design from the outset rather than consulted at the end or confined to an informatics silo. The stag hunt problem described earlier is, at root, a problem of credible assurance, and clinical leaders who are visibly shaping the change are one of the few sources of assurance the workforce will actually believe.

Let me be blunt about what this means for clinical education, and for medical education in particular. A training that produces doctors fluent in anatomy, physiology, biochemistry and pharmacology but unable to reason about data, algorithms or the systems through which care is actually delivered is not fit for the twenty-first century. The traditional basic sciences earned their primacy in an era when the limiting factor in care was the biological knowledge held in an individual clinician's head. That is no longer the only limiting factor, and in an age when AI can retrieve and apply biological knowledge on demand, the distinctive human contribution shifts toward exactly the things current curricula barely touch: how information flows, how systems fail, and how care is designed. None of this makes the basic sciences unimportant; it makes them insufficient. Clinical informatics is a clinical discipline in its own right, as much as public health medicine is, and the comparison is instructive because the two share the same essential move: lifting the clinical gaze from the individual patient to the system through which patients are actually served. Public health took the better part of a century to win that recognition. Clinical informatics does not have a century.

11.5 What the rest of us need to do

The public, as this book has argued, is no passive recipient of whatever healthcare AI the system produces. It is already an active force reshaping the landscape, and it has more power to drive the transformation this book argues for than it is generally encouraged to believe.

The most direct form of that power is political. The arguments in this book are not technical arguments that only specialists can evaluate. Instead they are arguments about how power is distributed in healthcare, who benefits from the current arrangement, and what it would take to change it. Those are arguments that any informed citizen can engage with and act on. Politicians who are asked by their constituents why validated patient-facing AI is not available through their health system, why the data generated by patients cannot be used to train AI that would benefit those same patients, and why the purpose-built consumer health products they already use are held to no meaningful clinical standard, face questions they need to answer. An informed public is the constituency that makes those questions politically salient.

The second form of power is as patients. Patients who arrive at consultations having used AI, who ask their clinicians to engage with the reasoning those tools have provided, who push back when they are told simply to ignore what the AI said, are changing the terms of the clinical encounter in ways that the institution cannot easily reverse. Given everything this book has said about the limitations of consumer AI, this is emphatically an argument for informed engagement rather than uncritical trust: using AI as a starting point for clinical conversations rather than a substitute for them, and expecting clinicians to meet that engagement constructively rather than dismissively.

11.6 The case for optimism

None of this is easy. The institutional forces this book has described are real, well-organised and have had a century to embed themselves. The path dependence is deep. The veto players are numerous. The incentive structures that reward the status quo are not going to dissolve because a book made the argument that they should.

But there are reasons for optimism that do not depend on ignoring these obstacles. The technology is ready in a way it has never been before with the gap between what AI can do in a research setting and what it can do in deployment having narrowed dramatically in the past five years. The models that are now available, both for clinical deployment and for consumer use, are capable of things that would have seemed implausible at the start of the decade. That capability is not going away, and it is not going to stop improving.

The demographic and financial pressures on healthcare systems are creating a crisis of sustainability that makes the status quo increasingly untenable. The NHS ten-year plan, to take the example closest to home, has explicitly acknowledged that the workforce expansion model of the past cannot continue, and has pointed to digital technology and AI as critical to a different model. The same arithmetic confronts every advanced system: American entitlement spending, European social insurance contributions and Asian dependency ratios are all telling their governments the same thing. None of this guarantees transformation, but it is a political context in which the arguments for transformation are easier to make than they have ever been, and one in which, as this chapter began by arguing, the public has already created facts on the ground that no amount of caution or guidance can manage away.

The patients who will benefit from a transformed healthcare system are already alive. Many of them are already using AI, imperfectly and without safeguards, not just because of convenience but also because the system has not provided anything better. The case for transformation is not abstract. It is the case for those patients getting care that is safer, more accessible, more equitable and more effective than what the current system reliably delivers.

This book began with the claim that healthcare systems were not built to improve healthcare in the sense that matters here, and every chapter since has traced how arrangements that evolved to coordinate complex, uncertain and high-risk activity became coupled to existing distributions of power, income and authority, and came to reproduce them, not through design or intent, but through the ordinary operation of their coordination structures. AI does not change that design by itself. What it does, for the first time, is create the conditions under which the design becomes politically visible and practically changeable. The public already knows what is not being delivered; it should also be able to see what could be, and the gap between the two is the measure of what is at stake. The fiscal pressure makes the status quo unsustainable rather than merely uncomfortable. And the analytical tools exist to understand where the resistance comes from and where the leverage is. That combination, visibility, pressure and understanding, is rarer than it looks, and it will not last. The question this book has been building toward is not whether transformation is possible. It is whether the people with the power to act will recognise the moment for what it is.

Bibliography

[1] W. Edwards Deming. *Out of the Crisis*. MIT Press, Cambridge, MA, 1986.

[2] Ashish Vaswani, Noam Shazeer, Niki Parmar, Jakob Uszkoreit, Llion Jones, Aidan N Gomez, Lukasz Kaiser, and Illia Polosukhin. Attention is all you need, 2017.

[3] Ray Kurzweil. *The Singularity Is Near: When Humans Transcend Biology*. Viking, New York, 2005. ISBN 9780670033843.

[4] Eric J. Topol. *Deep Medicine: How Artificial Intelligence Can Make Healthcare Human Again*. Basic Books, 2019. ISBN 9781541644618.

[5] John W. Ayers, Adam Poliak, Mark Dredze, Eric C. Leas, Zechariah Zhu, Jessica B. Kelley, Dennis J. Faix, Aaron M. Goodman, Christopher A. Longhurst, Michael Hogarth, and Davey M. Smith. Comparing physician and artificial intelligence chatbot responses to patient questions posted to a public social media forum. *JAMA Internal Medicine*, 183(6):589–596, June 2023. ISSN 2168-6106. doi: 10.1001/jamainternmed.2023.1838.

[6] Jim Oeppen and James W. Vaupel. Broken limits to life expectancy. *Science*, 296(5570):1029–1031, 2002. doi: 10.1126/science.1069675.

[7] Elizabeth A. McGlynn, Steven M. Asch, John Adams, Joan Keesey, Jennifer Hicks, Alison DeCristofaro, and Eve A. Kerr. The quality of health care delivered to adults in the United States. *The New England Journal of Medicine*, 348(26): 2635–2645, 2003. doi: 10.1056/NEJMsa022615.

[8] Martin N. Marshall, Paul G. Shekelle, Elizabeth A. McGlynn, Stephen Campbell, Robert H. Brook, and Martin O. Roland. Can health care quality indicators be transferred between countries? *Quality and Safety in Health Care*, 12(1):8–12, 2003. doi: 10.1136/qhc.12.1.8.

[9] Stephen A Martin, Minna Johansson, Iona Heath, Richard Lehman, and Christina Korownyk. Sacrificing patient care for prevention: distortion of the role of general practice. *BMJ*, 388:e080811, 2025. doi: 10.1136/bmj-2024-080811. Published 21 January 2025.

[10] David M. Levine, Jeffrey A. Linder, and Bruce E. Landon. The quality of outpatient care delivered to adults in the United States, 2002 to 2013. *JAMA Internal Medicine*, 176 (12):1778–1790, 2016. doi: 10.1001/jamainternmed.2016.6217.

[11] Lydia DePillis and Christine Zhang. How health care remade the U.S. economy. *The New York Times*, July 2025. Accessed: 2025-07-13.

[12] PwC EU Services EEIG and Open Evidence. Study on the deployment of AI in healthcare: Final report. Technical report, European Commission, Directorate General for Health and Food Safety, June 2025.

[13] Department of Health and Social Care. Fit for the future:

10 year health plan for England, July 2025. CP 1350, ISBN 978-1-5286-5807-2.

[14] Max Warner and Ben Zaranko. Implications of the NHS workforce plan. Technical Report R272, Institute for Fiscal Studies, 2023. IFS Green Budget 2023, Chapter 8.

[15] Hanwen Xu, Naoto Usuyama, Jaspreet Bagga, Sheng Zhang, Rajesh Rao, Tristan Naumann, Cliff Wong, Zelalem Gero, Javier González, Yu Gu, Yanbo Xu, Mu Wei, Wenhui Wang, Shuming Ma, Furu Wei, Jianwei Yang, Chunyuan Li, Jianfeng Gao, Jaylen Rosemon, Tucker Bower, Soohee Lee, Roshanthi Weerasinghe, Bill J. Wright, Ari Robicsek, Brian Piening, Carlo Bifulco, Sheng Wang, and Hoifung Poon. A whole-slide foundation model for digital pathology from real-world data. *Nature*, 630:181–188, 2024. doi: 10.1038/s41586-024-07441-w.

[16] Gabriele Campanella, Neeraj Kumar, Swaraj Nanda, Siddharth Singi, Eugene Fluder, Ricky Kwan, Silke Muehlstedt, Nicole Pfarr, Peter J. Schüffler, Ida Häggström, Noora Neittaanmäki, Levent M. Akyürek, Alina Basnet, Tamara Jamaspishvili, Michel R. Nasr, Matthew M. Croken, Fred R. Hirsch, Arielle Elkrief, Helena Yu, Orly Ardon, Gregory M. Goldgof, Meera Hameed, Jane Houldsworth, Maria Arcila, Thomas J. Fuchs, and Chad Vanderbilt. Real-world deployment of a fine-tuned pathology foundation model for lung cancer biomarker detection. *Nature Medicine*, 2025. doi: 10.1038/s41591-025-03780-x.

[17] Mattia Carletti, Jay Pandit, Matteo Gadaleta, Danielle Chiang, Felipe Delgado, Katie Quartuccio, Brianna Fernandez, Juan Antonio Raygoza Garay, Ali Torkamani, Ric-

cardo Miotto, Hagai Rossman, Benjamin Berk, Katie Baca-Motes, Vik Kheterpal, Eran Segal, Eric J. Topol, Edward Ramos, and Giorgio Quer. Multimodal AI correlates of glucose spikes in people with normal glucose regulation, pre-diabetes and type 2 diabetes. *Nature Medicine*, 2025. doi: 10.1038/s41591-025-03849-7.

[18] Artem Shmatko, Alexander Wolfgang Jung, Kumar Gaurav, Søren Brunak, Laust Hvas Mortensen, Ewan Birney, Tom Fitzgerald, and Moritz Gerstung. Learning the natural history of human disease with generative transformers. *Nature*, 2025. doi: 10.1038/s41586-025-09529-3.

[19] Zhenyu Yang, Xiaoxi Zeng, Yi Zhao, and Runsheng Chen. Alphafold2 and its applications in the fields of biology and medicine. *Signal Transduction and Targeted Therapy*, 8(1):115, 2023. doi: 10.1038/s41392-023-01381-z.

[20] Sarah Lewis, Tim Hempel, José Jiménez-Luna, Michael Gastegger, Yu Xie, Andrew Y. K. Foong, Victor García Satorras, Osama Abdin, Bastiaan S. Veeling, Iryna Zaporozhets, Yaoyi Chen, Soojung Yang, Adam E. Foster, Arne Schneuing, Jigyasa Nigam, Federico Barbero, Vincent Stimper, Andrew Campbell, Jason Yim, Marten Lienen, Yu Shi, Shuxin Zheng, Hannes Schulz, Usman Munir, Roberto Sordillo, Ryota Tomioka, Cecilia Clementi, and Frank Noé. Scalable emulation of protein equilibrium ensembles with generative deep learning. *Science*, 2025. doi: 10.1126/science.adv9817.

[21] World Bank. *Drug-Resistant Infections: A Threat to Our Economic Future*. International Bank for Reconstruction and Development / The World Bank, Washington, DC,

2017. License: Creative Commons Attribution CC BY 3.0 IGO.

[22] Jonathan M. Stokes, Kevin Yang, Kyle Swanson, Wengong Jin, Andres Cubillos-Ruiz, Nina M. Donghia, Craig R. MacNair, Shawn French, Lindsey A. Carfrae, Zohar Bloom-Ackermann, Victoria M. Tran, Anush Chiappino-Pepe, Ahmed H. Badran, Ian W. Andrews, Emma J. Chory, George M. Church, Eric D. Brown, Tommi S. Jaakkola, Regina Barzilay, and James J. Collins. A deep learning approach to antibiotic discovery. *Cell*, 180(4):688–702.e13, 2020. doi: 10.1016/j.cell.2020.01.021.

[23] Samuel H. King, Claudia L. Driscoll, David B. Li, Daniel Guo, Aditi T. Merchant, Garyk Brixi, Max E. Wilkinson, and Brian L. Hie. Generative design of novel bacteriophages with genome language models. Preprint at bioRxiv, September 2025.

[24] Christine Sinsky, Lacey Colligan, Ling Li, Mirela Prgomet, Sam Reynolds, Lindsey Goeders, Johanna Westbrook, Michael Tutty, and George Blike. Allocation of physician time in ambulatory practice: A time and motion study in 4 specialties. *Annals of Internal Medicine*, 165(11):753–760, 2016. doi: 10.7326/M16-0961. Published online 6 September 2016.

[25] Brian G. Arndt, John W. Beasley, Michelle D. Watkinson, Jonathan L. Temte, Wen-Jan Tuan, Christine A. Sinsky, and Valerie J. Gilchrist. Tethered to the EHR: Primary care physician workload assessment using EHR event log data and time-motion observations. *Annals of Family Medicine*, 15(5):419–426, 2017. doi: 10.1370/afm.2121. Published September/October 2017.

[26] Xinge Tao, Shuya Zhou, Kai Ding, Sairan Li, Yanzeng Li, Boyou Wu, Qirui Huang, Wangyue Chen, Muzi Shen, En Meng, Xiaowang Chen, Hong Hu, Jinchao Zhang, Jie Zhou, Lei Zou, Libing Ma, and Shasha Han. An LLM chatbot to facilitate primary-to-specialist care transitions: a randomized controlled trial. *Nature Medicine*, 2026. doi: 10.1038/s41591-025-04176-7.

[27] Scott J. Adams, Julián N. Acosta, and Pranav Rajpurkar. How generative AI voice agents will transform medicine. *npj Digital Medicine*, 8:353, 2025. doi: 10.1038/s41746-025-01776-y.

[28] Qiao Jin, Zifeng Wang, Charalampos S. Floudas, Fangyuan Chen, Changlin Gong, Dara Bracken-Clarke, Elisabetta Xue, Yifan Yang, Jimeng Sun, and Zhiyong Lu. Matching patients to clinical trials with large language models. *Nature Communications*, 15:9074, 2024. doi: 10.1038/s41467-024-53081-z.

[29] Janine Machin. AI physio app halves wait list for back pain treatment. BBC News, July 2025.

[30] Charlotte R. Blease, Cosima Locher, Jens Gaab, Maria Hägglund, and Kenneth D. Mandl. Generative artificial intelligence in primary care: an online survey of UK general practitioners. *BMJ Health & Care Informatics*, 31(1):e101102, 2024. doi: 10.1136/bmjhci-2024-101102.

[31] Jiyeong Kim, Kimberly G. Leonte, Michael L. Chen, John B. Torous, Eleni Linos, Anthony Pinto, and Carolyn I. Rodriguez. Large language models outperform mental and medical health care professionals in identifying obsessive-

compulsive disorder. *npj Digital Medicine*, 7(193), 2024. doi: 10.1038/s41746-024-01181-x.

[32] Kyle Lam, Julia Calvo Latorre, Andrew Yiu, Grace Navin, Alexander Tan, and Jianing Qiu. Physician input improves generative artificial intelligence models' diagnostic performance in solving complex clinical cases. *The Lancet Digital Health*, 7:100922, 2025. doi: 10.1016/j.landig.2025.100922.

[33] Youth Endowment Fund. Young people and violence: Annual vulnerability report 2025. Technical report, Youth Endowment Fund, 2025.

[34] Nick Obradovich, Sahib S. Khalsa, Waqas U. Khan, Jina Suh, Roy H. Perlis, Olusola Ajilore, and Martin P. Paulus. Opportunities and risks of large language models in psychiatry. *NPP – Digital Psychiatry and Neuroscience*, 2024. doi: 10.1038/s44277-024-00010-z.

[35] Elizabeth C. Stade, Shannon Wiltsey Stirman, Lyle H. Ungar, Cody L. Boland, H. Andrew Schwartz, David B. Yaden, João Sedoc, Robert J. DeRubeis, Robb Willer, and Johannes C. Eichstaedt. Large language models could change the future of behavioral healthcare: a proposal for responsible development and evaluation. *npj Mental Health Research*, 3(12), 2024. doi: 10.1038/s44184-024-00056-z.

[36] Julia Ive, Olatomiwa Olukoya, Jonathan P. Funnell, James Booker, Sze H. M. Lam, Ugan Reddy, Kawsar Noor, Richard JB Dobson, Astri M. V. Luoma, and Hani J. Marcus. AI assisted prediction of unplanned intensive care admissions using natural language processing in elect-

ive neurosurgery. *npj Digital Medicine*, 8:549, 2025. doi: 10.1038/s41746-025-01952-0.

[37] Timothy F. Bresnahan and Manuel Trajtenberg. General purpose technologies: 'engines of growth'? *Journal of Econometrics*, 65(1):83–108, 1995.

[38] Benjamin A Rodwin, Victor P Bilan, Naseema B Merchant, Catherine G Steffens, Alyssa A Grimshaw, Lori A Bastian, and Craig G Gunderson. Rate of preventable mortality in hospitalized patients: a systematic review and meta-analysis. *Journal of General Internal Medicine*, 35(7):2099–2106, 2020. doi: 10.1007/s11606-019-05592-5.

[39] Health and Society Team. Avoidable mortality in England and Wales: 2021 and 2022. Technical report, Office for National Statistics, June 2024.

[40] Anthropic. How people use Claude for support, advice, and companionship. Technical report, Anthropic, 2025.

[41] Shruthi Shekar, Pat Pataranutaporn, Chethan Sarabu, Guillermo A. Cecchi, and Pattie Maes. People overtrust AI-generated medical advice despite low accuracy. *NEJM AI*, 2(6), 2025. doi: 10.1056/AIoa2300015.

[42] Gunther Eysenbach, John Powell, Oliver Kuss, and Eun-Ryoung Sa. Empirical studies assessing the quality of health information for consumers on the world wide web: A systematic review. *JAMA*, 287(20):2691–2700, 2002. doi: 10.1001/jama.287.20.2691.

[43] Qian Chen, Yufan Jing, Yeming Gong, and Jie Tan. Will users fall in love with ChatGPT? a perspective from the triangular theory of love. *Journal of Business Research*, 186:

114982, 2025. ISSN 0148-2963. doi: 10.1016/j.jbusres.2024.114982.

[44] Donald O Hebb. *The organization of behavior: a neuropsychological theory*. Wiley and Sons, New York, 1949. ISBN 978-0-471-36727-7.

[45] Frank Rosenblatt. The perceptron: a probabilistic model for information storage and organization in the brain. *Psychological Review*, 65(6):386–408, 1958. doi: 10.1037/h0042519.

[46] Joseph A. Schumpeter. *Capitalism, Socialism and Democracy*. Harper and Brothers, New York, 1942.

[47] Thomas Kwa, Ben West, Joel Becker, Amy Deng, Katharyn Garcia, Max Hasin, Sami Jawhar, Megan Kinniment, Nate Rush, Sydney Von Arx, Ryan Bloom, Thomas Broadley, Haoxing Du, Brian Goodrich, Nikola Jurkovic, Luke Harold Miles, Seraphina Nix, Tao Lin, Chris Painter, Neev Parikh, David Rein, Lucas Jun Koba Sato, Hjalmar Wijk, Daniel M. Ziegler, Elizabeth Barnes, and Lawrence Chan. Measuring AI ability to complete long tasks. *arXiv preprint arXiv:2503.14499*, 2025. Model Evaluation & Threat Research (METR).

[48] Menglei Zhu, Hui Lin, Jue Jiang, Abbas J. Jinia, Justin Jee, Karl Pichotta, Michele Waters, Doori Rose, Nikolaus Schultz, Sulov Chalise, Lohit Valleru, Olivier Morin, Jean Moran, Joseph O. Deasy, Shirin Pilai, Chelsea Nichols, Gregory Riely, Lior Z. Braunstein, and Anyi Li. Large language model trained on clinical oncology data predicts cancer progression. *npj Digital Medicine*, 8:397, 2025. doi: 10.1038/s41746-025-01780-2.

[49] Thilo Hagendorff, Sarah Fabi, and Michal Kosinski. Human-like intuitive behavior and reasoning biases emerged in large language models but disappeared in ChatGPT. *Nature Computational Science*, 3:833–838, 2023. doi: 10.1038/s43588-023-00527-x.

[50] Marcel Binz, Elif Akata, Matthias Bethge, Franziska Brändle, Fred Callaway, Julian Coda-Forno, Peter Dayan, Can Demircan, Maria K. Eckstein, Noémi Éltető, Thomas L. Griffiths, Susanne Haridi, Akshay K. Jagadish, Li Ji-An, Alexander Kipnis, Sreejan Kumar, Tobias Ludwig, Marvin Mathony, Marcelo Mattar, Alireza Modirshanechi, Surabhi S. Nath, Joshua C. Peterson, Milena Rmus, Evan M. Russek, Tankred Saanum, Johannes A. Schubert, Luca M. Schulze Buschoff, Nishad Singhi, Xin Sui, Mirko Thalmann, Fabian J. Theis, Vuong Truong, Vishaal Udandarao, Konstantinos Voudouris, Robert Wilson, Kristin Witte, Shuchen Wu, Dirk U. Wulff, Huadong Xiong, and Eric Schulz. A foundation model to predict and capture human cognition. *Nature*, 644:1002–1009, 2025. doi: 10.1038/s41586-025-09215-4.

[51] Mahmud Omar, Vera Sorin, Jeremy D. Collins, David Reich, Robert Freeman, Nicholas Gavin, Alexander Charney, Lisa Stump, Nicola Luigi Bragazzi, Girish N. Nadkarni, and Eyal Klang. Multi-model assurance analysis showing large language models are highly vulnerable to adversarial hallucination attacks during clinical decision support. *Communications Medicine*, 5:330, 2025. doi: 10.1038/s43856-025-01021-3.

[52] Kenneth J. Arrow. Uncertainty and the welfare economics

of medical care. *American Economic Review*, 53(5):941–973, 1963.

[53] William J. Baumol and William G. Bowen. On the performing arts: The anatomy of their economic problems. *American Economic Review*, 55(1/2):495–502, 1965. ISSN 00028282.

[54] William J. Baumol, David de Ferranti, Monte Malach, Ariel Pablos-Méndez, Hilary Tabish, and Lilian Gomory Wu. *The Cost Disease: Why Computers Get Cheaper and Health Care Doesn't*. Yale University Press, 2012. ISBN 9780300179286.

[55] Thomas Piketty. *Capital in the Twenty-First Century*. Harvard University Press, Cambridge, MA, 2014. ISBN 9780674430006.

[56] Michael Freeman, Nicos Savva, and Stefan Scholtes. Economies of scale and scope in hospitals: An empirical study of volume spillovers. *Management Science*, 67(2):673–697, 2021. doi: 10.1287/mnsc.2019.3572.

[57] Daron Acemoglu and James A. Robinson. *Why Nations Fail: The Origins of Power, Prosperity, and Poverty*. Crown Publishers, New York, 2012.

[58] Francesco Filippucci, Peter Gal, Cecilia Jona-Lasinio, Alvaro Leandro, and Giuseppe Nicoletti. The impact of artificial intelligence on productivity, distribution and growth: Key mechanisms, initial evidence and policy challenges. OECD Artificial Intelligence Papers 15, OECD, 2024.

[59] Daniel Kahneman and Amos Tversky. Prospect theory: An analysis of decision under risk. *Econometrica*, 47(2): 263–291, 1979. doi: 10.2307/1914185.

[60] Raymond E. Miles and Charles C. Snow. *Organizational Strategy, Structure, and Process*. McGraw-Hill, New York, 1978.

[61] Hal R. Varian, Joseph Farrell, and Carl Shapiro. *The Economics of Information Technology: An Introduction*. Cambridge University Press, Cambridge, 2004.

[62] Julia Adler-Milstein, Sara G. Murray, and Robert M. Wachter. The market dynamics for third-party AI tools trying to compete with electronic health record developers. *JAMA*, 2026. doi: 10.1001/jama.2026.2394. Published online March 31, 2026.

[63] William Stanley Jevons. *The Coal Question: An Inquiry Concerning the Progress of the Nation, and the Probable Exhaustion of Our Coal-Mines*. Macmillan, London, 1865.

[64] Milton I. Roemer. Bed supply and hospital utilization: a natural experiment. *Hospitals*, 35:36–42, 1961.

[65] Robert M. Wachter. Making IT work: Harnessing the power of health information technology to improve care in England. Technical report, National Advisory Group on Health Information Technology in England, London, 2016.

[66] David Blumenthal. Launching HITECH. *The New England Journal of Medicine*, 362(5):382–385, 2010. doi: 10.1056/NEJMp0912825.

[67] Office of the National Coordinator for Health Information Technology. Adoption of electronic health record systems among U.S. non-federal acute care hospitals: 2008–2015. Data brief, US Department of Health and Human Services, 2016.

[68] Julia Adler-Milstein and Ashish K. Jha. HITECH act drove large gains in hospital electronic health record adoption. *Health Affairs*, 36(8):1416–1422, 2017. doi: 10.1377/hlthaff.2016.1651.

[69] Ajay Agrawal, Joshua Gans, and Avi Goldfarb. *Power and Prediction: The Disruptive Economics of Artificial Intelligence*. Harvard Business Review Press, Boston, MA, 2022.

[70] Timothy F. Bresnahan. Ajay agrawal, joshua gans, and avi goldfarb: Power and prediction: The disruptive economics of artificial intelligence. *Business Economics*, 59(2):120–122, 2024. doi: 10.1057/s11369-023-00337-z. Book review.

[71] Douglass C. North. *Institutions, Institutional Change and Economic Performance*. Cambridge University Press, Cambridge, 1990.

[72] Oliver E. Williamson. *The Economic Institutions of Capitalism*. Free Press, New York, 1985.

[73] Paul A. David. Clio and the economics of QWERTY. *American Economic Review*, 75(2):332–337, 1985. Papers and Proceedings of the Ninety-Seventh Annual Meeting of the American Economic Association.

[74] Paul Starr. *The Social Transformation of American Medicine*. Basic Books, New York, 1982.

[75] Ivan Waddington. *The Medical Profession in the Industrial Revolution*. Gill and Macmillan, Dublin, 1984.

[76] Mancur Olson. *The Rise and Decline of Nations: Economic Growth, Stagflation, and Social Rigidities*. Yale University Press, New Haven, CT, 1982.

[77] Miranda Laurant, Mieke van der Biezen, Nicky Wijers, Kanokwaroon Watananirun, Evangelos Kontopantelis, and Anneke J.A.H. van Vught. Nurses as substitutes for doctors in primary care. *Cochrane Database of Systematic Reviews*, 7:CD001271, 2018. doi: 10.1002/14651858.CD001271.pub3.

[78] American Medical Association. AMA successfully fights scope of practice expansions that threaten patient safety, 2023. Accessed 2025.

[79] Jacqueline Dunbar-Jacob and Jeffrey M. Rohay. State health and the level of practice authority for nurse practitioners. *Nursing Outlook*, 73(1):102319, 2025. doi: 10.1016/j.outlook.2024.102319.

[80] Michael D. Abràmoff, Philip T. Lavin, Marc Birch, Nilay Shah, and James C. Folk. Pivotal trial of an autonomous AI-based diagnostic system for detection of diabetic retinopathy in primary care offices. *npj Digital Medicine*, 1:39, 2018. doi: 10.1038/s41746-018-0040-6.

[81] Angus I. G. Ramsay, Nadia Crellin, Rachel Lawrence, Holly Walton, Stuti Bagri, Emma Dodsworth, Holly Elphinstone, Fergus Gleeson, Amanda Halliday, Kevin Herbert, Joanne Lloyd, Efthalia Massou, Raj Mehta, Stephen Morris, Pei Li Ng, Tracy O'Regan, Chris Sherlaw-Johnson, and Naomi J. Fulop. Procurement and early deployment of artificial intelligence tools for chest diagnostics in NHS services in England: a rapid, mixed method evaluation. *eClinicalMedicine*, 89:103481, 2025. doi: 10.1016/j.eclinm.2025.103481.

[82] Charles Kenney. *Transforming Health Care: Virginia Mason*

Medical Center's Pursuit of the Perfect Patient Experience. CRC Press, Boca Raton, 2010.

[83] Brent C. James and Lucy A. Savitz. How Intermountain trimmed health care costs through robust quality improvement efforts. *Health Affairs*, 30(6):1185–1191, 2011. doi: 10.1377/hlthaff.2011.0358.

[84] Patrick Kierkegaard. eHealth in Denmark: A case study. *Journal of Medical Systems*, 37:9991, 2013. doi: 10.1007/s10916-013-9991-y.

[85] Maria Olejaz, Annegrete Juul Nielsen, Andreas Rudkjøbing, Hans Okkels Birk, Allan Krasnik, and Cristina Hernandez-Quevedo. Denmark: Health system review. *Health Systems in Transition*, 14(2):1–192, 2012.

[86] Taavi Habicht, Marge Reinap, Kersti Kasekamp, Riina Sikkut, Liis Aaben, and Ewout van Ginneken. Estonia: Health system review. *Health Systems in Transition*, 20(1): 1–193, 2018.

[87] Robert M. Solow. We'd better watch out. *New York Times Book Review*, page 36, July 1987.

[88] Erik Brynjolfsson. The productivity paradox of information technology. *Commun. ACM*, 36(12):66–77, December 1993. ISSN 0001-0782. doi: 10.1145/163298.163309.

[89] Paul A. David. Computer And Dynamo: The Modern Productivity Paradox In A Not-Too Distant Mirror. The Warwick Economics Research Paper Series (TWERPS) 339, University of Warwick, Department of Economics, 1989.

[90] Erik Brynjolfsson, Daniel Rock, and Chad Syverson. The productivity J-curve: How intangibles complement general purpose technologies. *American Economic Journal: Macroeconomics*, 13(1):333–372, 2021.

[91] Daron Acemoglu and Pascual Restrepo. Automation and new tasks: How technology displaces and reinstates labor. *Journal of Economic Perspectives*, 33(2):3–30, 2019. doi: 10.1257/jep.33.2.3.

[92] Lidia Betcheva, Feryal Erhun, and Houyuan Jiang. Supply chain thinking in healthcare: Lessons and outlooks. *Manufacturing & Service Operations Management*, 23(6):1333–1353, 2021. doi: 10.1287/msom.2021.0992.

[93] Zoe Radnor and Sharon J. Williams. *Lean as a Healthcare Improvement Approach*. Cambridge Elements: Improving Quality and Safety in Healthcare. Cambridge University Press, 2025. doi: 10.1017/9781009423564.

[94] Eileen Kim, Vincent X. Liu, and Karandeep Singh. AI scribes are not productivity tools (Yet). *NEJM AI*, 2(12), 2025. doi: 10.1056/AIe2501051.

[95] Everett M. Rogers. *Diffusion of Innovations*. Free Press, New York, 5th edition, 2003. ISBN 9780743222099.

[96] Trisha Greenhalgh, Glenn Robert, Paul Bate, Fraser Macfarlane, and Olivia Kyriakidou. *Diffusion of Innovations in Health Service Organisations: A Systematic Literature Review*. John Wiley & Sons, 2008. ISBN 978-0-470-98727-8. doi: 10.1002/9780470987407. e-book edition.

[97] Lily C. Taylor, Niels Peek, Ari Ercole, Georgios Lyratzopoulos, and Juliet A. Usher-Smith. Enabling digital mul-

tifactorial risk assessment in primary care: an umbrella review and recommendations for design and implementation. *BMJ Health & Care Informatics*, 33:e101896, 2026. doi: 10.1136/bmjhci-2025-101896.

[98] H. David Banta. The diffusion of the computed tomography (CT) scanner in the United States. *International Journal of Health Services*, 10(2):251–269, 1980. doi: 10.2190/6D17-3UAU-RAM1-NVTR.

[99] U.S. Congress, Office of Technology Assessment. Policy implications of the computed tomography (CT) scanner. Technical report, U.S. Government Printing Office, Washington, DC, 1978.

[100] C. Challand, R. Struthers, J. R. Sneyd, P. D. Erasmus, N. Mellor, K. B. Hosie, and G. Minto. Randomized controlled trial of intraoperative goal-directed fluid therapy in aerobically fit and unfit patients having major colorectal surgery. *British Journal of Anaesthesia*, 108(1):53–62, 2012. doi: 10.1093/bja/aer273.

[101] J. Bruce Moseley, Kimberly O'Malley, Nancy J. Petersen, Terri J. Menke, Baruch A. Brody, David H. Kuykendall, John C. Hollingsworth, Carol M. Ashton, and Nelda P. Wray. A controlled trial of arthroscopic surgery for osteoarthritis of the knee. *The New England Journal of Medicine*, 347(2):81–88, 2002. doi: 10.1056/NEJMoa013259.

[102] Alexandra Kirkley, Trevor B. Birmingham, Robert B. Litchfield, J. Robert Giffin, Kevin R. Willits, Cindy J. Wong, Brian G. Feagan, Allan Donner, Sharon H. Griffin, Linda M. D'Ascanio, Janet E. Pope, and Peter J. Fowler. A randomized trial of arthroscopic surgery for osteoarthritis of the

knee. *The New England Journal of Medicine*, 359(11):1097–1107, 2008. doi: 10.1056/NEJMoa0708333.

[103] Michelle M. Mello and Troyen A. Brennan. The controversy over high-dose chemotherapy with autologous bone marrow transplant for breast cancer. *Health Affairs*, 20(5): 101–117, 2001. doi: 10.1377/hlthaff.20.5.101.

[104] H. Gilbert Welch and Juliana Mogielnicki. Presumed benefit: Lessons from the American experience with marrow transplantation for breast cancer. *BMJ*, 324(7345):1088–1092, 2002. doi: 10.1136/bmj.324.7345.1088.

[105] Richard A. Rettig, Peter D. Jacobson, Cynthia M. Farquhar, and Wade M. Aubry. *False Hope: Bone Marrow Transplantation for Breast Cancer*. Oxford University Press, New York, 2007.

[106] Qilu Li, Peilin Li, Haijing Hao, Rema Padman, Hewitt Gao, J. Travis Gossey, Jiang Bian, and Yiye Zhang. The impact of leadership on AI deployment study outcomes in healthcare: an integrative analysis. *npj Digital Medicine*, 8:799, 2025. doi: 10.1038/s41746-025-02177-x.

[107] Haiyang Yang, Tinglong Dai, Nestoras Mathioudakis, Amy M. Knight, Yuna Nakayasu, and Risa M. Wolf. Peer perceptions of clinicians using generative AI in medical decision-making. *npj Digital Medicine*, 8:530, 2025. doi: 10.1038/s41746-025-01901-x.

[108] Jason W. Burton, Mari-Klara Stein, and Tina Blegind Jensen. A systematic review of algorithm aversion in augmented decision making. *Journal of Behavioral Decision Making*, 33(2):220–239, 2020. doi: 10.1002/bdm.2155.

[109] Pierre E. Heudel, H. Crochet, Q. Filori, T. Bachelot, and J. Y. Blay. Artificial intelligence in medicine: a scoping review of the risk of deskilling and loss of expertise among physicians. *ESMO Real World Data and Digital Oncology*, 11, 2026. doi: 10.1016/j.esmorw.2026.100693.

[110] Krzysztof Budzyń, Marcin Romańczyk, Diana Kitala, Paweł Kołodziej, Marek Bugajski, Hans O. Adami, Johannes Blom, Marek Buszkiewicz, Natalie Halvorsen, Cesare Hassan, Tomasz Romańczyk, Øyvind Holme, Krzysztof Jarus, Shona Fielding, Melina Kunar, Maria Pellise, Nastazja Pilonis, Michał Filip Kamiński, Mette Kalager, Michael Bretthauer, and Yuichi Mori. Endoscopist deskilling risk after exposure to artificial intelligence in colonoscopy: a multicentre, observational study. *The Lancet Gastroenterology & Hepatology*, 10(10):896–903, 2025. doi: 10.1016/S2468-1253(25)00133-5.

[111] David Leslie, Anjali Mazumder, Aidan Peppin, Maria K Wolters, and Alexa Hagerty. Does AI stand for augmenting inequality in the era of covid-19 healthcare? *BMJ*, 372:n304, 2021. doi: 10.1136/bmj.n304.

[112] Ashraf Fawzy, Tianshi David Wu, Kunbo Wang, Matthew L. Robinson, Jad Farha, Amanda Bradke, Sherita H. Golden, Yanxun Xu, and Brian T. Garibaldi. Racial and ethnic discrepancy in pulse oximetry and delayed identification of treatment eligibility among patients with Covid-19. *JAMA Internal Medicine*, 182(7):730–738, 2022. doi: 10.1001/jamainternmed.2022.1905.

[113] Sylvia E. K. Sudat, Paul Wesson, Kim F. Rhoads, Stephanie Brown, Noha Aboelata, Alice R. Pressman, Aravind Mani,

and Kristen M.J. Azar. Racial disparities in pulse oximeter device inaccuracy and estimated clinical impact on Covid-19 treatment course. *American Journal of Epidemiology*, 192 (5):703–713, 2023. doi: 10.1093/aje/kwac164.

[114] Ziad Obermeyer, Brian Powers, Christine Vogeli, and Sendhil Mullainathan. Dissecting racial bias in an algorithm used to manage the health of populations. *Science*, 366(6464):447–453, 2019. doi: 10.1126/science.aax2342.

[115] Judy Wawira Gichoya, Imon Banerjee, Ananth Reddy Bhimireddy, John L Burns, Leo Anthony Celi, Li-Ching Chen, Ramon Correa, Natalie Dullerud, Marzyeh Ghassemi, Shih-Cheng Huang, Po-Chih Kuo, Matthew P Lungren, Lyle J Palmer, Brandon J Price, Saptarshi Purkayastha, Ayis T Pyrros, Lauren Oakden-Rayner, Chima Okechukwu, Laleh Seyyed-Kalantari, Hari Trivedi, Ryan Wang, Zachary Zaiman, and Haoran Zhang. AI recognition of patient race in medical imaging: a modelling study. *The Lancet Digital Health*, 4(6):e406–e414, 2022. doi: 10.1016/S2589-7500(22)00063-2.

[116] Bojana Velichkovska, Hristijan Gjoreski, Daniel Denkovski, Marija Kalendar, Irene Dankwa Mullan, Judy Wawira Gichoya, Nicole Martinez, Leo Celi, and Venet Osmani. Bias in vital signs? machine learning models can learn patients' race or ethnicity from the values of vital signs alone. *BMJ Health & Care Informatics*, 32:e101098, July 2025. doi: 10.1136/bmjhci-2024-101098.

[117] Sam Rickman. Evaluating gender bias in large language models in long-term care. *BMC Medical Informatics and Decision Making*, 25:274, 2025. doi: 10.1186/s12911-025-03118-0.

[118] Catalina Gomez, Ruolin Wang, Katharina Breininger, Corinne Casey, Chris Bradley, Mitchell Pavlak, Alex Pham, Jithin Yohannan, and Mathias Unberath. The explainable AI dilemma under knowledge imbalance in specialist AI for glaucoma referrals in primary care. *npj Digital Medicine*, 8:706, 2025. doi: 10.1038/s41746-025-02069-0.

[119] Feiyang Yu, Alex Moehring, Oishi Banerjee, Tobias Salz, Nikhil Agarwal, and Pranav Rajpurkar. Heterogeneity and predictors of the effects of AI assistance on radiologists. *Nature Medicine*, 30(3):837–849, 2024. doi: 10.1038/s41591-024-02850-w.

[120] Ethan Goh, Robert Gallo, Jason Hom, Eric Strong, Yingjie Weng, Hannah Kerman, Joséphine A. Cool, Zahir Kanjee, Andrew S. Parsons, Neera Ahuja, Eric Horvitz, Daniel Yang, Arnold Milstein, Andrew P. J. Olson, Adam Rodman, and Jonathan H. Chen. Large language model influence on diagnostic reasoning: A randomized clinical trial. *JAMA Network Open*, 7(10):e2440969, 2024. doi: 10.1001/jamanetworkopen.2024.40969.

[121] Shan Chen, Mingye Gao, Kuleen Sasse, Thomas Hartvigsen, Brian Anthony, Lizhou Fan, Hugo Aerts, Jack Gallifant, and Danielle S. Bitterman. When helpfulness backfires: LLMs and the risk of false medical information due to sycophantic behaviour. *npj Digital Medicine*, 8:605, 2025. doi: 10.1038/s41746-025-02008-z.

[122] S. Bedi, Y. Jiang, P. Chung, S. Koyejo, and N. Shah. Fidelity of medical reasoning in large language models. *JAMA Network Open*, 8(8):e2526021, 2025. doi: 10.1001/jamanetworkopen.2025.26021.

[123] Arjun Mahajan, Ziad Obermeyer, Roxana Daneshjou, Jenna Lester, and Dylan Powell. Cognitive bias in clinical large language models. *npj Digital Medicine*, 8(428), 2025. doi: 10.1038/s41746-025-01790-0.

[124] Paige Nong, Julia Adler-Milstein, Nate C. Apathy, A. Jay Holmgren, and Jordan Everson. Current use and evaluation of artificial intelligence and predictive models in US hospitals. *Health Affairs*, 44(1):90–98, 2025. doi: 10.1377/hlthaff.2024.00842.

[125] Dennis Bontempi, Osbert Zalay, Danielle S Bitterman, Nicolai Birkbak, Derek Shyr, Fridolin Haugg, Jack M Qian, Hannah Roberts, Subha Perni, Vasco Prudente, Suraj Pai, Andre Dekker, Benjamin Haibe-Kains, Christian Guthier, Tracy Balboni, Laura Warren, Monica Krishan, Benjamin H Kann, Charles Swanton, Dirk De Ruysscher, Raymond H Mak, and Hugo JWL Aerts. Faceage, a deep learning system to estimate biological age from face photographs to improve prognostication: a model development and validation study. *The Lancet Digital Health*, 2025. doi: 10.1016/j.landig.2025.03.002.

[126] OpenAI. AI as a healthcare ally: How Americans are navigating the system with ChatGPT. Technical report, OpenAI, January 2026.

[127] King's Health Partners and Responsible AI UK and The Policy Institute at King's College London. The use of AI in UK healthcare: Public perceptions and healthcare priorities. King's College London, May 2026.

[128] Nuffield Trust and Royal College of General Practitioners. Over 1 in 4 GPs use AI at work but national policy failing

to keep up with pace of change. Nuffield Trust, December 2025. Mixed-methods research combining the annual GP Voice Survey with online focus groups. Accessed 13 July 2026.

[129] Beatriz Costa-Gomes, Pavel Tolmachev, Eloise Taysom, Viknesh Sounderajah, Hannah Richardson, Philipp Schoenegger, Xiaoxuan Liu, Matthew M. Nour, Seth Spielman, Samuel F. Way, Yash Shah, Michael Bhaskar, Harsha Nori, Christopher Kelly, Peter Hames, Bay Gross, Mustafa Suleyman, and Dominic King. Public use of a generalist LLM chatbot for health queries. *Nature Health*, 1:689–696, 2026. doi: 10.1038/s44360-026-00117-x.

[130] Hirotaka Takita, Daijiro Kabata, Shannon L. Walston, Hiroyuki Tatekawa, Kenichi Saito, Yasushi Tsujimoto, Yukio Miki, and Daiju Ueda. A systematic review and meta-analysis of diagnostic performance comparison between generative AI and physicians. *npj Digital Medicine*, 8:175, 2025. doi: 10.1038/s41746-025-01543-z.

[131] Kobi Hackenburg, Ben M. Tappin, Luke Hewitt, Ed Saunders, Sid Black, Hause Lin, Catherine Fist, Helen Margetts, David G. Rand, and Christopher Summerfield. The levers of political persuasion with conversational AI. *Science*, December 2025. doi: 10.1126/science.adi3436.

[132] Harriet Sherwood. 'I felt pure, unconditional love': the people who marry their AI chatbots. *The Guardian*, July 2025.

[133] Arthur Tang, Neo Tung, Huy Quang Nguyen, Kin On Kwok, Stanley Luong, Nhat Bui, Giang Nguyen, and Wilson Tam. Health information for all: do large language

models bridge or widen the digital divide? *BMJ*, 387: e080208, 2024. doi: 10.1136/bmj-2024-080208.

[134] NHS England. NHS backs AI notetaking to free up more face-to-face care. NHS England press release, January 2026. Launch of the self-certified registry of ambient voice technology suppliers, 16 January 2026; evaluation across 17,000 patient encounters. Accessed 13 July 2026.

[135] NHS England. NHS accelerates artificial intelligence rollout to cut waiting times and improve care for millions. NHS England press release, July 2026. Announces NHS App AI triage tool rollout to 200,000 patients within 12 months and all app users by April 2028, within a £10bn three-year technology programme. Accessed 13 July 2026.

[136] Royal College of Physicians. RCP engagement with MHRA consultation on the regulation of AI in healthcare. Royal College of Physicians consultation response, March 2026.

[137] Skills for Health. AI in healthcare: What clinicians and NHS leaders need to know in 2026. Skills for Health, April 2026. Reports 89% of clinician non-users of AI citing professional liability and medico-legal risk as the dominant adoption barrier. Accessed 13 July 2026.

[138] Cass R. Sunstein. *Laws of Fear: Beyond the Precautionary Principle*. Cambridge University Press, Cambridge, 2005.

[139] Jessica D. Workum, Sade J. Krijgsman, Ildiko Vajda, R. M. van Stokkum, Jan van den Brand, Diederik Gommers, Ari Ercole, and Michel E. van Genderen. When are large language models medical devices? Navigating the MDR and

AI Act for healthcare applications. *BMJ Health & Care Informatics*, 2026. In press.

[140] Tom Moberly. Doctors must stop using unregistered AI scribe tools, says NHS England. *BMJ*, 389:r1302, 2025.

[141] Youssof Oskrochi, Elliott Roy-Highley, Keith Grimes, and Sam Shah. Digital health technology compliance with clinical safety standards in the National Health Service in England: National cross-sectional study. *J Med Internet Res*, 27:e80076, October 2025. ISSN 1438-8871. doi: 10.2196/80076.

[142] Stephen Gilbert, Hugh Harvey, Tom Melvin, Erik Vollebregt, and Paul Wicks. Large language model AI chatbots require approval as medical devices. *Nature Medicine*, 29 (10):2396–2398, 2023.

[143] Stephen Gilbert, Tinglong Dai, and Rebecca Mathias. Consternation as Congress proposal for autonomous prescribing AI coincides with the haphazard cuts at the FDA. *npj Digital Medicine*, 8:165, 2025. doi: 10.1038/s41746-025-01540-2.

[144] Ipsos. Health and AI: Public attitudes in Britain. Technical report, Ipsos, January 2026. Ipsos survey of UK adults.

[145] Ajay Agrawal, Joshua Gans, and Avi Goldfarb. *Prediction Machines: The Simple Economics of Artificial Intelligence*. Harvard Business Review Press, Boston, MA, 2018.

[146] Massimiliano Ferrara, Giampaolo Viglia, and Jose Carlos Romero. Strategic tensions in organizational GenAI adoption: A game theory modeling of internal resource competition, workforce dynamics, and value management.

Technological Forecasting and Social Change, 227:124653, 2026. doi: 10.1016/j.techfore.2026.124653.

Index

www.ingramcontent.com/pod-product-compliance
Lightning Source LLC
LaVergne TN
LVHW021742071126
851857LV00039B/593
* 9 7 8 1 0 6 6 7 2 6 4 0 0 *